A New Look at Canadian Indian Policy

Respect the Collective—Promote the Individual

by Gordon Gibson

Fraser Institute
2009

Date of issue: January 2009
Printed and bound in Canada

Library and Archives Canada Cataloguing in Publication

Gibson, Gordon, 1937–
A new look at Canadian Indian policy : respect the collective—promote the individual / Gordon Gibson.

Includes bibliographical references.
ISBN 978-0-88975-243-6

1. Indians of North America--Canada--Government relations. 2. Indians of North America--Legal status, laws, etc.--Canada. 3. Subsidiarity. 4. Indians of North America--Canada--Politics and government. I. Fraser Institute (Vancouver, B.C.) II. Title.

E9-2.G43 2008 322.1197'071 C2008-907617-6

Contents

Foreword

In what follows, I argue that the estate of the Indian people of Canada is the most important moral question in federal politics. The responsibility flows directly to each of us as voters. This book talks about what we, Canadians generally, can do to understand this and what governments can do to discharge their responsibilities.

In that sense this is not a book that one should read to learn about Indians.[1] There are many persons far more knowledgeable on that topic, most particularly the people concerned. Equally, this is not a book on what Indians ought to do. Opinion on that topic is a book that each Indian must write for him- or herself. Rather, my topic is what mainstream society ought to be doing in our Indian policy.

I say that the standard model for thinking about Indian policy is fundamentally wrong, giving too much weight to the collective and too little to the individual. But opposition to basic change is immense, the resistance fuelled by habit, thoughtlessness, guilt, the implied loss of intellectual capital that always follows a major re-thinking, and threats to the cash flow and status of workers in the largest failed area of government responsibility in the country. For that reason alone, proposals for change will face criticism, in which honest debate will be difficult in the short term. Some commentators will say—with reason—that this book challenges some of the most basic assumptions of established Indian policy. This challenge would not be necessary if established Indian policy was working well, for Indians or anyone else.

1 See "On language," pp. 18–29, for a note on words and language. In particular, the concepts of "Indian" and "aboriginal" are importantly different.

The recommendations are grounded in the author's perception of reality. Others will see different facts on the ground and have strongly differing views. I respect that. Let us talk.

First, why do I say the standard model is fundamentally wrong? In brief, because it presumes and enforces a relationship between the Indian individual and relevant collectives (both Indian and state), which relationship is biased against individual freedom and choice. This relationship, I say, has produced the adverse social outcomes—in health, education, life span, incomes, housing, substance abuse, violence, imprisonment and so on—universally criticized by all.

The relationship between the individual and the collective has been the major force in human life from time immemorial but the character of that relationship has evolved over time. Through most of recorded human history, the collective (whether religious or temporal or both) has been in the ascendency in the affairs of ordinary people. Individual liberty was reserved for the leadership. Then came the idea of western liberalism, growing gradually for around two-hundred years now, that to empower all individuals with sufficient information and options is to allow everyone to make the most of their individual lives.

From the beginning it has been clear that the individual by himself is virtually nothing while together we can make progress. Experience has led to the establishment of social institutions that can add guidance and assistance to the individual lot while at the same time upholding the social system itself. Ideas of trust and the predictability of the rule of law are the most basic. This is not the place for an essay on social development but it can be said with confidence that this field is subject to constant debate. In our time, different ideas of the relationship between the individual and the collective underlie the tensions between the secular west and Islam. In western societies, some now worry that too much freedom or, more precisely, the irresponsible exercise of freedom can lead to trivial licentiousness.

In one dark corner of this long and wide-world drama, a special case of the relationship between individual and collective has been playing out in Canada, especially for the past 150 years, in the lives of native Indians. In this particular corner, the collective assumes an importance unthinkable in the mainstream. Indian policy, imposed by the mainstream on some Canadians—"Indians"—has built for them a world that is both a fortress and a prison. The effects on the individuals within that system have been profound.

I believe that there is a growing concern about this. If so, there is an opening to a better future—indeed it has slowly been unfolding for years through individual actions. But in spite of good will, pernicious and counter-productive incentives remain to burden an entire people, not just as trailing legacies of the past (like residential schools) but as current active goals of governments and other entities in the system. That is the study of this book. In the longer term, things will sort themselves out for the better as long as we remain a free and liberal society. The only question is how many lives will be wasted in the waiting period, and that is important. The best way to shorten that time frame for betterment is to honestly discuss the issues.

What we are doing now is profoundly immoral. The fatal defects in outcomes are not redeemed by the fact that the intentions are in general of the best. The problems in this area are similar to those discussed in the more recent literature on foreign aid (e.g., Easterly, 2006; Calderisi, 2006), which discusses in essence the problems of trying to set other people's priorities. In our own little Canadian Third World we are guilty of the same mistakes, as what follows will describe.

⚶ ⚶ ⚶

A word about the arrangement of the book, and then the author, and then those he must thank.

The introduction, "Where we begin," supplies a thumbnail sketch of historic context and current statistical and other realities. The first chapter amplifies the historic context and devotes considerable space to a description of the words we use in discussing policy. Some of these are ambiguous, some are highly charged, and most of them suffer from difficulties of one sort or another. Yet they are the words we have, so it is important to begin by seeking the greatest possible clarity and objectivity in their use. In a supplementary note to this chapter, the importance of the *McIvor* case and the implications of C-31 are described as being most important to the long-term demographics.

Chapter 2 gives an overview of the history of the Indian peoples and the law that controls their lives. It was Prime Minister Mackenzie King who said that Canada has too much geography and not enough history, by which I think he meant the accumulated social depth of a country like England or the United States, both of which he admired. The Indian people of Canada, by contrast, have a great deal of history, much of it unhappy, which in many cases daily informs their lives to an extent quite unimaginable to most of us. At the same time, judging by land claims, they have too little geography. Many in the mainstream would prefer to forget history and to focus on the future. That simply will not work in a reconciliation process with people who feel very strongly about their history. We must not only examine it, but understand it.

As to law, most of us in the mainstream cannot imagine (nor would we tolerate) the daily basics of our lives being dictated by remote and uncontrollable law but that is the estate of the Reserve Indian. Mainstream law deals with us as individuals. Indian laws deal with Indians as members of a collective and has done since the "nation to nation" basis was established after contact by the British. Indians are singled out in our Constitution and, based upon that, an immense edifice of Indian law has been erected by Parliament and, since 1982, by the courts.

The current consensus is that action as to directive law in respect of Indians should be minimized by the mainstream level and enacted only by Indians. But laws do not only give direction; they may also confer rights, and rights have an impact upon others. A significant body of aboriginal rights has been embedded in our mainstream law in theory and will increasingly grow from that in practice as courts elaborate these things. We need to understand that in some detail.

The third chapter addresses concepts, organizations, and life on the ground. The concepts begin with a description of the different form of citizenship contemplated for Indians and takes an initial look at the tension between the individual and the collective. The necessary features and possible variations of a viable parallel society are canvassed.

National organizations, voluntary (e.g. Assembly of First Nations) and statute-based (e.g. financing and statistical organizations) are described, along with a discussion of "direct action." A bit of the American experience, especially the lessons of the Harvard project, is then related to Canada. Some of the aboriginal thought of Calvin Helin, Jean Allard, and Clarence Louie is noted as a modern reaction to the standard model adopted by the Royal Commission on Aboriginal Peoples (RCAP) and the Assembly of First Nations (AFN).

Chapter 4 enters into the philosophy of the relationship between the individual and the collective, beginning with the major questions and a taxonomy of collectives. The thinking of Gerald Taiaiake Alfred and Tom Flanagan (as polar positions on this topic) is described with a deeper exploration of the thinking of Alan Cairns, Charles Taylor, and Will Kymlicka on such matters as the internal and external relationships of the collective, the dilemma of the liberal confronted with illiberal possibilities of his belief, Bradford Morse on the inherent right, and the United Nations' indigenous proposals. The chapter concludes with the view that whatever one's philosophical conclusions, the force of history and a moral contract require that a genuine version of the parallel society remain on offer in order to hold out meaningful choice for the individual.

Chapter 5 enters into the details of the modern treaty process and governance. Treaties have been adopted as the means of resolving major outstanding questions, and it is only reasonable to expect that the major gains being won by tribes in this process will in due course force the re-opening of existing treaties negotiated in the circumstances of a hundred years and more ago, at the very least in the area of self-government. This is thus a very important area.

Treaty policy is set to meet the institutional needs of elites and collectives; the interests of the individual are secondary and may, or may not, be accommodated. This is true even though ratification customarily requires a referendum. This is explained, along with the benefits and problems of what has come to be the standard treaty model. Suggestions, some quite basic, are proposed for improvement.

"Self-government" is seen as a sort of silver bullet to solve the problems of Canadian Indians. But available data is skimpy and certainly mixed. Very small governments with relatively large powers have inherent challenges that will be described and weighed. A continuing argument, begun in the previous chapter, is made for the application of subsidiarity to these questions.

The final chapter asks "Where to from here?" The "default scenario" (that is, "business as usual") is described and assessed as wanting. The moral responsibility of the mainstream is re-visited and the sad case of Kashechewan discussed as an example. The general response to our moral duty is outlined as a two-track process of empowering individuals and reshaping mainstream institutions to make them more welcoming and open to Indians' aspirations.

A direct payment of "treaty money" is discussed (a sort of modified Guaranteed Annual Income) which would, in part, re-direct funds from Chief and Council to individuals and, in part, add new funding for off-Reserve purposes. The case is made for much more extensive provincial involvement in the off-Reserve world.

New and needed legal relationships are discussed. Indian power has earned a new seat at the social table and there is an analysis of how far it is similar to other new actors—trade unions and the environmental movement—of the past century. Just as the accommodation of the earlier new actors has matured from a litigious to a routine process of regulation, so, it is argued, should Indian questions be accommodated by new machinery. We are heading down the US road of extensive court supervision of the new "black power" player in that country; and there is a better way.

The book concludes with a renewed call for subsidiarity, some constitutional musings, and a statement of why, in the view of the author, the approach of this book fits well into the new kind of nation that Canada is becoming.

⚘ ⚘ ⚘

Writing this book has been a humbling experience. In the first place, the subject matter is complex and deep, freighted with emotion, and intensely involves the personal lives of hundreds of thousand of human beings. Moreover, generalizations are difficult as outcomes from the impact upon individuals of Canadian Indian policy span a broad range from the happy to the unbearably sad. One is driven to averages, which are sad enough.

Next, as time passes, things change. While this book has been in preparation the Kelowna Accord has appeared briefly in the headlines, been celebrated, and then effectively vanished. A few new treaties have been concluded. Manifestations of direct action, perhaps most famously Caledonia in Ontario but in other places across the land, have commenced and some are still in progress. Small but important individual advances have been made in education. A status Indian has been appointed as Lieutenant Governor in British Columbia, following another in Ontario. The federal government has made a major official apology in respect of the history of Residential Schools and a "Truth and Reconciliation Commission" is now at work. So the topic, hard to get your arms around even at a moment frozen in time, is in fact a moving target as well. But with all this flux, there is no doubt that there is a very great deal that can be said.

The writer first learned of Canadian Indians from his father. My Dad spent his early years as a logger and fisherman on the West Coast of Vancouver Island, at that time a very isolated part of Canada. Most of his co-workers and friends were Indians. As I grew up (I was born in 1937), it was in an atmosphere where my family acknowledged some difference between Indians and others but not in any of the important dimensions of humanity. Indians were always just other people.

Apart from a few years in independent business, my first real job was in Ottawa working for the Hon. Arthur Laing, then Minister of Northern Affairs. I had the privilege of travelling extensively in the Arctic, learning about the people then commonly called Eskimos. I was Mr. Laing's Executive Assistant when he gained the added responsibility of Indian Affairs in 1966. That involved me at once in what was even then a huge bureaucracy and all of the policy files. Perhaps more importantly, it introduced me to Len Marchand, an aide who had come over from the former Minister. Len went on to become a Member of Parliament and, as I recall, the second Indian member of the Senate after British Columbia's Guy Williams (whose appointment was recommended by Mr. Laing).

I went to work for Pierre Trudeau in 1968 as his Executive Assistant. That job involved scheduling the Prime Minister's time and I well recall the enormous amount of it he invested in developing the famous (or infamous) white paper of 1970 (Canada, 1969) that became a turning point in Indian history. Richard Gwyn in his book, *The Northern Magus*, reported that Trudeau spent more time on the Indian file that year than any other topic and I can believe that. I was still in the Prime Minister's Office when the white paper went down in flames and Prime Ministerial attention turned to Quebec, never to return to this file except as a part of constitutional negotiations.

During these years in Ottawa, it was a part of my job to meet with and study the views of many of the leaders of the time, including the young, strong, and influential Albertan, Harold Cardinal of the National Indian Brotherhood and Kahntineta Horn and Andrew Deslisle of the Quebec Mohawks.

I returned to British Columbia where as an MLA for North-Vancouver Capilano I learned something of the proud Squamish Nation. My friend Percy Paull honoured me with a talking stick. I noted that Indian affairs were totally ignored in the Legislature of the day. This was then exclusively an "Ottawa" problem.

Leaving direct politics at the end of the 1970s, I began writing about public policy, deeply immersed in the constitutional turmoil of the 1980s. Little noticed by most at the time was the aboriginal content of the constitutional amendments of 1982 and the two, largely failed, Indian-government constitution conferences that followed. But no serious public-policy writer could fail to track the fact that a new topic was moving to the front burner. My business relationships in the 1980s led to significant involvement with the leadership of the wealthy Samson Band of Hobbema, just south of Edmonton. I remember in particular Vic Buffalo and Roy Louis for their articulate and sincere thought.

While most eyes were focused on Quebec separatism as we moved through Meech Lake and the Charlottetown Accord, serious students knew that a new force of Indian nationalism was also at work in this constitutional process, the more effectively because it was under the radar of the headline writers. I wrote my first substantial column on the topic in the *Globe and Mail* in 1990 and have never left it for long since. Towards the end of that decade, the *Delgamuukw* decision revolutionized both Indian law (a revolution arguably begun by Sparrow in 1990) and through that period this non-lawyer gained a non-degree in Indian studies because of an intense personal interest in aboriginal law.

The truly landmark Nisga'a Treaty did not become final until 2000 but I wrote extensively on its development for the three previous years. Three monographs on this topic were published by the Fraser Institute. There was a personal tinge too: I had served with much pleasure in the Legislature with Frank Calder, the Nisga'a Chief who started it all (in recent history—the claim goes back more than a century) and came to know him as a fine man.

In 2001, I organized a series of debates and lectures on Indian policy for Simon Fraser University that included a memorable discussion between Alan Cairns and Tom Flanagan. The "hook" was the referendum on treaty policy promised and delivered by the new Liberal government of British Columbia but the content was far broader and can still be found on the university's web site at <http://www.sfu.ca/referendum/>.

For the three years after the Nisga'a Treaty, I turned most of my attention to democratic reform, though I did participate in the Treaty Annuity Working Group, organized by Jean Allard in Winnipeg under the umbrella of Wayne Helgeson and the Social Planning Council. Through a conference and extended correspondence this group helped examine the expanded "treaty money" approach to a sort of a guaranteed annual income, popularized by Allard in his Big Bear's Treaty. This relationship gave me the opportunity to come to know Leona Freed, the spark plug of a Prairie women's group working for greater accountability of Band governance.

Some three years ago, I began work on this book after watching with growing dismay the apparent paralysis of the treaty process in British Columbia and the relentlessly unhappy statistics across the country on average social outcomes. In my work on democratic reform, I had been developing a model of the "political marketplace" of governments and bureaucracies, which of course is so very different from the free market that governs most of our lives in the mainstream. Free markets are voluntary and we seek to make them transparent, accountable, and competitive. Political markets are non-voluntary and coercive, seriously lacking in transparency, accountability, and competition. That is the system that governs Indian policy.

Any examination of the evolution of governance over the centuries must note the gradual building of political forces that often results in a sudden, tectonic shift. Power shifts tend often to be abrupt rather than gradual, and long past time because of the extraordinary defence mechanisms and the power of inertia for any *ancien régime*. So it is with Indian policy, it seemed to me. Equally, any examination of governance in the West cannot overlook the rise in the power of the individual in his/her relationship to the social collective and I concluded that this might be a useful perspective for the examination of Indian policy in Canada and a possible means of resolving the tensions between an aboriginal parallel society and the mainstream, tensions partly historic but also partly created by post-Confederation law and policy.

⚘ ⚘ ⚘

The result is this book, and I must thank many people for their assistance. My first debt is highly practical, namely to the people who made it possible. That list begins with the John and Lotte Hecht Foundation of Vancouver, which has financially supported this venture for long past the original due date, as an idea for a short paper gradually expanded into something much longer. Michael Walker, then Executive Director of the Fraser Institute, was supportive from the outset and his successor, Mark Mullins, has continued that.

Early on in my thinking in the 1980s and 1990s, with no idea of this book in mind but simply a desire for better understanding, I sought out many Indian leaders to obtain their perspectives. None of the names I will mention has seen this manuscript and they might well differ with it, perhaps even intensely, but that will not prevent me recording a debt to some who are now deceased and some who may recall me but vaguely if at all, for the time they spent with a then simply curious writer about public policy. I begin with the aforementioned Len Marchand, and add Stan Dixon of the Sechelt, Wendy Grant (as she then was), Ed John, Joe Mathias (now deceased), and Bill Wilson, all of the Summit,[2] Ernie Crey and Doug Kelly of the Sto'lo, Stewart Phillip of the Union of BC Indian Chiefs, Nelson Leeson of the Nisga'a and, especially, Herb George (Satsan) with whom I had the pleasure of several public philosophical debates that we enjoyed so much that we briefly contemplated a joint provincial tour.

Controversial figures were included: Gail Sparrow, once Chief of the Musqueam and Meaghan Walker-Williams of the Cowichan had a highly

2 An umbrella group of bands and tribes in British Columbia.

individualistic approach and I had very extensive correspondence especially with the latter. Miles Richardson, Chief Commissioner of the BC Treaty Commission was very helpful back then, as were a couple of conferences organized by the Commission and available in their archives, especially "Speaking Truth to Power." More recently, I owe a debt for their time to Chief Kim Baird as she developed the Tsawwassen Treaty and Manny Jules of Kamloops, architect of much of the new national Indian infrastructure, especially in the finance field. I would add correspondence with Taiaiake Alfred in which he elaborated his philosophical work.

Stephen Hume, a columnist for the *Vancouver Sun*, is deeply knowledgeable in these matters and I appreciate our many e-mail debates.

Except in the past two years, none of these encounters (and many others including persons met at numerous conferences that I have not recorded) were arranged with this book in mind but together they served to give me a beginner's education of what the Canadian system looks like to a person of Indian identity and a clear understanding of the tremendous power of the impact of the laws and policies of the mainstream society.

Lawyers are exceedingly important in this field and have been generous with their time. I would mention Tom Isaac, Keith Clark, Michael Goldie, Chris Harvey, and Keith Lowes. Jim Aldridge, lawyer for the Nisga'a, was especially helpful on that treaty. John Weston kept me closely informed on the progress of the current case known as Chief Mountain, which may figure importantly in the future.

Several persons have been good enough to review some or all of this text. I would mention Harry Swain, a former DIAND Deputy Minister. Certain anonymous persons currently in government have been of great assistance, regrettably always within the four corners of their oaths of secrecy. Former BC Attorney General and Aboriginal Relations Minister Geoff Plant provided insights. Alan Cairns and Will Kymlicka gave extensive comment on the philosophy chapter. I am grateful to Hamar Foster of the University of Victoria who read the section on law and saved me from many errors. Of course, I do not burden him or any of the others with responsibility for my remaining views, and each of these would have (or actually have) written very different books. Their kindness is the more greatly appreciated because of that.

My greatest thanks must go to my two distinguished peer reviewers, Paul Tennant and John Richards. In addition to a careful reading of this manuscript, both of these men have been kind enough to talk and correspond with me continually over many years as my thinking, so raw at the beginning compared to theirs, was able to develop.

Some of the ideas in this book will be controversial and I implicate none of the above in that, or in any errors of fact or approach that may remain. Indeed, I am sure that every single one of them will disagree with parts, perhaps important parts, of the work. Such faults as there are, are mine. But I do credit them very much for such merit as the reader may find in what follows.

GFG
September 30, 2008

A NEW LOOK AT CANADIAN INDIAN POLICY

Where we begin

Certain events and results are well known. North America has been populated by humans for many thousands of years. About 400 years ago, Europeans began to arrive in numbers in what they called the "New World." The first British Colony was established at Roanoke (1586/7), followed more successfully by Jamestown (1607) and, in 1610, the first British Colony in what would become Canada at Cuper's Cove, in modern-day Newfoundland. The first French colony was established at Port-Royal, in what is now Nova Scotia, in 1605.

The newcomers found indigenous peoples in organized societies. Some of the economies were based on hunting and gathering and some were agricultural. No doubt all of the parties wondered how to relate and the response would vary considerably. Some contact was peaceful, and some violent (Mann, 2005). During the seventeenth century, the newcomers interacted increasingly with the indigenes. Minor settlements were established. Trade in animal, forest, and agricultural goods grew, and some military alliances were struck in pursuit of European rivalries extended to America. During the eighteenth century, trade and alliances continued. Land acquisition by newcomers grew apace, some by way of agreement and some by displacement.

The New World gradually became economically important to Europeans and the colonies expanded rapidly. In 1763, Britain issued a Royal Proclamation (George III) that governed, *inter alia*, intercourse with the native peoples to control expansion and require fair dealing. In this and other ways, a convention of dealing with natives as members of collectives was firmly established.

In 1776, American independence was declared and established 1783. Thereafter the Proclamation was superseded in United States. That country saw many eastern tribes displaced, rapid westward expansion, and the beginning of the Indian Wars. The technological, military, and organizational advantages of the settlers generally prevailed in cases of indigenous resistance once secure logistical bases had been established in the New World. During the nineteenth century, the United States completed its consolidation of territory from sea to sea. The Indian Wars ended with complete victory for the settlers and Indians were placed in "Reservations." Treaties with Britain—the Convention of 1818 and 1846 Treaty of Oregon—settled North American boundaries. The military usefulness of Indian allies ended.

During these centuries and throughout North America, the indigenous population was dramatically weakened by disease, economic and physical displacement, cultural competition, and war (Diamond, 1999). A "Reserve" system was instituted in much of what was to become Canada. An Indian policy, partly seeking assimilation and partly effecting geographical isolation and minimal sustenance was adopted. In 1867, Indians were singled out in the Canadian Constitution as charges of the federal government. This identification and differential legal, financial, and other treatment continues unabated (and often exacerbated, though in different ways) to this day.

In 1876, the Indian Act was enacted. Indians effectively ceased to be legal persons and mostly disappeared from public view for almost 100 years. Traditional political organization was suppressed and replaced by rule from Ottawa and very limited versions of local democracy. The shift in the balance of power was complete. By the beginning of the twentieth century, the heirs of the aboriginals living in North America at contact had become a totally subject people, effectively by force (though little actual fighting took place in Canada).

Vigorous prosecution of Treaty[1] arrangements in Ontario and the Prairie provinces saw Indians "surrender" almost all of the land base in those areas. Duly authorized signatures were obtained. Treaties were few in the Atlantic, Quebec, and British Columbia but the effective result (of dispossession) was the same, as was the effective compensation (that is, small parcels of land, minimal government services, and stewardship). The newcomers declared, or often merely assumed, legal title to most of the country though some of that would in due course be challenged.

Sometime before or around the turn of the twentieth century, the aboriginal population reached its nadir, probably at less than 100,000 members, forming perhaps only 1 in 70 (or 1.5%) of an exploding Canadian population. Numbers then began to grow again.

1 Agreements by way of "Treaty" became the formal way of honoring the nation-to-nation process established by the Royal Proclamation (George III).

In the early twentieth century, restrictions on Indians and erosion of their land base continued. Laws forbidding mobility, free association, and access to legal counsel were put in place. Matters continued to evolve. A residential schooling system was set up for some. The mid-twentieth century saw recognition of Indians as legal persons for the purposes of voting. But the beginning of widespread application of the cash-welfare system to Reserves effected a newly debilitating revolution in lifestyles, as incentives to work decreased.

By the late twentieth century, Indians began to re-appear in political discussions. A revolutionary and unilateral white paper proposing that Indian status be eliminated and the collective abandoned in favor of the individual and full ordinary citizenship was rejected. Courts began significant interventions in making Indian law. Politicians and bureaucrats gradually abandoned the policy field (but not finance) in favor of an evolving complex of Indian activists, academics, courts, and a growing aboriginal bar. Attention shifted from outcomes and realities to process and entitlements.

Costs and public attention (though not public understanding) escalated dramatically. Improvement in the estate of individual Indians remaining within the Reserve system did not keep pace but official policy remained focussed on building on that system. At the same time, a significant number (now about two-thirds) of aboriginal descendents began to separate from the Reserve system and integrated into—or at least co-existed with—mainstream Canadian society.

Over a period of about 300 years, the previous multiple societies occupying North America were overcome, overwhelmed, and mostly destroyed by a massive wave of European immigration through a combination of war, displacement, and disease. Established arrangements of politics and custom were ended. The descendants of the aboriginals were sequestered into small and mostly isolated areas of land and largely ignored except when causing inconvenience. Most traditional anchors for the human spirit—traditional values, property, economics, political organization—were eliminated or severely diminished.

While there were individual exceptions and many of them, the gradual change to a culture of despair, defeat, and social disintegration led to average lives that by reference to the mainstream society were short, diseased, poor, uneducated and inward, with an unhealthy focus on the past and victimhood. The treatment of Indians was essentially governed by unilateral decisions made by the newcomers and, particularly, by their governments.

While all of this was going on, mainstream North America was producing the most prosperous and culturally vital society in the history of mankind. At the same time according to the Assembly of First Nations, "the United Nations Human Development Index (HDI) ranks Canada 8th on the HDI scale while First Nations rank 63rd" (2005, June 27). Very significantly, Canada has in the past generation seen a massive new wave of immigration, this time from Asia. This cohort has no connection with the above events and little concern for them. This will have major political significance, as the latest set of newcomers has no emotional connection with the previously summarized history.

Some statistical indicators of the average Indian estate as of today are shown in "Some statistics" (p. 7). It is important to note that all of the numbers there are averages. Some individuals, some groups are far better off than the average. The estate of others is worse. But the averages tell a story that should not be ignored, though it usually is. That story is the greatest moral issue in contemporary Canadian public policy.

All of the above is vaguely known to most Canadians and it is a source of background worry and guilt. Perhaps it is not in the foreground because we appear to be on a path that never seems to change. However, this situation is not destiny. It had been created by choices—choices of others in the past, of our governments and, ultimately, of all of us today. The story can be changed by other choices.

NOTE

Some statistics

Life expectancy at birth for Status Indians[1] is estimated at 70 years, compared to the Canadian average of 77 years. Infant mortality among Status Indians on reserves stands at 7.2 per 1,000 live births, compared to a rate of 5.2 for Canada (Gour, 2005). The suicide rate in the Indian population is over double the national rate and at least five times greater amongst young people.[2]

The prevalence of lone-parent families among Status Indians is twice that of the national population. Less than half of all Aboriginal children under 15 live in a married-couple family, compared to three-quarters of other children (Hull, 2001). The pregnancy rate for girls younger than 15 who live on reserves is about 18 times higher than for the same age group in the national population (Health Canada, 2000). At least six times as many on-reserve, Status Indian children are in the care of the state as is the case in the national population.[3]

About 70% of all Canadians, but only about 55% of Indians living off reserve and only about 40% of Indians on reserve, have attained a high-school certificate. Only 30% of reserve students enrolled in Grade 12 are graduating high school (Gour, 2005). Less than 10% actually graduate from Grade 12 in 12 years (Breaker and Kawaguchi, 2002).

---

1 "Status Indians" or "Registered Indians" (the terms are synonymous) are those persons who are registered with Ottawa. This is a legal rather than an ethnic or identity concept, although the overlaps are very considerable. The legal differences are so material that important consequences flow from the definition.

2 About 28 per 100,000 compared to about 13 per 100,000. Among men between the ages of 15 and 24, the rates are 126 per 100 compared to 24 per 100,000; among young women, the rates are 35 per 100,000 compared to only 5 per 100,000 (Health Canada, 2003).

3 Farris-Manning and Zandstra, 2003. Almost 6% of on-reserve, Status Indian children are in care. Up to 40% of all Canadian children in care are Aboriginal.

Aboriginal youth are far more likely to offend, and this is reflected in an incarceration rate eight times higher than that of non-Aboriginal youth (Latimer et al., 2004; Clatworthy and Mendelson, 1999). The proportion of Aboriginal adults in the federal inmate population is also at least eight times greater than their proportion in the general population.[4] Aboriginals make up 65% of Vancouver street kids (Smith, Saewyc, Albert, MacKay, Northcott, and McCreary Centre Society, 2007).

The unemployment rate on reserves is almost four times the national rate, and one-and-a-half times the rate for Status Indians off reserve. The incidence of household low income is 40% for Status Indians but only 12.5% for others.[5] The median income of Indians on reserve is about two-thirds that of those off-reserve, and less than half that of non-Aboriginal Canadians (Treasury Board of Canada, 2005). On reserve, Status Indians depend on government transfers for a third of their income. Off reserve, Status Indians depend on government transfers for a fifth of their income. Other Canadians depend on government transfers for only 12% of their income. On reserve, the proportion of Indians who receive social assistance is about twice that amongst the general population.

The natural growth rate (that is, excluding immigration) of Status Indians is seven times higher than the Canadian rate.[6] About half of the Status population is under 25 years old, compared to a third of the Canadian population.[7] The aboriginal share of the total Canadian population is projected to increase to around 4% by 2017, from 3.4% in 2001. In Saskatchewan and Manitoba, the

4 Boe, 2002. According to Correctional Investigator of Canada, "the best estimate of the overall incarceration rate for Aboriginal People in Canada is 1,024 per 100,000 adults ... the comparable incarceration rate for non-Aboriginal persons is 117 per 100,000 adults" (Office of the Correctional Investigator of Canada, 2006: Aboriginal Offenders.

5 According to the 2001 Census. As to unemployment data, the figures are 27.7%, 7.2%, and 19.8% for reserve, mainstream, and off-reserve, respectively.

6 The Canadian natural growth rate is 0.3, according to Statistics Canada. The natural growth rate of Status Indians is 2.1 (Gour, 2005).

7 According to Canada, Indian and Northern Affairs Canada, 2006b. The median age of what Statistics Canada defines as the "North American Indian" population was 24 years in 2001, projected to 26.6 in 2017. Comparable figures for the total Canadian population are 37.1 and 41.3 years, respectively (Statistics Canada, 2005).

population share of 14% in 2001 is expected to rise to around 20% by 2017. About a quarter of the population in these two provinces aged under 14 is aboriginal; by 2017, around a third is expected to be (Statistics Canada, 2005). The population of Status Indians, however, is and will be lower. According to the 2006 Census, the number of Canadians claiming aboriginal identity was 1,1172,790 while the "Status Indian"[8] population was only 623,780, or about 53% of the larger number.

8 According to Statistics Canada, "the expression 'Registered Indian' refers to those persons who reported they were registered under the Indian Act of Canada. Treaty Indians are persons who are registered under the Indian Act and can prove descent from a band that signed a treaty. The Registered Indian counts … may differ from the administrative counts maintained by the Department of Indian Affairs and Northern Development, with the most important causes of these differences being the incompletely enumerated Indian reserves and Indian settlements as well as methodological and conceptual differences between the two sources." In fact, the difference may be material. Using data from Canada, Indian and Northern Affairs Canada (2006b), the author calculates that the administrative number may now be as large as 770,000. Moreover, in the 2006 census, 698,000 Canadians identified themselves as "North American Indian," So the cited percentage, although based on official numbers, is likely low.

NOTE

The population implosion? The recent rise and long-term projected decline of the Registered Indian population

The *McIvor* case is the latest development in the legislated and judicially determined rules for Registered Indian status(see page 32). It is under appeal with an unknown outcome. But even without that decision, the demographic impacts of C-31 were immense. What is not usually understood is that, while the new rules (which were essentially intended to implement gender neutrality, though *McIvor* questions the success of that) initially gave rise to a very significant increase in legally defined Indian population, C-31 will in the longer run lead to a very significant population decline. Here are some of the more striking conclusions in the standard study on this topic, *Re-assessing the Population Impacts of Bill C-31* (Clatworthy, 2001).

For the first 15 years the new rules under C-31 led to a population of about 175,000 greater than otherwise would have been the case. (It is important to understand that this population surge was as a result of law, not fertility.) Reinstatements accounted for about 106,000 and new births that otherwise would not have been registered, about 59,000. Significantly, about 70% of the surge was off Reserve, tilting the balance between town and Reserve, partially in terms of residence but also arguably in the importation into Status of a new, previously off-Reserve, cohort more influenced by the mainstream view.

Populations will build for about two generations (50 years) adding about 327,000 persons above the number to be expected under the old rules, and peaking at about 1.08 million. Growth on Reserve is expected for 65 years. The populations on and off Reserve are expected to peak at 811,000 and 317,000, respectively.

After about 2050, total population entitled to Registration peaks, gradually descending from 1.08 million to about 770,000 (more or less today's number) in 2100. During this time of course, Canada's total population will have grown tremendously. The political implications are obvious. The on-Reserve fraction of Registered Indians in 2100 would be much higher than today, at about 84%. This is among other things the result of higher "out-marriage" (that is, marriage to other than a Registered Indian) and lower fertility rates off Reserve.

After three generations (75 years) the number of non-Registerable descendents of today's Registered population would become a majority. A slight adjustment to the rules (some, but not all) of the sort sought by *McIvor* could add about 60,000 persons immediately and a further accretion of 126,000 over the first generation, at which time the impact of the change would dwindle.

Of course, such long-term forecasts as Clatworthy's are highly subject to variables, not just the usual demographic sort such as fertility and aging but the much-harder-to-predict cultural trends such as out-marriage, a central determinant of Registered populations. But, if they are close to accurate—and this is careful research—the questions raised are explosive.

The view of the Assembly of First Nations is clear:

> By 2010, nearly one in five First Nations children will no longer be eligible for status under the terms of the Indian Act ... in the eyes of the government they are no longer "Indians," even if they live a traditional life in their traditional community ... The federal government cannot and must not legislate the extinguishment of our citizens, whether based on gender, age, or the "wrong" lineage of First Nations ancestry. (Assembly of First Nations, June 28, 2005)

The language is inflammatory and nonsense. The government has not legislated the "extinguishment" of anyone. It simply sets the rules as to who is a legal Indian. But what one may predict with great confidence is that this will be a major political battle over the next few years, as it cuts to the very core of the power of the System.

The politics will be strange. Indians will be split—some seeing the danger of too many more faces at the same-sized table, while others—elites, the ones we will mostly hear from—will want to grow their flocks. If mainstream politicians react in the same way as they did to the immigration lobby over the past generation, the caps will come off. But at some point the mainstream voter will say, "enough!"

For this writer, the moral response is clear. Whenever the government has a chance, it should reduce the legal differences between Canadians, and certainly not cause such differences to grow. Governments should celebrate what we have in common and leave it to the individual to celebrate diversity, with neither penalty nor subsidy.

CHAPTER 1

Intent and context

This book begins with the widely shared view that the circumstances of Indians in Canada are unacceptable.[1] It will attempt to explain this situation in historic and contemporary terms, which explanation will in itself suggest useful changes in policy.

Though occasional excursions into fine points of law and policy will be unavoidable, this is not intended as a reference for academics. Its purpose is rather to assist the ordinary citizen in thinking about the greatest moral question today in Canadian public policy and to lay out in simple terms the questions we need to consider if we wish to demand improvements of our political representatives.

The words "simple terms" are not intended to suggest that the underlying reality is simple. This world is a very complex place with a deep and rich variety everywhere you look, best understood and lived and improved by those persons directly involved.

That is exactly the point: the impact of policy is highly site-specific and individual. Our Indian policy to date deals insufficiently with that point, as is inevitable with any approach directed mainly at the collective rather than those individuals trapped in that policy mesh. We have not simply failed to

---

1 For clarity and because of very significant differences in the legal environment, the discussion will focus mainly on Status Indians rather than the larger population of "aboriginal" persons as described in the section, "On language," at the end of this chapter. This is a very important distinction. Non-Indian aboriginals are far better off on the average and not burdened (or, in rare cases, advantaged) by the very different legal and financial circumstances of Indians. Only Indians are explicitly cursed by official policy.

help Indians help themselves, notwithstanding much time and money and good intentions. Far worse: we have proactively buttressed a pattern of perverse legal and financial incentives making self-help far more difficult than needs be. As a result, the gap as between the Indian median circumstances and those of the mainstream is not minor; it is scandalous.

The book will come to the conclusion that the cause is within our control and that therefore remedies are as well. Of course, causation has acted over generations and improvement will take time too. Human beings do not easily change their thinking. The essential remedy is added choice for individuals. Since the implications of this are revolutionary in the world view of current Indian policy, some considerable space will be devoted to what that means.

A major premise of this work is that Indians are ordinary human beings just like everyone else in Canada, not merely in the biological sense but in their hopes, fears, needs, incentives, and so on. Many might find the statement of such a premise redundant, almost a tautology, but in fact an examination from this point of view immediately lays bare many problems with current official Indian policy. In particular, such an examination must question the "parallel society" advocated by governments and many Indian elites.[2]

Current government policy maintains that Indians are such fundamentally different people from the rest of us that a separate society is required, though with very considerable interaction with the mainstream, as an unavoidably practical matter. A separate society will not be the advice of this study but the approach will be canvassed as an alternative that cannot be ignored since it is supported widely and in good faith. I will conclude that the option of a "parallel society" must be on genuine offer, failing which the "choice" I propose will be meaningless.

Supporting current Indian policy requires a departure from ideas that are deeply embedded in the foundation of Canada. In the rest of our social considerations, we are most insistent that variation along the common axes of diversity—ethnicity, gender, religion, cultural heritage, and so on—should have nothing to do with rights, freedoms, the treatment of persons by the state, or economic, social, or political organization. The view of this

2 Note that the idea of a "parallel society" is very different from the multicultural concept of a "cultural mosaic." In the latter case, the idea is that of preserving diversity in a single, united, and comprehensive whole; the former contemplates a separate society.

work is that Indians are entitled to, and should receive, the same consideration. Those supporting our current policy disagree.

Of course, at the cost of some tension and misunderstanding, two or more fundamentally different systems of social organization can be maintained in one state. Faith-based groups, such as the Hutterites of Canada or the Amish of the United States are smaller but obvious and durable examples. These are examples within stable, tolerant democracies but successful empires throughout history have also provided examples. The British, Roman, and Ottoman empires, for instance, allowed for sub-societies based on territorial boundaries, without at the same time ever allowing any question as to who had the last word. Sub-units within a dominant society based on culture or ethnicity rather than territory are also known, with a mixed record. The "overseas Chinese" and Jews around the world have maintained coherent social organizations, not without persecution however and almost always without explicit constitutional sanction. Black America and Hispanic America are clearly different from majority America, with the proviso that the dominant sentiment in each of these groups wants "in" rather than "out". Sometimes ethnic or cultural sub-units—Kurds in the Middle East, the Irish, the Palestinians—seem to want *separate* rather than *co-* existence. The myriad cultures of Russia, China, and South Asia can range from one end of this continuum to the other. There is no suggestion of particular similarities between these cases. The examples are simply to indicate that parallel societies, or aspirations thereto, are not uncommon, so we must consider the idea with respect.

To move in a useful way from beginning to end will require an analysis not just of where we are but of how we got here. Many problems in human relationship are "path dependent." To take two intractable issues of our time, Northern Ireland and Palestine, solutions have been severely constrained by historical baggage of conflict and suffering. In other words, history matters. It is impossible to dismiss the past. The challenge is to avoid becoming its prisoner. Many who would discuss Indian issues in the twenty-first century would prefer to look only to the future. That is convenient for the mainstream sides of the table. It theoretically makes the questions easier and more amenable to rational discourse and trade-offs. But any search for agreement must address the concerns of all sides of the table and that will necessarily summon up the past. This cannot be avoided, so considerable time will be spent on the topic.

The analysis will require a consideration of certain words, and how we use them for, in this field as many, words can be our servants or our masters.

A part will be devoted to that end. Philosophers have weighed in on these issues over the centuries, from Lockean ideas of land tenure and the fascination of Rousseauvian Europe with the "noble savage" to the latter day thinking of such as Cairns, Taylor, Kymlicka, Alfred, and others. As government policy makers tend to be dealers in second-hand ideas, we will have to look at some of these first-hand sources.

At the beginning, too, we should acknowledge that there is serious fault to be found today, not "back then." The traditional, comfortable myth is that, while terrible things were done, they were done in the past. In fact, the prime fault that must concern us lies not in the past, nor with bad people, nor with the victims of this story, the ordinary Indian people. Rather the fault lies directly with the mainstream society of today, which means most of the readers of this book. It lies in particular with the Indian System, a dense complex of talent and money that has evolved in part to advance the cause of ordinary Indians but now in addition has assumed major commercial importance.

The concept of "fault" is not meant to imply guilt, merely error. Guilt implies knowingly malign behavior or egregious failure to address problems or to exploit or oppress other human beings. While some of this surely exists, it is not within the target area of this study. I seek here rather to explore the unintended consequences of well-intentioned policies.

At this beginning too, I will state a guideline that the remedies to be proposed are not designed to be subtractive in any sense. There will be no challenges to Indian claims of rights and title, or arguments to change or dispense with any given way of life in any given place, nor any challenge to the financial implications thereof. These are all discussions that must be had because we live in a world of limited resources and the allocations of those resources among human beings with competing claims for health and education and economic security will always be a matter for discussion. But these are issues of politics. Our political system works reasonably well in most fields but in this area of policy it has failed us. To sort out why, we have to go beyond politics to philosophy, to find a better way of thinking about these things. That done and certain new principles added, we can again entrust the important decisions about resource allocation to the political system, where they belong.

In attempting to suggest a framework for thought about this issue, a statement of limitations and humility is essential. The author is not an Indian and I do not pretend to speak for Indians, any more than, not being a woman, I can speak for women. Though once a child I am now old and can no longer speak for children, except by way of fond memory. Some non-Indian scholars have so immersed themselves in this study that they can make some claim to "speak," though they are few. There are Indian writers who have had much to say and their number grows. All of these voices form a part of the puzzle and are entitled to a respectful hearing. I claim nothing more than that respectful hearing, my expertise limited to a considerable knowledge and study of Canadian politics, public policy, the "art of the possible," and an ability to sometimes see old questions from a different view.

This author explicitly recognizes that there are many roads to the top of the mountain and that he knows few of them. The expertise in solutions for individual groups or persons is distributed across the country. This book gives some advice on what to do but is mostly about how to think about the issues. But that is not nothing—indeed, it addresses a fundamental barrier to progress. Not only are there many roads to the top of the mountain, there is often lack of agreement on which mountain is the right one. And of course, some roads lead not to the top but over a precipice.

The differences as to the "right road" are real. While it is a very difficult question for our increasingly rights-focused society to contemplate, Indian collectives are not always in agreement with the Canadian mainstream on even such fundamental issues as gender and human rights, let alone the primacy of the individual. There is genuine and sincere debate.

The different views on rights are supported by constitutional law as well. It is often not well understood that the Charter of Rights and Freedoms contemplates this very question and provides (as per the descriptive note for Section 25): "Aboriginal rights and freedoms [are] not affected by Charter."[3] That is to say, Indian tradition and custom trumps the Charter for those individuals living under Indian governments. (The exception is s. 28, equality of gender, which applies equally to Indians.) In fact, law and the Constitution are driving forces in Indian society to an extent totally foreign (and surely

---

3 Section 25. The guarantee in this Charter of certain rights and freedoms shall not be construed so as to abrogate or derogate from any aboriginal, treaty or other rights or freedoms that pertain to the aboriginal peoples of Canada including

a) any rights or freedoms that have been recognized by the Royal Proclamation of October 7, 1763; and

b) any rights and freedoms that may now exist by way of land claims agreements or may be so acquired.

unacceptable) in mainstream society. For this reason, a section on the good and bad of Indian law will be an essential part of this review.

This book will deal but briefly with the usual remedies proposed by reformers: improved education, health, housing, and employment. Yes, they are essential parts of the answers but there is simply no point in another book adding to the literature about these things. Everyone agrees, and has for years. Funds have been appropriated in very significant amounts. This must continue. But progress has not been satisfactory. The real question is not about the money but about why the results have been so inadequate, even shocking?

One remedy will be canvassed at greater length. It is a standard claim that, if the mainstream society would get out of the way and provide the resources, Indian self-government will constitute the magic bullet to resolve problems. Questions of law ("the Inherent Right" to self-government), capacity, and of approach (that is, what sort of self-government) arise here. Because of serious insistence by Indian elites who have much to gain from "self-government" and serious resistance from the mainstream community (based on equality views of Canadian society) this issue has become an important bottleneck, arguably far more important than intrinsic merit would support. There may be a way around this impasse.

On language

Before beginning the main discourse, it is good to talk about words. We think with words. The cumulative wisdom of language generally informs and guides our thought but individual words can mislead. Consider for example how the phrase "two-tier medicine" has poisoned the health-care debate for years. The area of Indian policy is also burdened with such problems.

Indian and aboriginal

Begin with the word, "Indian." Historically it was a misnomer bestowed by the eventually dominant, newcomer Europeans on those inhabiting North America at time of contact. The quest those days was to find routes and ways to exploit the "Indies" and "Indian" stems from a major geographic misunderstanding. The label has been firmly cemented by centuries of usage and law.

From the beginning, the word was not used simply as a relatively neutral geographic or ethnic label, like, say "Greek" or "British." "Indians" were considered by the then Europeans to be not only indigenous but also inferior. While the particular connotations have changed over the years, the overall negative implication remains. Historically there has been an implication of difference in some basic human sense, a racist connotation similar in kind to the nineteenth-century American use of "Negro." For these reasons, the most basic word in the vocabulary for our study, "Indian," is in itself a reminder of another, less liberal time. It is also for now unavoidable, both because it is embedded in our basic law and Constitution and because alternate descriptors to be considered below have even greater defects. It is a measure of how far our Indian policy has drifted from propriety that we are caught in this linguistic trap.

"Indian" is also misleading in that the word covers such a wide variety of circumstance. The conditions and social outcomes for reserve and urban Indians are very different, even if many of the people concerned often move back and forth. As in most communities, there are rich and impoverished; there are the highly educated on the one hand and the illiterate on the other, and so on. Nonetheless, the word "Indian" has a definable core content grounded in law, identity, culture, and inheritance and the three other most commonly used words are enemies of clear thought.

"Aboriginal" is often used as a less offensive euphemism for "Indian." This is understandable—we Canadians do not like to offend. I would argue, however, on that score that reform is apt to come sooner if the words we use necessarily confront us with the problems we would rather overlook. "Aboriginal" is also a much more inclusive term intended to cover Inuit,[4] Métis, and vaguely defined others as well. Moreover, the census definition of "aboriginal" is based on self-identification. For the census, you are an aboriginal if you say you are and by this definition there are 1,172,790 "aboriginals" in Canada. The legal and material circumstances of these groups can vary so immensely that the word should be used with great care.

As a political reality for non-Indian aboriginals seeking the benefits of Indians (land, hunting rights, social services), there is a great value in

4 Legally "Indians" for constitutional purposes but never included in the Reserve system prevalent in the South. The settlements were so small and remote and the land so barren that no further isolation was thought required. Though the arguments of this paper generally apply, the Inuit of northern Canada have their own special problems and opportunities in addition. The "opportunities" include a quasi-provincial government controlled by Inuit, which after 15 years does not seem to have improved education or employment or diminished suicide rates.

blurring the distinction. An understandable goal of those concerned with Métis claims is to attempt to bootstrap entitlements by comparison and association with the entitlements of Indians. While understandable, it does not assist clear thought because Status Indians have rights that are importantly different from those of Métis.

Culture and identity

It is perhaps worth an excursion at this point to distinguish between "culture" and "identity" in describing groups. The descendents of North American aboriginals present at contact have in fact been deeply shaped by the technological, industrial, consumer, and cultural evolution of North America. Television, the automobile or skidoo, junk food, and many other elements of our civilization including above all the language (mostly English but some French) cannot be denied. Scholars may differ as to the cultural overlap between mainstream Canadians and most southern "aboriginals" however defined, but surely it exceeds 90% and is much higher than the cultural commonality of a new immigrant from Vietnam or Honduras. So cultural differences may erode. This has no necessary connection with "identity." "Identity" is who you think you are and such views may be very firmly held even in the absence of major cultural differences.

It is very important to understand why the words "Indian" and "aboriginal" should not be used interchangeably or as synonyms as it too often done. The only people with a significant and different bundle of legal and financial rights based on race in Canada are Indians. Non-Indian aboriginals do not have the land title and legal rights of Indians (except for some minor and difficult-to-establish hunting rights). Non-Indian aboriginals do not enjoy the special access to medical, educational, and other social services of Indians. Non-Indian aboriginals are not treated as collectives at law, nor is the state support for a "parallel society" concept seriously applied to them. These are immense differences.

The conflation and confusion inherent in the commonly used word "aboriginal" is useful to some Indian leaders as it causes the mainstream society to believe that Indians constitute a much larger fraction of the population of Canada than is really the case, the real number being a bit over 2%. (Equally there are incentives for leaders to inflate the number of persons on reserve as, for many programs, cash follows head counts.) And the conflation and confusion is useful to the non-Indian aboriginal leadership because it assists them in their constant efforts to gain the legal entitlements of Indian status. But the confusion and conflation is not helpful to the sincere analysis of public policy and the word will be used here only when talking of identity or constitutional aboriginals or when common usage has established a new meaning. (For example, "aboriginal rights" stem from the rights of aboriginals in Canada at contact, all of whom were what the Constitution calls "Indians" today.)

It is interesting how the word "Indian" is increasingly avoided by the mainstream. A fine example is available on the web site of Indian and Northern Affairs Canada (INAC). In the comprehensive alphabetical index, there are only five topic areas beginning with the word "Indian" but 17 beginning with the word "aboriginal." Even this does not begin to describe the actual usage. "First Nation" (see below) has only four index entries but in actual parlance and the recent literature, "Indian" is avoided like the plague and "aboriginal" and "First Nation" are widely used, the former often improperly.

"Native" is another much-employed, but ill-defined, euphemism. All persons born in a place or even long-time residents are "natives" in the ordinary sense of the language. The same problem applies to the word "indigenous," as in "indigenous peoples." We are all from somewhere and all of us ultimately must trace our ancestors back to the same small group of *homo sapiens* that began to migrate out of central Africa. Aside from the important issue of vested historical and communal property rights (to be dealt with extensively later), a Scottish family that arrived in Ontario four generations ago is surely as "indigenous" as an Indian family that arrived in British Columbia hundreds of generations ago.

The law of Canada is very explicit on this point. The full benefits of citizenship, without any distinction whatsoever, are available to all citizens however or whenever that status may have been acquired. The idea implicit in "indigenous"[5] is a direct challenge to that concept, which, if entertained, needs use-specific justification.

"First Nations" is an increasingly common descriptor and has its positional usefulness. "First" has strong connotations of primacy, claim, and legitimacy. "Nation" has in ordinary language the connotations of permanence, viability, credibility, and sovereignty. Successfully putting the two together as a label for a group of people achieves a commanding height of language. It is true that the use of "nation" in this context is valid in the dictionary's sense of a cultural group: the "Kurdish nation" is an example, a far larger and stronger community than any Canadian Indian tribe by an order of magnitude. But this is a secondary use in English, though it is certainly

5 Particularly as used by the United Nations; see Chapter 4 *re* the Declaration.

true that North American tribes have referred to themselves as "nations" for centuries, in common with colonial bureaucrats.

It is my guess that, when most Canadians hear or read the word "nation," their minds import the primary, ordinary meaning described above. One recalls the rather angry debate as to whether Quebec should be called a "nation" or not, for exactly that reason. (Of course, at that time the reason for the extraordinary concern was the fear of validating the separatist cause by using a word with implications of sovereignty.) The confusion is exacerbated by the increasingly common application of the phrase to individuals, not just a group. We see descriptions like, "... a First Nation ..." did such and such, referring to a person.

There is disagreement on how many Indian "nations" there are in Canada. Even if the number is set as low as the estimate of 60 by the Royal Commission on Aboriginal Peoples (RCAP) (based on mostly long-gone patterns of language use), the population of the average "nation" would be only 11,000. Such a population base is much smaller than that required for the primary meaning of the word "nation," suggested above as permanent, viable, credible, and sovereign international entities.

"First Nation" helps with white guilt and veils ongoing questions. To understand the impact of words, try this experiment: in every government (federal, provincial, or Indian) statement, replace the words "First Nation" with the word, "Indian." Many people would find this usage grinding, grating, even offensive. This is because "First Nation" allows us mentally to avoid what is really happening here: people are being distinguished on the basis of a particular kind of exclusion, in this case closely correlated with inheritance and the Constitution.

This book will not use "First Nation" except where the phrase appears in a quotation or legal title. Of course, people are entitled to use whatever words they can convince others to accept but in this case there is another legal word that serves a partly similar purpose, namely "Band," This is a concept inhering in the Indian Act that contaminates it from the outset but at least it has a clear meaning. However the word "Band," while being set out in law, has its problems as well. The creation of Bands by Ottawa was arbitrary and often unjustly divided historic groups and always ended up in severely delimiting the territory of Band members. It is a difficult word with some bad history. A more useful and neutral word that will be used from time to time is "tribe." More employed in the United States, this concept is broader than "Band" and more closely approximates the idea sought in the secondary meaning of "nation," but without the confusing accompanying baggage.

There is a mirror image of "First Nation" that many academics like to use for non-Indians, that is, the rest of us. That would be "settler society." The implied connotations of late arrival and colonialism are obvious. These words too are not helpful. Indeed, today's Indians are themselves descendents of an earlier "settler society." It is better not to use words that imply guilt or raise hackles, unless that is the intent. "Settler society" will not be used here, except in reference to the distant past. "Mainstream" will be the word for Canadian society generally.

There is a further and even more important reason for this suggested usage. Canadian society over the past two generations has been changed almost beyond recognition by a new wave of Asian immigration. The idea behind "settler society" relates to the descendants of the Caucasians who came from Europe. That group is now but a part of the face of Canada, and in the main cities that drive our culture and politics, that group will soon be a minority. "Settler society" loses its meaning in such circumstances. Our two main words—"Indian" and "mainstream"—both have their defects but, since we have to use words, these two are the most neutral and precise available.

Race

The expressions "race" and "race-based" may sometimes be employed in discussing Indian policy but this is not good practice as "race," as used in ordinary parlance, is frequently a "hot button" that riles the emotions. In part this is because of the unhappy experiences with race in North American history, in part because of residual prejudice (though this is sometimes over-stressed for debating purposes), and in part because discrimination on the basis of race is forbidden in both our legal and moral concepts of human rights.

It is also true that who is an "Indian" for the purposes of the big book in Ottawa may have nothing to do with ancestry. In the past, white women became "Indian" by marriage whereas full-blooded Indian women lost that legal status upon marrying a white man. Today's law is less blatant but no less confused, and will be described later. As a contemporary development, a judgment issued in the BC Supreme Court as at this writing would add hundreds of thousands of Canadians to the "Indian" status in law.[6] This judgment has been appealed but gives further illustration of the dangers of putting too much stock in "race" if the definition of "Indian" in law is so arbitrary as to be hugely changeable by the courts or Parliament.

6 *McIvor v. The Registrar, Indian and Northern Affairs Canada*, 2007 BCSC 827. See The McIvor decision, page 30, for a full description.

However, it is true that major elements of Indian policy are "race-based" in concept. The *Indian Act* itself is exactly such a case, as is s. 91(24) of our Constitution. I cite the comments of Justice Ian Binnie of the Supreme Court of Canada (SCC) in the hearing of *R. v. Kapp* when he said: "Because the Constitution contemplates race based legislation, 91, [sic], and I mean the *Indian Act* is race based legislation and there are benefits and there are burdens and there are exclusions"; and then later of s. 91(24) in particular: "But it is by definition race based authorization. That's all it is" (*R. v. Kapp*, SCC 31603, Dec. 11. 2007: transcript). In concurring with the eventual judgment in that case Bastarche, J. said of the burden on non-aboriginal fishermen: "It is also clear that the disadvantage is related to racial differences" (*R. v. Kapp*, 2008 SCC 41). The discrimination against (and occasionally in favor of) Indians under 91(24) may or may not have been "race based" at the time, in our current context. In 1867, writers often spoke of the "English race," for example. The word appears to have acquired a harder edge since that time and, in my opinion, is usually best avoided as unclear and inflammatory.

In any event, not all of the matters touching Indians that are controversial in the newspapers can be properly thus categorized, even if the meaning of the word, "race" were clear. In particular, so-called race-based entitlements (or oppressions) should not be confused with inherited entitlements. As a major example, it is normal in our society that owned property is heritable and often—even usually—conveyed to descendents. There is nothing "racial" about this. It is simply a question of one's forbearers, of whatever race.

Note that "aboriginal title" (which really means *Indian* title as no other aboriginals have it) is a special issue in British Columbia. It is only now being defined as a result of inaction over 150 years and is huge in importance; but it is not a racial matter. The courts have been quite clear that there always was a collective, common-law right to title in the lands of British Columbia by the historic aboriginal occupants and no party to any litigation has made any serious objection to this. The only debate has been over whether that aboriginal common-law title was extinguished by valid government action, and the courts have found that not to be the case so that aboriginal title—within boundaries largely yet to be defined—exists in British Columbia and is not race related.[7]

7 A potentially explosive issue that has never been tested and probably never will be in Canada is whether the doctrine of conquest could be made to apply. In international law, conquest is conclusive in transferring both sovereignty and title as well, insofar as the conqueror may wish to do that. The US Supreme

The same may be said for other heritable rights such as the taking of wildlife under certain circumstances. Again, these rights are private property (and in this case, as with land, collective property as well). Some people may feel that it is "not right" that some other people should, by inheritance, have special privileges over what is otherwise public property but that fact is a matter of law, not race, and no different in principle than wealthy persons owning salmon streams in the Maritime provinces or old Crown grants that conveyed title to subsurface mineralization, now normally a public asset.

On the other hand, policy-based entitlements such as the "Aboriginal Fishing Strategy," the commercial sales program for some Indian salmon fishermen in British Columbia litigated under Kapp (*R. v. Kapp*, 2008), was clearly set up by the federal government as a matter of policy rather than inherited entitlement.[8]

There are other special privileges that are also inherited and that have become "property" by way of treaties. That applies, of course, to treaty lands but also to specific entitlements to tools or clothing or small cash payments. More controversial is the gray area of such things as special health or educational entitlements for Status Indians, and here there is a genuine disagreement between Indian leaders and the Crown. The Crown maintains that many of these entitlements are a matter of policy and voluntary Crown action, rather than treaty entitlements. But, as noted above with respect to the Aboriginal Fishing Strategy, to the extent they are mere policy they can properly be called discrimination for or against Indians, rather than inherited rights.

Court came to that conclusion in finding tribes to be "domestic dependent nations" pursuant to conquest. Most Indian spokespersons in Canada insist their ancestors were never conquered and no government has been prepared to argue that a century of complete subjugation amounts to the same thing. The British Columbia government came close in claiming that title was extinguished by way of colonial land ordinance. This was accepted by the trial judge in *Delgamuukw*, who found title to have been extinguished "by necessary implication" of Colonial Land Ordinances. That argument was over-ruled by the BC Court of Appeal and dropped by a new British Columbian government when it took the case to the Supreme Court of Canada.

8 There is an inherited entitlement to salmon (see R. v. *Sparrow (1990)*, S.C.R. 1075) but that is non-commercial and limited to fish for food, social, and ceremonial purposes.

It is a debate. Does a treaty entitlement to a "medicine chest"[9] translate to a modern-day entitlement that goes beyond ordinary Medicare? The answer has linguistic consequences. If the entitlement is a mere policy, it is surely discriminatory in concept because it is accessible only to "Status Indians," a term that for all the confusion retains at its core a strong correlation with the "race" of 1867. But if the entitlement flows from a treaty or the common law, it is inherited property.

This may seem too much emphasis on mere words but the symbolism is important. Many people see core health-care services as central to our definition of what it means to be a Canadian and differential entitlements based on mere policy are potentially destructive to Alan Cairns' notion (see Chapter 4) of necessary shared citizenship. It is a messy business, as indeed the entire debate about Indian policy will be until Indians are considered to be ordinary people under the law. ("Ordinary people" of course have every right to heritable entitlements but not to the "race-based" kind.)

Traditional territory

Another phrase to be watched with care is "traditional territory," referring to the claimed range of use (including hunting) or occupancy by aboriginals at contact. The problem is not in this neutral description: all of habitable Canada can be fairly described as "traditional territory" in this sense. Rather the problem lies in current usage by white politicians, especially in British Columbia and other non-treaty parts of Canada. When claims are not settled, all of the "traditional territory" is the usual opening position of the Indian side of the table. That would be any sensible negotiator's demand, sitting in that chair.

I speak rather of the other side of the table. Politicians making speeches in the ballroom of the Hotel Vancouver who open by giving thanks for "being in the traditional territory of the Coast Salish Nations" (for example) may thereby be raising unrealistic expectations among the seekers of current rights to land, but using cheap words rather than ceding hard title. It is a very direct implication of existing entitlement and another example of the dangerous tendency of politicians in this and other areas to buy temporary peace with fine words. If politicians are going to use this phrase, the meaning should be specified as defined powers in defined areas. Anything else misleads to confusion.

---

9 Inserted in one treaty only.

Indian Industry

I should make reference to one phrase that is coming into common usage, which I will not employ because it has unhelpful negative connotations. That phrase is "Indian Industry." I agree that no disrespect need be intended by the words. One could equally speak of an "education industry" or a "health industry." The effect and the intent of the description is to bring a set of preoccupations that are held out as noble in nature into the more factual perspective of the self-interest of the individuals concerned. One of the greatest insights of Public Choice theory[10] is that, in politics just as in commercial enterprise, the self-interest of practitioners is of great importance in the decisions they make. That does not mean the decisions are wrong. It does mean they are subject to examination under the wise investigator's rule of *cui bono*—"who benefits?"—from any given approach.

That said, there is no doubt that the connotation of "Industry" is negative, in the sense of ascribing a predominantly commercial purpose to what is a very mixed set of motives and activities. I prefer and will use the words "Indian System" to describe that huge complex of persons, practitioners, and policies that is built around the singling out of Indians in our Constitution and all that flows therefrom.

I have been unable to come up with any good estimate of the size of the System. It is certainly large, in the tens of thousands of actors. This number excludes ordinary Status Indians themselves, who for the System are the *raison d'être* and targets of its policy. Rather the System includes all Indian politicians, their lawyers and other advisors, the federal and provincial bureaucracies engaged, the related ties of the courts and lawyers and consultants to government and business in the field, and others whose primary income or status stems from the fact of the inclusion in the Constitution of s. 91(24) (1867) and ss. 25 and 35 (1982).

A glimpse of the top of the iceberg may be seen in *A Guide to Aboriginal Organizations and Services in British Columbia* 2007/2008 (British Columbia, Ministry of Aboriginal Relations and Reconciliation, 2007. The are 115 pages of detail with well over 1000 organizations listed. The involved personnel would clearly number into the many thousands. This is a very big business. There is even at least one clipping journal serving the System, an invaluable

10 The foundational work is *The Calculus of Consent; Logical Foundations of Constitutional Democracy* (Buchanan and Tullock, 1962). A more recent work for lay readers is *Beyond Politics: Markets, Welfare and the Failure of Bureaucracy* (Mitchell and Simons, 1994).

reference. The *BC Media Monitor: First Nations Edition* (Cornerstone Planning Group, serial) is a twice-monthly publication with around 50 BC news items in each issue.

There is no reason to believe that the practitioners in this industry are any better or worse people than those found in any other. The point is, every industry has its unique incentives and self-interests that tend to be followed. The numbers are large. Federal expenditures exceed $10 billion annually. All tribes plus provincial governments and large businesses have their own legal, administrative, and program departments. To this must be added the large costs of consultation and negotiation.

These numbers are not cited as criticisms. As to the annual federal expenditures, Indians like other citizens receive health benefits, education, and welfare and these are always big numbers. As to the cost of treaties, they are "forever" documents and have to be done right. The point is simply that the "Industry" is a large one and, like all such economic clusters, has its own internal drivers.

Parallel society

At various points in this book, I will use the phrase "parallel society." Indeed, one of my conclusions will be that the mainstream has created for itself a moral obligation to hold out at least a variation of this concept to Status Indians as a genuine life choice. In Chapter 3, I define the concept and characteristics of a viable parallel society at some length. For now, it is sufficient to understand the idea as an autonomous, self-governing set of entities within the Canadian nation, self-defined as to membership (but based upon an idea of "Indianness" or "aboriginality") and with a land base, financial resources, and institutions adequate to support an on-going an identity and lifestyle for its citizens that is different from the mainstream. The Assembly of First Nations sometimes uses the words "Third Order of Government" for the institutional component. The idea is the core recommendation of the Royal omission on Aboriginal Peoples.

Given political, financial and demographic realities, it is clear that any such parallel society would have to be interdependent with the mainstream but the emphasis is on independence. It is clear that there are other major difficulties here, not only with philosophical ideas of citizenship and the views most Canadians hold about equality, but also with the extremely powerful cultural influences of the modern world. But "parallel society" remains a good descriptor of the aspirational goals of many Indian leaders and academics.

Inherent right

To round out this short lexicon attention should be drawn to the words "inherent right." This is the System's nomenclature for the idea of an inherited and never-ceded national sovereignty said to lodge in Indian communities, yielding an "inherent right to self-government."

While it is implicit in Western ideas of freedom that we all have an "inherent right" at an individual level to govern ourselves, the System's claim is less obvious. We will return to this debate in Chapter 4. It turns upon questions about the "rights" of a collective, as distinct from an individual, and is only a claim, not a proven entitlement. For now, one is advised to treat the phrase with an open mind and also to consider that findings of the Supreme Court of Canada in this area have been overall very sceptical and narrowly cast.

NOTE

The *McIvor* decision

The *McIvor* decision is having a significant impact on demographics. At the same time, the case deserves highlighting because of the strong case illustrations it gives to other realities of Indian policy making.

The full name of the case is 2007 BCSC 827 *McIvor v. The Registrar, Indian and Northern Affairs Canada*, Madam Justice Ross presiding. On the surface, it is a specific case seeking a declaration of gender equality in Indian law but in fact it tells us much more. The plaintiffs, Sharon Donna McIvor and her son, Charles Jacob Grismer claimed that aspects of An Act to Amend the Indian Act, 1985, were unconstitutional. The Act is generally referred to by its House of Commons name, Bill C-31. The alleged unconstitutionality was differential treatment applied to the transmission of Indian status through the male and female hereditary lines. The arguments are extremely technical. In the end, the judge agreed with the plaintiffs and the case has been appealed, presumably because of its huge importance. The decision, if upheld, could add between 25,000 and 700,000 persons to the Indian Register.[1] Many—perhaps most—would not have Band membership.

Those are the bare facts. The principles are even more important. The first thing to be noted is that the lives of Indians are hugely governed by law, to a degree that would surely be unacceptable in the mainstream. This case shows that fact at its most basic, asking, "Exactly who is an Indian?" The answer to that question, immaterial to most of us, is absolutely central to the lives of hundreds of thousands of people.

The second point to be noted is that a very considerable number of people who have some Indian ancestry but are not Status Indians would like to become so. Outsiders might be surprised, given the statistics cited about the life outcomes of average Indians, but that is an inadequate perspective. The aspiring Indians wish to improve their lives. The reasons vary from personally

1 This extraordinarily broad range was put forward by the Crown at trial, depending upon how much of what the Plaintiffs are seeking might finally be awarded by the Court. Unattributed media speculation has been in the 200,000 range.

very important cultural intangibles to the very concrete realities of access to enhanced health plans and secondary education, plus in many cases, tax exemptions, the right to live on Reserves, and the social status conferred within an Indian community.

The case takes us through history, reminding us that discrimination against females was once the custom in the settler society: witness the aphorism of the famous eighteenth-century British legal expert, William Blackstone: "Husband and wife are one person and the husband is that one." The record is more mixed in Indian history but, in any event, mainstream law until 1985 clearly discriminated against Indian women. C-31 was an attempt to remedy that condition and was years in the making, finally introduced by Minster David Crombie.

The Minister's purpose was threefold. The Bill was to end gender discrimination. It was to restore status to those who had lost it as a result of discriminatory provisions. And very importantly, it was to move the power to decide who is or is not a member of a Band (and therefore in theory entitled to the benefits of Band property and assets) away from Ottawa and to the individual Bands. The amendments were controversial. The considerable expansion of the number of persons with Indian status was seen by some Bands as a threatened dilution of their property rights if new members were to be admitted. The change in the status of women was controversial in some areas and even some Indians who supported it felt that the change in law should not be imposed upon the tribes. But according to Minister Crombie it was the very best package that could be done in the circumstances and the Bill become law. However, according to the decision of Judge Ross, certain discrimination continued, was incompatible with the Charter (Constitution Act, 1982) and was therefore struck down and the aggrieved persons are entitled to status.

For the future it is important to note, as does the judge at paragraph 261, that "[i]t is not contested that the regime for registration in its application going forward is a gender-neutral scheme." Rather, it applies only to persons born before 1985. Thus, the long-term forecasts of the gradual disappearance of legal Indians absent legislative change presumably remain valid, but will have to be modified as to timetable if the current surge in the number of legal Indians is sustained on appeal.

In addition, the possibility of many thousands of new legal Indians with no even theoretical territorial attachment is something that has never been considered. Among other things, it would give the System a serious challenge as to how to claim to speak for persons not affiliated with any Indian government, when of course the System is based on territory and Indian government. More thought will have to be given to this matter.

CHAPTER 2

History and law

Most people feel their history more than they know it. Details are apt to be sketchy and often closer to grand myth than plain fact. Felt history tends to be highly selective, malleable, and manipulable. All this said, what people believe their history to be is of importance in their lives, both personal and political. This is true of everyone, everywhere.

For people on a successful, forward-looking life path, history matters less. And naturally, for those for whom the future is less encouraging, more attention may be paid to history and the past. Persons or groups experiencing failure or even unsatisfactory results in current circumstances often seek the reason in past grievances. A culture of victimhood is far easier to live with than explanations that rest on inadequacy or even bad fortune. When history builds on success and sets up a virtuous circle, it inspires confidence for tomorrow. But a history of misery can set up a vicious circle where failure is used to confidently predict more of the same.

The point of these observations is that, if we wish to understand others and gain their respect in return, parties to such a relationship must pay full attention to the things that others feel important. The same obligation rests on everyone, which tends to unavoidably expand the scope of dialogue. Not only is this approach necessary; it should be welcomed as a means to deepen eventual agreements or better inform disagreements.

In this chapter, we begin with a recital of history and law, from the view of an outsider. Any history is necessarily selective and generalizations as to the overarching meanings are those of the author. Others will have different views but what follows is an attempt in good faith at objectivity, realizing that the many diverse facets of history may be seen differently by others.

For the reader who wishes to pursue historical detail, there is a rich literature. Only a very broad outline is required for our purposes here. For an academic expert's short history of Indian events in British Columbia, a previously unpublished cumulative account to 2008 by Prof. Paul Tennant of the University of British Columbia offers another perspective for British Columbia (see The Indian Land Question in British Columbia, p. 237).

When European adventurers began their incursions into North America some 500 years ago, they found the continent to be already occupied. Indeed, it is reasonable to suspect that it was fully populated on a sustaining basis, given the local technology and infrastructure of the time. Certainly indigenous people were to be found from the Arctic Ocean to the Caribbean and beyond, organized into many small governments (often with larger links and alliances) and economies, mostly but by no means entirely societies of hunters and gatherers.

The British, French, and Spanish were the most active Europeans in North America; for our purposes, Britain is the only important player. Spanish influence was mostly well south of Canada[1] and French influence ended with the signing of the Treaty of Paris in 1763. That document marks the high-water mark of the rule of Britain over almost all of North America contacted by that time. Only two decades later, that country was to lose its far richer colonies lying to the south of Canada, by revolution.

The year 1763 was important as well for the issuance of the Royal Proclamation of that year, pursuant to the peace signed at Paris and, more directly, to Pontiac's Rebellion later that year led by former allies of the French (relevant sections are reproduced in The Royal Proclamation of 1763, p. 76). This is an act of great importance in Indian law and policy and is worth study for what it tells us of the times and of Imperial thinking. The intent was to shut down further expansion westward from the Thirteen Colonies into Indian Country and to allow a breathing space for the further development of settlement policy. But it also formalized a well-established practice, namely the treating with Indians on a nation-to-nation basis.

The British military establishment was always small compared to the Empire's far-flung acquisitions and possessions, and supply lines were long. It just made good sense to establish peaceful arrangements with indigenous peoples where possible, and even military alliances if (as with the French and Spanish in North America) imperial conflicts were playing out in the local

---

1 With the exception of Vancouver Island and the introduction of the horse to the Americas.

area. Such a diplomatic and official relationship was necessarily nation to nation. The Proclamation made clear that this type of relationship was also to extend beyond military matters, to the alienation of land title and territory, with individuals excluded from the process on both sides. The purpose was entirely pragmatic. Official relationships were not to be undermined or influenced by the actions of individuals pursuing their own interests.

The status and seizure of Indian lands had been much debated in Europe. The doctrine of *terra nullis* held that unoccupied lands were free for the taking. The difficulty was that occupancy of the continent (albeit light and often nomadic) was an obvious contrary fact that on moral grounds would preclude simple taking. The British philosopher John Locke developed a theory that the ownership of land could not arise from mere occasional use but rather required the input of labor, claim, and continuous use and occupancy (Arneil, 1996). This view was convenient to European ends but the British did not fully act on that theory for practical reasons. Some of the land obviously was occupied, by numerous tribes that could choose to cooperate or resist.

Moreover, in the earlier times deals could often be made by private persons with Indian individuals or small groups to give some color of legitimacy to land takings, perhaps without the general assent or even knowledge of the tribes concerned. Thus as the Proclamation noted, "great Frauds and Abuses ... to the great Prejudices of our Interests" had resulted. Of course, the Proclamation law in what was to become the United States was only temporary, soon swept away by the American Revolution and the later Indian Wars. (Even in the United States, during the early nineteenth-century the Proclamation remained influential in the Indian jurisprudence of US Supreme Court.)

This much must be underlined: the Proclamation was a clear acknowledgement of some sort of Indian "burden on title" (as the courts were later to describe it). International law was clear that good and full title could be achieved by conquest but that was not the general British practice in North America. They sought agreement.

In Canada, the imperial writ held as policy even after the American Revolution and was put into practice even in areas (such as British Columbia, at least initially) not covered by the Proclamation. Lands were to be acquired on the bases of treaty and cession.[2] If the "burden on title" argument is

2 British Columbia was an important exception to the role of the Proclamation, not lying within the described boundaries. After the few, small "Douglas

important, there is an even more essential point in all of the above. It became firmly established in the law of Canada that dealings with Indians were not to be individual. Indians were to be treated with only as a part of a collective.

The founding doctrines

Thus two patterns of behavior adopted for practical reasons: first, nation to nation and, second, collective rather than individual treatment of Indians became the principles that remain the bedrock of policy today, having in the 250 succeeding years been reviewed only once, in the rejected white paper of Pierre Trudeau (Canada, 1969). Indians in Canada were not to be seen primarily as individuals, in contrast to all other human beings in the developing tradition of the Enlightenment. The importance of this for all that follows, for everyone, cannot be over-estimated.

The other bedrock principle of Indian policy was to be established in the aftermath of the War of 1812. While the Treaty of Oregon was not to set the southern borders of British Columbia for another 34 years, the frontier between eastern United States and Canada was essentially peaceable and secure. The military usefulness of the Indians to the British was at an end. Their nuisance factor remained, namely Indian occupancy (even if sparse, but often on choice lands) as an impediment to colonization.

The means of resolving this problem was to gather Indians on to small parcels of land and keep and isolate them there. Often (but by no means always, exceptions being most of the Atlantic, much of Quebec, and most of British Columbia) this was done by means of formal written Treaties leading to the creation of Reserves and certain other entitlements. The idea essentially was to get the Indians off most of the land to open it up for others.[3]

Treaties" local policy changed and lands were simply taken. In the then-separate colony on the mainland of British Columbia where Douglas was also Governor for a time, events were overtaken by the Gold Rush. All of this gave rise to the BC Land Question, still being worked out today.

3 The fact that much of the country is not covered by settlement treaties is of great importance. Claims to remedy this are of course most advanced in British Columbia but eastern Canada should not be ignored. The Marshall-Bernard case (*R. v. Marshall*; *R. v. Bernard* [2005]) that applies will be mentioned later but, as a

The popular characterization of Indian policy thenceforth is that of "assimilation" but that is rather less than half a truth. It is true that the law provided for the acquisition of full citizenship by those Indians who (in effect) renounced their people and their past by way of so-called "enfranchisement" and it is also true that the educational and socialization policies of the Department of Indian Affairs were designed to "civilize" Indians. Many of these programs were so insensitive, even brutal, that the concept of "assimilation" gained a very bad name in Canada at the same time the superficially similar idea of the "melting pot" was becoming received wisdom in the United States. In any event, the actual operational policy was not assimilation. It was isolation.[4] Out of sight, out of mind, out of the way, Indians ceased to be a barrier or even a factor to the fullest exploitation of Canadian territory by others.

Like the collective idea, isolation was also tackled in the failed white paper (Canada, 1969). The two ideas survived that process and, as we shall

---

general view of interest, I pass on the comment of a former very senior federal official with direct responsibilities in this area who wrote to me as follows.

> The question of eastern Canadian treaties and extinguishment deserves some attention. The famous Micmac Treaties of 1725 and 1752, as examples, are often cited by whites as evidence of surrender and extinguishment, whereas they are in fact and form typical 18th-century treaties of navigation and commerce, such as were commonly used among European countries at the end of one or another of their interminable wars. Nobody ceded anything—they just agreed that they would go back to the norms of ordinary commerce. I fearlessly predict that one day the Micmacs will take these to court, arguing that aboriginal title still exists in full and undiluted form, and that the treaties were merely armistice agreements between militarily similar groups—and that the Supremes will agree, thereby tossing all of the land titles in the Maritimes into the air. In Quebec, or at least the southern portions of the province that were actually settled, the legal theory is that aboriginal title was extinguished by the King of France before 1759, so there is nothing more to be discussed. Best of luck …

4 Some argue that isolation was in fact an intended way-station en route to assimilation, keeping Indians free of corrupt white influences while attempts were made to Christianize and "civilize" them prior to full integration into the wider society. Whatever the rationale, isolation and the freeing of land for development was the result.

see, have since been continued and re-invented, this time, strangely, as intended worthy goals, in the concept of the "parallel society."

It is very difficult for those of us in comfortable, growing, urban Canada today to imagine the historic despair of a shrinking, locked up, and oppressed people, away from opportunity, numbers dwindling, often dramatically through disease. But we should imagine it as well as we can and then consider that there is such a thing as collective memory passed on between generations, which persists in considerable vitality to this day.

Hived off in small communities, mostly remote, Indians largely disappear from the history of Canada until the 1960s and, indeed, were at one time on their way to disappearing from history through depopulation. Of course, there were events that caught the public attention: the two Riel Rebellions had close Indian connections, for example. There were occasional uprisings in British Columbia as well,[5] but mostly things were quiet, to the outside world.

A watershed moment

The Canadian colonies formed their union in 1867, in the twin shadows of the British Empire and the American Civil War. As a federal state, the new country required a constitution to delineate the responsibilities of the federal and provincial governments. The central government was to inherit the great responsibilities of the Colonial Office and the provinces were to acquire mere local matters. Recall that the relationship with Indians had always been nation to nation, of a quasi-diplomatic and military nature. No one thought much of Indians at all by 1867. It was natural to relegate such former colonial responsibilities as might be entailed to the central power and thus there was added to Section 91 (enumerating the jurisdiction of the central government in Ottawa) the seven fateful words of s. 91(24): "Indians and lands reserved for the Indians."

It was a watershed moment. There would be no discussion today of matters Indian in Canada were it not for Section 91(24) of the constitution. Millions of otherwise ordinary Canadians over the years have been made to pay dearly for that bit of what we would today call racism inserted by the Framers.

But people must be judged according to their times and, at the time of Confederation, the general thought was that local governments or

5 See the appendix, "The Indian land question in British Columbia," p. 237.

commercial interests were much more likely to exploit the native peoples of North America than would be a distant imperial administration with loftier principles and larger goals. That was the spirit behind the Royal Proclamation of 1763 and it was carried over into the Canadian federation by assigning Indian interests to the Crown federal. Serious debate as to whether the continued singling out of Indians should have been considered at all would have been a good thing but did not fit the times.

Whatever the reasons, the dreadful words were there. As a thought experiment, suppose they had been omitted? Try to imagine the world today. We have changed a great deal since 1867. The British and Canadian societies of that date, while by no means to be despised compared to that which had gone before, were among other things sexist, racist, and bigoted. White Anglo-Saxon Protestants ruled the roost. Catholics and Jews were tolerated, but only just. Women were inferior to men, and Chinese and Indians inferior to just about everyone.

But Indians were the only class, kind, or race fortunate or unfortunate enough to be mentioned in the Constitution.[6] Almost 140 years later, Catholics and Jews and women and Chinese have progressed with the world and live in Canada as anyone else. Indians have not and do not, to anything like the same extent. We should think about that, and wonder about the connection.

This is the only discrimination based on race or ethnicity or heredity authorized by the Constitution. Its incorporation into the basic law provided the necessary foundation for today's notion of a "parallel society," a state within a state, based upon race.

It is not too much to say this: Section 91(24) condemned millions of people in the ensuing years to lives much lesser than they might have been, by singling out "Indians" as different from others on the basis of race. We know today on the basis of the human genome that they are not different in any material way. But they are still treated differently.

Section 91(24) made it possible to deny Indians the vote[7] and imprison them, literally, on reserves. (The permission of the Indian Agent was required

---

6 There were of course references to the Catholic religion and the French language, but this is a different issue.

7 This extended to the provincial level. One of the first acts of the British Columbian Legislature after entering Confederation was to make it clear that Indians had no vote. This followed a pattern in the province once Governor

to leave.) It made it possible to seize children and place them in far-away schools or to seize goods or to prohibit freedom of assembly and association or to forbid the hiring of lawyers.

The micromanagement of people's lives was a routine part of the system. An essentially communist society was established where the ownership of real property on an individual basis was impossible because the Crown claimed title to all land, albeit "in trust" for the collective. Little was expected of these people and it is worth underlining that the subtle, corrosive discrimination of low expectations is one of the most destructive acids that can be dropped upon anyone, especially when it is racially based. If there is important racist sentiment in the land today, it is exactly that of low expectations.

The implications of s. 91(24) were made manifest with the passage of the Indian Act in 1876. The Act treated Indians as wards of the state. Such real property as they occupied was controlled by the government. While exempt from paying taxes, they were also denied the right to vote. It is important to understand how pervasive was this system of tutelage and how this changed Indian lives and customs. A functioning political and economic culture was totally upended. The economic part is obvious if for no other reason than the severe restrictions on mobility. Other distortions such as those introduced by a welfare system were to come much later.

Voice and exit

But it is the political part that is perhaps more important. Two dimensions in particular need emphasis. They are comparable to the factors of "voice" and "exit" familiar to political scientists (Hirschman, 1970). The "exit" component is the "political market" factor of mobility, which acts as a sort of check on local government. Under pre-Reserve conditions, tribal political units were subject to losing (or gaining) membership if a given leadership was working much better or worse than might be expected. One should not overstate this: kinship no doubt remained the most powerful influence. But, there was a certain discipline imposed on Indian leaders by the right of

---

Douglas had left. Douglas respected Indians, had an Indian wife, and made 14 treaties settling land and rights. It appears that Douglas was not a good keeper of records and the reserves set aside under his administration were left vulnerable to reductions after his retirement (see Foster et al., 2003.

Douglas' successors adopted a new policy that included the widespread confiscation of lands without warrant and, in the 1860s, even a denial of land pre-emption rights available to all others.

members or whole families to move from one band to another (most likely within the same tribe). Occasional collective acts of inter-tribal violence also changed the status quo.

The right of mobility was ended by the Indian Act. Indians were assigned to Bands, Bands were assigned to Reserves, and that was that. Mobility ended. This is a stunning change in political terms, and even harsher from the human point of view. Today, we value freedom. There are few more essential attributes of freedom in the developed world than mobility rights. Consider yourself and family restricted to living all of your life on a few hundred acres.

As to "voice," the Indian Act imposed a style of majoritarian democracy and a strengthened executive branch (within limits allowed by the Indian Agent) on communities that traditionally had a more consensual form of decision making. It became easier, because of the newly imposed governance structure, to divide the community between the "ins" and the "outs." Simple majorities need pay less attention to minority interests than consensual models. Indeed, much of our modern law and jurisprudence grapples with this very problem of minority rights.

The combination of these two political changes encouraged the growth of a new kind of controlling elite, often based on family lines. Of course, as in every society, kinship had always been a factor in power relationships. In communities with a vibrant private-sector economy and private property rights, this would be less important. In communities where much of the work is government work and most of the cash flow and most of the property is controlled by government (in this case, the collective), this becomes crucial. As long as the Indian Agent had *de facto* governance, these issues mattered less (though of course the personal agenda of the Agent might cause its own problems). With the transfer of virtually all power under the Indian Act from the government in Ottawa to Indian governments they came to matter a great deal indeed.

On the early legal front, evolution was slow up until about 1973. The main case was *St. Catherines Milling* of 1888 before the Judicial Committee of the British Privy Council,[8] which resolved a dispute between federal and provincial governments as to jurisdiction over ceded lands.[9] The

8 The Judicial Committee of the British Privy Council was the ultimate court in those times.

9 The judges referred to the "Indian title" on unceded lands as a "mere burden," an estate that was to grow in importance about 85 years later in the first Nisga'a

courts had little to say for the next 90 years in this area (with the notable exception of *R. v. Drybones*, [1970] S.C.R. 282. There was a reason for this quietude. In those days, under the doctrine of sovereign immunity the Crown could not be sued without its consent, which governments routinely denied to Indian plaintiffs. So Parliament was supreme and Indians were mostly quiet.

Not entirely though. Indian agitation over land claims, especially in British Columbia, where it will be recalled almost none of the province was covered by treaty, led to commissions of review, some addition to and subtraction from Reserves, continuing dissatisfaction and finally the passage of an amendment to the Indian Act in 1927 forbidding Indians from hiring lawyers or assembling in groups without special permission for land claims purposes.

The modern era

The unintended consequences of welfare

World War I, the Great Depression, and then World War II effectively diverted all of the nation's political energies elsewhere until the late 1940s. In the post-War era, however, more modern social and political theories began to be applied. Welfare was introduced to Reserves, with a profound impact on life. What had essentially been a subsistence, non-cash, economy now had some cash. This led to changes in working patterns and consumer, health, and dietary habits, the most dramatic being substance abuse. According to John Richards,

> [t]he great expansion of social programs by Ottawa and the provinces since the end of World War II has induced many Aboriginals to change their lifestyle, to rely increasingly on government transfer income, and to work at less arduous traditional activities. Aboriginal reliance on social assistance increased in the 1950s when publicly funded relief become available. It further increased during the 1970s as Ottawa accepted the strategy of institutional parallelism and increased fiscal transfers to bands. For the past two decades, on-reserve welfare beneficiaries have on average exceeded 40% of the on-reserve population. For

---

case. But even in 1888, this "burden" was an interest in land covered by s. 109 of the then Constitution.)

> comparison, over the past three decades, the peak for the comparable statistic among the off-reserve (Aboriginal and non-Aboriginal) population occurred in the mid-1990s, at 10%; by 2001 it had fallen back to 6%. (Richards, 2006: 43–44)

In other words, incentives were dramatically changed in already dispirited communities by way of welfare, though from the government's point of view it was acting in a socially progressive manner.

Residential schools

The residential schools history over this period is too complex to be properly canvassed here. While there were certainly some good intentions along with some positive results (some people speak well of their school experience and some parents wanted their children there), there were many negative results. The strongly prevailing view today is that, not only was the experience a disaster for those it affected directly, but its effects echo through the generations as a direct cause of dysfunction in Indian communities. No objective dialogue will be possible on this issue for many years. A recent formal apology and compensation process from the federal government may assist in gradually turning injured eyes forward.

The right to vote

The right of the federal vote was restored to Indians in 1960 though the theoretically corresponding obligation of taxation was not imposed.[10] The protection of Indian land holdings from seizure for any purpose including non-payment of taxes was deemed so fundamental as to require the continuation of this exemption (which is contained not in the Constitution as many believe, but in a simple section [s. 87] of the Indian Act.[11]

---

10 Tom Flanagan (2000: 105) makes the point *re* the famous dictum of "no taxation without representation," that the obverse is also true: that is, one is very differently motivated in casting one's vote if one does not pay taxes. The focus of the citizen shifts from the pain of taxes to the quest for benefits and favors.

11 There will in due course be a constitutional issue as to whether Indian Title lands, neither "Reserve" nor "surrendered" in the words of s. 87, which may be acquired by litigation and not by Treaty explicitly conferring an exempt status, may in fact be taxable. It is an intriguing question.

The philosophical revolution begins

The 1960s were a time of change and upheaval throughout North America, and this percolated into Indian policy. The Hawthorn Commission (Hawthorn, 1966/67) was appointed and reported. The core idea of this work will be described in more detail in chapter 4, with particular attention to the work of Alan Cairns, one of Canada's most distinguished political scientists, who was the chief researcher to the Commission. The idea of "Citizens Plus"[12] first surfaced there but was widely derided in a time when "equality" (as championed by Martin Luther King) was the preferred goal.

The *Hawthorn Report* was ahead of its time in proposing measures for the individual Indian. Tom Flanagan reports on and quotes Hawthorne in his *First Nations, Second Thoughts*:

> Specifically, *Hawthorn* recommended spending money on housing and welfare on Reserves to obtain a minimum standard of living, but only that. The major expenditures should come in areas like education, job training and counselling, and off-reserve housing: "What is suggested is that, insofar as the economic development of Indians lies primarily in wage and salaried employment, and that for most Indians such employment lies beyond commuting distance of their reserves, a large and increasing part of an expanded Indian Affairs budget should be used to support Indians who wish to leave their reserves." (Flanagan, 2000: 178; citing Hawthorn, 1966/67: 165)

Flanagan then goes on to say: "In the same vein, Hawthorn urged that Indians should receive health, education and welfare services from provincial authorities. Not only would the quality of services be better than those previously provided by federal authorities, but a provincial system of benefit delivery would promote the integration of Indians into Canadian society." (Flanagan, 2000: 179).

These are remarkably modern sentiments from 40 years ago and the System that opposes such ideas so strongly today did not exist back then. It is fascinating to muse how history might have unfolded had the federal government implemented these policies rather than seeking the "big bang" of the white paper.

---

12 This is described in more detail in chapter 4 but the general idea is that history and the law gives extra rights to Indians and equity requires that these be recognized.

The "white paper"

In 1970 came an initiative that changed everything in unintended ways, being the first serious re-thinking of Indian policy in at least 100 years. Pierre Trudeau's government saw all Canadians as equal and worried about the anomalous status of Indians. After some consultation—not enough, as it turned out—and a tremendous amount of Cabinet work the government produced the *Statement of the Government of Canada on Indian Policy* (Canada, 1969), the famous "white paper" that has since become a negative symbol of the supposed assimilative intentions of Canada's white society (as it largely then was), even though the document explicitly rejects assimilation as the goal.

Every serious student of these questions should read the white paper, both because of the good it contains and for its fateful error. The paper outlined a plan that would have forcibly emancipated Indians. Some brief extracts will give the tone.[13]

> The Government believes that its policies must lead to the full, free and non-discriminatory participation of the Indian people in Canadian society. Such a goal requires a break with the past. It requires that the Indian people's role of dependence be replaced by a role of equal status, opportunity and responsibility, a role they can share with all other Canadians.

In a later, background section the reasons were more fully described:

> The legal and administrative discrimination in the treatment of Indian people has not given them an equal chance of success. It has exposed them to discrimination in the broadest and worst sense of the term—a discrimination that has profoundly affected their confidence that success can be theirs. Discrimination breeds discrimination by example, and the separateness of Indian people has affected the attitudes of other Canadians towards them.

Noble intentions and a clear admission of error, but the remedy was to be as directive as anything in the past. There was a certain nod to humility: "Many years will be needed. Some efforts may fail, but learning comes from

---

13 The white paper is available in HTML at <http://www.ainc-inac.gc.ca/pr/lib/phi/histlws/cp1969_e.html> and in PDF at <http://www.ainc-inac.gc.ca/pr/lib/phi/histlws/cp1969_e.pdf>; these versions are searchable, but not paginated.

failure and from what is learned success may follow. All the partners will have to learn; all will have to change many attitudes." No doubt this sentiment of mutual accommodation was sincere, but the underlying issue of who is right here shortly follows: "Indian people *must be persuaded*, *must persuade themselves*, that this path will lead them to a fuller and richer life" (emphasis supplied). Then, came a statement that is as sadly true today as it was when written nearly 40 years ago, an assessment of the shortfall from continuing "business as usual":

> The Government could press on with the policy of fostering further education; could go ahead with physical improvement programs now operating in reserve communities; could press forward in the directions of recent years, and eventually many of the problems would be solved. But progress would be too slow. The change in Canadian society in recent years has been too great and continues too rapidly for this to be the answer. Something more is needed. We can no longer perpetuate the separation of Canadians. Now is the time for change.

The change was to be effected by a six point plan.

> The government believes that the framework within which individual Indians and bands could achieve full participation requires:
> 1 that legislative and constitutional bases of discrimination be removed;
> 2 that there be positive recognition by everyone of the unique contribution of Indian culture to Canadian life;
> 3 that services come through the same channels and from the same government agencies for all Canadians;
> 4 that those who are furthest behind be helped most;
> 5 that lawful obligations be recognized;
> 6 that control of Indian lands be transferred to the Indian people.

What was being proposed here was a revolution. That it was well meant is indisputable. In theory, it described a "win/win" for everyone and provided for a special effort and cost by Canadian taxpayers to make it so. It was admitted that this would take some time, but not much.

> Some changes could take place quickly. It is expected that within five years the Department of Indian Affairs and Northern Development

> would cease to operate in the field of Indian affairs; the new laws would be in effect and existing programs would have been devolved. The Indian lands would require special attention for some time. The process of transferring control would be under continuous review.

Later sections recognized the need for special arrangements for lands, presumably out of concern from the preservation of the land base.

Cabinet documents in those days often set up a couple of stark alternatives and then proposed a "third option" that was cast as the obvious conclusion. This document said the choices were (1) a continuation of Reserves, or (2) assimilation, or "a third choice—a full role in Canadian society and in the economy while retaining, strengthening and developing an Indian identity which preserves the good things of the past and helps Indian people to prosper and thrive."

The Chiefs of Canada rose up against these propositions. Pierre Trudeau had made a fatal error. He had neglected to provide for those Indians—and there were many—who simply wished to continue to live under the security of the familiar old system, whatever its defects. The Government of Canada was in essence proposing to overnight rip up a contract with Indians that the government had fashioned over 100 years.

This was unacceptable both politically and in equity. As to the latter, governments have no right to change fundamental rules quickly, for anyone, except by consent or in an emergency. Neither exception applied here. As to the politics, the Chiefs, acting through the National Indian Brotherhood and effective activists such as Harold Cardinal of Alberta with his counter "Red Paper" raised such a stir that the government simply backed off. Trudeau was never a man to withdraw from a fight on a central issue but this one was peripheral to him. It was an idealistic concern. He thought he was doing the right thing; but if the supposed beneficiaries were not interested, well the famous shrug.

The results of this failed policy initiative can hardly be over-emphasized. An evolving process of gradual improvement in Indian affairs was nipped in the bud by an attempt to "do it all" in one big bang. This having failed, the public, having done its best through its (then very popular) government, gave up and moved on, as did the media. The field was abandoned to interested parties, all with their own axes to grind, and has remained a "client captured" field of government policy ever since—arcane, complex, a notoriously difficult file, and a place for experts and those directly involved.

Suppose the white paper had never been brought forward? There has been a "Fourth-World nationalism" of indigenous groups around the world, which like Third-World nationalism has arguably succeeded in part by the "white guilt" felt by the First World over its colonial policies. This might have had some impact on Canada but accommodation might also arguably have been easier had not Trudeau (with the best of intentions) stirred up this hornet's nest.

The Ottawa public service in particular was traumatized by these developments. They had never before experienced "Indian Power." They had gone from complete control of Indians to flak-catching impotence overnight. The bureaucrats began off-loading areas of responsibility and potential blame as quickly as possible, sending both money and responsibility to Band governments. There was a common sense in this. It is illogical to accept responsibility for things beyond the scope of one's powers. But an unfortunate result was that any locus of accountability became increasingly difficult to find. The development of Indian policy thenceforth and continuing until today passed into the hands of the courts and the Indian System. The latter term needs definition, but first the courts.

Enter the courts

There was to be one major decision by the Supreme Court of Canada (SCC) prior to the new powers conferred by the Constitution Act, 1982 and a constant stream thereafter. The first was *Calder v. Attorney-General of B.C.* delivered in 1973. This related to the hundred-year-old land claim of the Nisga'a tribe in north-western British Columbia. Chief Calder (with whom I was privileged to serve in the British Columbian Legislature) sought a declaration of possessory title in the large Nisga'a traditional territory. The seven-member bench split three to three on Nisga'a title, the seventh member declining to rule on a technicality. The Nisga'a had come within an ace of a declaration of ownership of the Nass Valley, a significant portion of the province.

At that time, Parliament could still have over-ruled the court had Ottawa actually lost this case (before the Charter, Parliament was supreme in all areas and could have passed a law retroactively extinguishing and continuing Indian title). No such action was taken but the decision added to the traumatized bunker mentality in Ottawa.

Everything changed again in the aftermath of the Constitution Act, 1982.[14] If the discrimination of 1867 was a more-or-less absent-minded con-

---

14 It is interesting that two of the initiatives of Pierre Trudeau thought more or less incidental at the time, the white paper and the Indian portion of the 1982

tinuation of British practice, the race-based amendments of 115 years later were hardly so morally innocent. That major overhaul of the Constitution was a matter of careful thought in all of its aspects, though there is good evidence that the results becoming apparent a generation later would have surprised and troubled the modern framers.[15]

As is well known, the Constitution Act, 1982 ended the absolute collective supremacy of Parliament and the Legislatures acting in their jurisdictions and established the superior authority of the constitution. It is the Supreme Court of Canada that is charged with deciding when the constitution trumps Parliament and there is no appeal from their rulings except for some important Charter rights subject to the so-called "notwithstanding clause." The Indian law sections of the *Constitution Act, 1982* are not subject to "notwithstanding."[16] Thus, the Supreme Court is the ultimate maker of Indian law in Canada today in any area where it chooses to state that the constitution applies. This has led to much work for lawyers.

To re-state for convenience, Sections 25 and 35 read as follows:

> s. 25. The guarantee in the Charter of certain rights and freedoms shall not be construed so as to abrogate or derogate from any aboriginal, treaty or other rights and freedoms that pertain to the aboriginal peoples of Canada including
>
> any rights and freedoms that have been recognized by the Royal Proclamation of October 7, 1763; and
>
> any rights or freedoms that now exist by way of land claims agreements or may be so acquired.

> s. 35. (1) The existing aboriginal and treaty rights of the aboriginal peoples of Canada are hereby recognized and affirmed.
>
> (2) In this Act, "aboriginal peoples of Canada" includes the Indian, Inuit and Métis people of Canada.

---

amendments, were to become so influential in Canadian politics today. Along with s. 91(24), they remain the modern drivers of Indian policy.

15 While this comment may be made with respect to other sections of the Charter as well, the documentation is especially clear as regards Indian law. See "What was the intent of the framers of Section 35?" p. 78.

16 As is the case with much of the Charter; "notwithstanding" applies only to s. 2 and ss. 7 to 15.

> For greater certainty, in subsection (1) "treaty rights" includes rights that now may exist by way of land claims agreements or may be so acquired.
>
> Notwithstanding any other provision of this Act, the aboriginal rights referred to in subsection (1) are guaranteed equally to male and female persons.

There follows a s. 35.1 committing to a constitutional conference including aboriginal representatives before any constitutional amendments touching ss. 25, 35, and also s. 91(24), noted above.

While Section 25 has to date been but lightly litigated, its plain English meaning is that, if parts of the Charter offend traditional aboriginal practices, those parts of the Charter are not enforceable as against Indian governments. For example, the British Columbia Supreme Court has ruled (Williamson, J. in *Campbell et al. v. AG BC/AG Cda & Nisga'a Nation et al.*) that Section 3 of the Charter guaranteeing a vote to everyone is not applicable on Nisga'a territory and s. 25 was one of three stated reasons. In the recent *R. v. Kapp*, the Court divided sharply (albeit six to one) on the import of s. 25 and we will no doubt hear more of this.

For present purposes, the important point to note is that, while the usual wording in modern treaties states that the Charter applies to Indian governments established under such treaties, this is misleading to the layman. The fact is that all of the Charter applies including s. 25, which in a sort of "Catch 22" removes from Indians *vis-à-vis* their governments any of the standard protections that can be argued to be inconsistent with "any aboriginal, treaty or other rights and freedoms that apply to the aboriginal people of Canada." Thus, curiously, the Charter itself provides another example of how our law limits the rights of Indian individuals, while buttressing the rights of the collective.

S. 35 has had most of the attention. The framers thought it an innocuous section put in for political correctness and, indeed, in the final drafting Premiers Lougheed and Bennett attempted to remove all doubt by inserting the word "existing" to qualify "aboriginal rights." Their intent was that no new law be invented as a result of this clause. They did not reckon with the ingenuity of the Supreme Court of Canada.

It is essential to understand the power of the Court in Indian law. Quite simply, since 1982 it has been the final authority. As noted, the famous "notwithstanding" clause does not apply to ss. 25 and 35. The sections are open to very broad interpretation. And the insistence of the framers on the word, "existing"? The Court has simply ignored the plain meaning of the word, treating new rights that they create as though they had already been "existing," though perhaps latent, in 1982 and now unearthed and discovered by the Court.

Parliament and the Legislatures are no longer supreme in this area. This has led to two unfortunate and no doubt unexpected effects. First, governments figuratively throw up their hands when courts give directions on Indian law that are otherwise questionable as sound policy and take the easy way out. This means spending money and conferring special status as required. (This is the "easy way out" because governments can solve problems using other people's money rather than their own, scarce, political capital. And in general, politicians know that voters have a higher opinion of judges than of them, and thus they avoid fights with the courts.) Second, if governments wish to evade political responsibility for controversial policies they may wish to adopt for whatever reason, they may claim such actions to be "mandated by the courts" even if such statement is questionable. Few readers are lawyerly enough to challenge it.

Sometimes this led to a flat lie. The "Pilot sales program" instituted by the Mulroney government in 1992 and continued by the Liberals allows for the commercial sale of salmon caught by certain Indians on the Fraser River during special fishery openings denied to whites, Japanese (traditional salmon fishers), and so on. These "openings" take precedence in the hierarchy of access to the fish so that some years ordinary commercial fishers sit on the shore watching Indians take the only commercial catch available.

The federal government traditionally defended this practice in its political stance on the basis that it is mandated by *R. v. Sparrow* (1990), a SCC decision that stated that Indians have a right to a food fishery for personal and social purposes. But no commercial fishing priority whatsoever was conferred by *Sparrow*. The federal claim was indeed simply not true. The ordinary commercial fishers have been sacrificed, first perhaps as a part of a grand Mulroney strategy to gain an Indian buy-in to the Charlottetown Accord[17] and thereafter continued by the Liberals to keep peace on the river, in reaction to Indian threats of violence.

Endless court challenges by the commercial fishermen have only this year been resolved and it has cost them dearly from their own pockets while the government used taxpayers' money to oppose them. The Supreme Court

17 The surprising creation of the Territory of Nunavut with a population of only 22,000 was another such consideration.

of Canada heard the latest challenge in the Fall Session, 2007 and, in the end, concluded that discrimination in the fishery on the basis of race is a policy act of government protected under the affirmative-action power of the Charter, s. 15(2). This policy is not, however, a requirement of the Court. The point this illustrates: the Constitution Act, 1982 gives the federal government a convenient cover of deniability of authority in many cases by claiming the direction of the Court. Very few citizens or members of the media understand the law sufficiently to question such claims.

This practice has spilled over to the related actions of provincial governments as well. Thus have democratic authority and responsibility been further eroded, again leaving the Indian System to fill the vacuum—for someone must make decisions.

A multiplicity of judgments by the Supreme Court followed the 1982 amendments. *Guerin v. The Queen* (1984), a wholly correct ruling, held Ottawa accountable for incompetent administration of Indian assets. *Sparrow*, as noted, provided for a food fishery. But *R. v. Van der Peet* (1996) made it clear that this did not convey a commercial privilege, except in the very rare circumstances cited in *Gladstone v. Canada (Attorney-General) (2005)*.

The cases cited in the previous paragraph are all from British Columbia, which has had particularly strong Indian leadership in recent years. It will be recalled that in British Columbia treaties had never been signed[18] and the "land question" had heated up after the *Calder* decision. British Columbia in fact has been the pace-setter in Indian policy from about 1990 to the present.

Not that eastern Canada had been entirely without developments. On the positive side, the James Bay and Northern Quebec Agreement, 1975, had settled[19] claims and development rights (especially hydro) in an immense territory in Quebec. On the negative side and also in Quebec, the "Oka" uprising, 1990—a standoff between the military and Mohawks in the community of Oka triggered by municipal seizure for a golf course of land claimed by Indians—resulted in death and transfixed the country for days. The Mohawks won their land-claim point and more in the end, and governments had been badly beaten up politically. From Oka onward, money and concession became the default response to Indian demands. The Oka warriors so successfully unbalanced Ottawa that for years thereafter and to this

---

18 Except for the small "Douglas treaties" and Treaty 8 in the northeast corner of the province.

19 Though not conclusively, as it emerged later.

date it would scuttle from any apprehended confrontation. That continues to this day. Cigarette and other smuggling across the St. Lawrence, illegal tobacco sales on Reserves, and illegal gambling operations are all ignored by the authorities for fear of trouble were the law to be enforced. The moral and political high ground had, for the time, been definitively won by the Indian side.

The motivation of governments, especially Ottawa, shifted more than ever to the avoidance of trouble from questions about the merit of policy.[20] This was reinforced by the military-type confrontation with the RCMP at Gustafsen Lake in 1995, and by the Ipperwash occupation, also 1995, which resulted in the death of Band member Dudley George and an eventual commission of inquiry appointed by a subsequent government. These cases were in many ways the physical analogue to the intellectual case of the white paper. Serious embarrassment on each occasion led to policy paralysis in the governments concerned, and a fear of confrontation in any matter whatsoever. For example, a subsequent, highly questionable, manifestation and occupation in the Ontario town of Caledonia (Six Nations Mohawks, Ontario) has therefore simply been allowed to fester for two years (as of this writing) rather than being dealt with by way of law enforcement. The balance of power had shifted.

National policy in this area was now more than ever out of the control of anyone. This statement includes the "System," because of course that complex is not an organized entity capable of being directed by anyone, or responsible to, and held accountable by, anyone. Such a chaotic situation is not *prima facie* bad—"free markets" operate efficiently under certain conditions—but in this case the free-market disciplines of transparency, competition, and constructive incentives do not exist. What emerged became a true

---

20 The political weakness of the Mulroney government in power at the time had a lot to do with this. Beset on all sides, the government had no stomach for conflict with media-popular Indians. And, as a part of the immense investment of resources in the attempt to secure both re-election and the (ultimately failed) Charlottetown Accord constitutional-amendment package, for which the government wished to achieve Indian support, very large cash and policy concessions were made, including vaguely defined but clearly major dimensions of self-government, assignment of Fraser River salmon, and arguably the creation of Nunavut. The Liberals supported these views and the successor Liberal government continued them even after the failure of the Accord, in for example, a statement *re* the "Inherent Right" (to self-government).

policy jungle, which is part of the root problem. There might be quite general agreement on this description of unacceptable chaos were there a way of polling the System; but agreed remedies would be harder to find.

British Columbia takes the lead

In British Columbia, other developments were afoot, which were to lead to a revolutionary new Indian policy, though this was little recognized at the time. This was set out in the report of a tripartite task force—federal, provincial and "Summit"[21]—convened to address an increasingly unsatisfactory situation. As the *Report of the British Columbia Claims Task Force* itself notes, political and legal activity on the part of the tribes had been increasingly visible and successful. Moreover, said the task force, "direct action," little seen in British Columbia until this time, was now at work:

> Direct action returned to prominence during the mid-1970s with rallies, sit-ins and road and rail blockades. These actions were aimed as much at unsatisfactory conditions on the reserves as at the land question. During the 1980s, a new round of direct action began, both to assert aboriginal title and, in some cases, to halt specific resource development projects in First Nation territories.
>
> In a number of instances court injunctions suspended resource development pending the outcome of disputes over aboriginal title. As well, in response to increasing political activity by aboriginal people at the national level, the Constitution Act, 1982 included provisions which recognized and affirmed aboriginal and treaty rights and called for a First Minsters' conference to address aboriginal constitutional issues. The province continued to deny the existence of aboriginal title, and declined to negotiate with First Nations. The resulting impasse was as unsettling to some non-aboriginal groups and interests as it was dissatisfying to the First Nations. (British Columbia, Ministry of Aboriginal Relations and Reconciliation, 1991)

---

21 The "Summit" was a new grouping of some but not all of the tribes of the province—about 60%—formed for the purpose of representing Indian interests in anticipated treaty negotiations. Other Indian organizations, notably the Union of BC Indian Chiefs based in the Interior of British Columbia, declined to take part, claiming sovereignty as a non-negotiable issue.

These very pressures had led to the striking of the Task Force. Without for the moment opining on their wisdom, the recommendations were truly historic and, unlike the equally momentous proposals of the white paper, were to actually govern public policy for years to come. The *Report* made 19 recommendations, of which the most salient are the following.

New relationship

There was to be a "new relationship." Seemingly innocuous, this was in fact a repudiation of past policy as the new relationship clearly implied the continuation and validation of a separate Indian society. In historical perspective, as compared to the old "assimilation" or "isolation," this was a significant milestone on the road to the establishment of a continuing "parallel society."

Treaty discussions

Lightly structured treaty discussions were to be held, with any and all matters to be on the table. "Stages" of negotiations were identified; a Treaty Commission established to oversee the process; funding and negotiators were to be provided. While not explicit in the recommendations *per se*, treaties were clearly seen as the route to resolution of all questions. No overall time lines were laid out.

Without clear guidelines, time lines, or targets for success, the process was a guaranteed long-term exercise in the making, with the built-in incentives for all of the decision makers concerned weighing more in favor of continued negotiations than in favor of quick resolution or, indeed, any resolution.

Representation and overlapping claims

The tribes were to decide themselves on their representation and on issues of overlapping claims.

Non-aboriginal interests

"Non-aboriginal interests" were to be represented by governments. This representation has never really been accepted as satisfactory by either private or municipal interests, in very major part because of non-transparency and the highly secretive nature of government decision-making in this area, and the suspicion that governments really had a different agenda here than that of their citizens.[22] This lack of representative legitimacy

22 See chapter 5 for a discussion of why such suspicions are rational given the incentives of those at the table.

remains a serious bone of contention in British Columbia and undermines public support for agreements coming out of the discussions.

Interim measures agreements

"Interim measures agreements" were provided for to deal with issues or resources under dispute pending final settlement. The obvious and fair reason was to try to prevent wastage of the assets (for logging, mining, etc.) being negotiated during the process. The overlooked (or undiscussed) but very important side effect of thereby removing pressure to settle was not mentioned.

The New Democratic Party (NDP) took office in British Columbia in 1991 just after the release of Task Force's *Report* and, as described above, the federal government was in a weakened situation with respect to virtually all significant political questions in the country. Thus it was with alacrity that the Report and its provisions were adopted, as an apparently constructive (and at the beginning, low-cost) means of "doing something." However, expectations were also raised, which were not to be met.

The tripartite British Columbia Treaty Commission was put to work in 1993 to facilitate modern treaties in the province. Respectable progress was being made over a five-year period, though dramatically interrupted by the standoff at Gustafasen Lake in 1995. This proved to be an aberration and talks continued.

Then came *Delgamuukw v. British Columbia*, the single most important Indian law decision of the Supreme Court of Canada to date, handed down in December, 1997. Named for one of the plaintiffs, the case heard a claim by two Indian groups, the Gitskan (now, Gitxsan) and the Wet'suwet'en, seeking a declaration that they owned both land title and sovereign governmental authority in a large portion of north-central British Columbia. It will be recalled that most of British Columbia was not covered by treaty, and thus the matter of title could have been, and was, considered an open question, though sovereignty was thought a bit of a stretch by most.

The case resulted in the lengthiest trial to that time in British Columbia's history. Chief Justice MacEachern of the Supreme Court of British Columbia heard evidence both in the territory claimed and in Vancouver for more than 360 court days stretching over three years. Extensive expert evidence was called as well as oral recollections of history and the singing of traditional songs (to demonstrate occupancy and so on).

At the end of the day, MacEachern essentially rejected the Indian argument. He recognized a good claim to title in small areas as well as a general fiduciary duty of the Crown to the Indians concerned. However, as to title over the province in general, he ruled that belonged to the Crown by "necessary implication" of Colonial land ordinances and that any claim to governmental authority had been extinguished by the extension of British sovereignty. The British Columbia Court of Appeal overturned MacEachern's single most important ruling (that is, that Indian title had been extinguished before Confederation, so what was there really left to talk about?) but left most of the rest of the judgment undisturbed and the question of title uncertain.

Matters were left in abeyance for some time, since the governments of the day had a decision that was acceptable as far as the federal government in Ottawa was concerned and, though not acceptable in the view of the current provincial government in Victoria, perhaps surmountable by negotiations. The abeyance failed to produce results at the bargaining table and eventually the Supreme Court of Canada was asked and agreed to hear the appeal and rendered a judgment in December, 1997. The Supreme Court ruled that the trial-court process was flawed by insufficient deference to oral evidence and used that as a reason to set aside Chief Justice MacEachern's ruling in its entirety, while at the same time remarkably noting that many of his conclusions might be validated had the case been heard properly.

The Supreme Court went on to provide a conceptual and philosophical framework for Indian title that it said continued to exist in British Columbia, without defining any locations or boundaries. Notwithstanding the fact that the question of oral evidence had no bearing whatsoever on the claim to governance (sovereignty) and that all necessary arguments were before it on this matter, the court declined to affirm the trial judge's finding of extinguishment of sovereignty.

Those are the bare facts at law, but more should be said to illuminate the massive and unpredictable impact of the law and politics in this area. As to politics, after the MacEachern decision, which was agreeable to the Social Credit government (since it essentially resolved the Land Question in the province), an NDP government was elected in the province. It took the position that the judgment was too harsh and ordered negotiations. When these failed, it engaged new lawyers and instructed them in the response to the appeal by the Plaintiffs to abandon the (fundamental) finding of Colonial extinguishment and take a far softer position in other areas. The shift was so surprising that the British Columbia Court of Appeal took the most unusual step of itself engaging the first, dismissed set of lawyers to act as *amicus curia*.

Eventually, the Supreme Court of Canada was sympathetic to the Indian appeal. Lawyers do not second guess judges if they wish a successful career, but a layman's insight is that the court was uncomfortable with the crushing impact on the Indians' negotiating position in the Treaty Commission process were the lower courts to be upheld and so seized upon a rather questionable reason (that is, alleged insufficient consideration of oral evidence when on the clear record there had been a plenitude of such) to set the judgment aside and invent its own version of how negotiations on Indian title should be framed. This version guides the process to this day.

Their reasons for declining to rule on the sovereignty issue are harder to guess. It has certainly remained as a worry for governments, which may have been the Court's intent, as well as inducing Indian nationalists to believe and maintain that sovereignty is an achievable goal.[23] In any event, the net effect was to continue and accelerate the pursuit of "third order" sovereignty at treaty tables in British Columbia, which remains a major stumbling block.

The effect on treaty negotiations was predictable. The balance of power had been hugely manipulated by judicial fiat and the the process came to a halt for some years as the parties readjusted their thinking.

The exception of course was the work on the Nisga'a Treaty, which had been underway for 20 years. With the confusion elsewhere in negotiations, a provincial NDP government philosophically disposed to treaties and a federal Prime Minister, once a Minister of Indian Affairs, wishing to add this to his roster of accomplishments, and given that the fact that the lands concerned were little known and far from major population centres, progress was achieved by way of concession and the Nisga'a Treaty was ratified by British Columbia in 1999 and by Ottawa in 2000.

---

23 However other SCC cases, especially *Mitchell v. MNR*, 2001, pose difficult challenges for the sovereignty argument, notwithstanding *Campbell*, see below, never validated by appeal. In *Mitchell*, the full seven-member bench ruled against a claimed Indian right to carry goods unimpeded across the border between Canada and the United States but two judges, Justices Major and Binnie, went further and suggested a quashing of sovereignty: "Since the claimed aboriginal right did not survive the transition to non-Mohawk sovereignty, there was nothing in existence in 1982 to which s. 35(1) protection of existing aboriginal rights could attach ... To extend constitutional protection to the respondent's claim would overshoot the purpose of s. 35(1)" (*Mitchell v. MNR*, 2001: summary concurring judgement). This is a clear "shot across the bow." Even *Delgamuukw* reiterated the Court's view in *R. v. Pamajewon*, [1996] that "rights to self-government, if they existed, cannot be framed in excessively general terms" (Paragraph 170).

The Nisga'a Treaty provided for a constitutionally protected parallel society in northwestern British Columbia on about 2000 square kilometers of land, about 5% of the original claim. This was accompanied by a cash settlement of about $200 million, plus access to salmon, and wildlife-management powers in a much wider area, plus forestry advantages. Regular financial support by the federal government for the Niaga'a Nation was continued and, indeed, increased by $3 million *per annum* to cover the new costs of self-government. Most significantly, a separate government was established with constitutional sovereignty in 14 heads of power, including such important ones as citizenship, education, and child care.[24] The responsibilities were huge when set against the capacity of about 2,500 persons, most of them young, on the lands at the time.

The Treaty was made explicitly subject to the Charter but this is of questionable meaning (except for gender equality) because of the Charter's escape clause for Indians, s. 25. Provision was made for democracy but persons off the lands were given effective voting power of about one tenth that of residents. (This latter provision is in the Nisga'a Constitution rather than the Treaty.)

There is no doubt that this treaty was a landmark event. It cost a lot of money—about $100 million in legal, consulting, and negotiating fees—and established a template for future settlements. No rigorous third-party, external evaluation of the success of the Nisga'a experiment has been published to date.

The Nisga'a Treaty was received with mixed feelings in British Columbia. The general sense of "white guilt"[25] in respect of Indian policy led to approval by a slight polling majority in spite of general unease because of a very strong consensus, according to other polls of the day, that all Canadians should be treated equally. This latter sentiment led to a court challenge of the constitutionality of the Treaty by three members[26] of the then-Liberal opposition in the provincial legislature. They noted that the Treaty, under

24 For further details, see Canada, Indian and Northern Affairs Canada, 2004a; for comment by this author, see Gibson, 1999a, 1999b. There is a rich literature on this treaty, mostly supportive.

25 The guilt is indeed mostly "white," in the sense of being felt by white persons, and is not generally applicable to the very large and growing number of so-called visible minorities from Asian rather than European backgrounds who will become increasingly influential in Canadian politics.

26 Gordon Campbell, Geoff Plant, and Mike DeJong. *Campbell et al. v. AG BC/AG Cda & Nisga'a Nation et al.*, 2000; generally known as *Campbell.*

the terms of s. 35, became a protected part of the Constitution. The essential claim of the plaintiffs was that the Treaty, by assigning elements of sovereignty to a third order of government and failing to treat non-Nisga'a within the territory equitably in defiance of the Charter, amounted to a change in the Constitution. In particular, the federal and provincial governments together hold the entirely of available sovereignty and the treaty pretends to give some of that to the new Nisga'a government. This, they said, cannot be done through the back door of s. 35 but only through the front door of the amending formula.

The case was heard by Judge Williamson of the Supreme Court of British Columbia. In a truly extraordinary ruling, he held that there was no problem with the elements of sovereignty conferred on the Nisga'a government because this had not been subtracted from the federal and provincial governments. Instead, the British had held back just enough sovereignty at the time of Confederation to allow the Nisga'a Treaty constitutional room. As to denial of Charter rights to others (the right of a non-Nisga'a in the area to vote on local government matters), this was sanctioned, said the judge, by the provisions of s. 25 as well as by the fine print of s. 3 (which refers only to federal and provincial elections) and the fact that there are other examples in Canada where residents cannot vote for one reason or another.

The plaintiffs appealed but were then elected to government. A section of the Treaty requires that no party to the Treaty should question its terms. Campbell, Plant, and DeJong decided they were bound by that provision, and there the matter ended. This unusual judgment remains the law in British Columbia, though it may be changed by another Nisga'a challenge case, *Sga'Nisim Sim'Augit (Chief Mountain) v. Canada* (commonly referred to as *Chief Mountain*), which has now been in the court system for seven years and has yet to be heard substantively due to truly disgraceful dilatory measures by the three governments concerned. (Again, as at this writing, the plaintiffs in *Chief Mountain* have just won the right to proceed.)

To complete this brief survey of developments in British Columbia before returning to the rest of the country, in law the leading recent case has been *Haida Nation v. British Columbia (Ministry of Forests)*, which has established clearly that the Crown (but not private parties) has a considerable duty of consultation, to which we shall return, before authorizing any activity that might infringe on Indian rights or title on claimed (as distinct from proven) Indian land. However, the court also held that this is not a fatal barrier to development even over Indian objections as long as consultation is followed by reasonable accommodation, compensation, or both, if appropriate, and the works are in the public interest, which is rather broadly defined. *Haida* has been settled by the Supreme Court of Canada.

More recently, a decision was rendered in the case, *Tsilhqot'in Nation v. British Columbia* (commonly referred to as *William*), being a claim to aboriginal title in the Chilcotin country. The case lasted five years, cost $30 million, and provides the first court analysis of the meaning and extent of aboriginal title, defined in the first instance by *Delgamuukw*. In the end, the Supreme Court of British Columbia, Vickers J., opined that title had been proven to about 2,000 square kilometers but made no award because the plea was not congruent with the discovered title area. Very importantly, Justice Vickers opined that aboriginal title land is essentially federal land, not provincial, a material event in a province where claims cover almost the entire area. In addition, Justice Vickers recalled to everyone's attention to an aspect of *Delgamuukw* more or less hidden from the public for 10 years by political and media inattention, namely that aboriginal title cannot be extinguished and is not extinguished by provincial grant of fee simple title. This is political dynamite, as ordinary British Columbians hold their properties in exactly such fee simple. If their title is not good, or is lawfully burdened by aboriginal title, there will be either a solution to that problem or a crisis.[27] The decision has been appealed but the fee-simple matter follows the SCC's precedent so closely that it is hard to see how that part can be reconsidered without the Court swallowing its words, as it can do (see *Marshall I*, below).

Elsewhere in Canada

Elsewhere in the country, the law was also unfolding in important ways. *R. v. Pamajewon* made it clear that whatever might be the content of Indian sovereignty and any "inherent right," it was limited and (as per this case) did

27 See, however, Isaac, 2006. This distinguished Vancouver lawyer holds that fee title is unlikely to be disturbed in general. As a brief summary of a much more complex argument: "In any event, whether Aboriginal title has been extinguished or not, it is clear that the granting of fee simple interests, by the federal or provincial Crown, is a justifiable infringement of such title" (2006: 58). This does not, however, deal with the question of compensation (a usual remedy for infringement) nor with the many "less than fee" interests such as leases or licenses. In addition, the courts may choose to treat differently remote and detached fee parcels such as those involved in *Tsilhqot'in Nation (William)*.

not include the right to establish and regulate casinos. *R. v. Powley* went on a more expansionist course, opening Indian-type rights to Métis but under quite narrow definitions. *Mitchell v. MNR* was a case concerning the alleged rights of Indians to move anything freely across the border with the United States. This claim was denied, with a strong concurring judgment suggesting the Court will not look favorably in the future on Indian sovereignty claims in general.

The "*Marshall*" cases in New Brunswick demonstrated with great clarity what mischief a well-meaning but confused Court can wreak by ill-considered words. In *R. v. Marshall* ([1999] 3 S.C.R. 456; *Marshall I*), which was about the right to fish for eels, the Court ruled that a very old treaty of peace and friendship (which actually on its face dealt largely with limiting Indian rights to trade other than at specified "truck houses") somehow in fact guaranteed every Indian a sufficient access to the resource base of the province for an adequate living. It was a splendid example of the Supreme Court's inventiveness and bands in New Brunswick seized on this as a general license of exploitation for all of the fish, rocks, and trees of the province.

The highly lucrative and regulated lobster fishery was the first to be attacked under this theory, leading to violent confrontations with commercial fishermen. The injustice was no different in kind from the situation earlier described in British Columbia but, in this case, the violence on both sides did not allow the politicians or even the Court to ignore the situation. In an embarrassing reconsideration (*R. v. Marshall* [1999] 3 S.C.R. 533; *Marshall II*), the Court swallowed its words whole and said in effect, "No, no—we were just talking about eels."[28] But a great deal of damage had been done in racial relations and another generation of young Indians had been led to believe they owned the resources of the country. In *Marshall-Bernard,* the last round of the *Marshall* trilogy, this belief was finally rejected by the Court, which rejected a claim for the free aboriginal taking of trees on a commercial basis. *Marshall-Bernard* seemed to put quite severe constraints on aboriginal title,[29]

---

28 Defenders of the Court properly note that the original judgment stated clearly that aboriginal rights could be regulated but the message obviously was not clear enough.

29 *R. v. Marshall*; *R. v. Bernard* [2005] 2 S.C.R. 220, 2005 SCC43. In the summary of judgment by the Chief Justice, the Court explained that there must be evidence of occupation to claim title and that occupation must be pre-sovereignty, "physical," and "exclusive": "Typically, this is established by showing regular

but Vickers J. in *Tsilhqot'in Nation (William)* worked with that in his finding of an expansive area for a semi-nomadic people and further litigation will certainly be required.

Much ill will and uncertainty was caused by *Benoit v. Canada*, a ruling by the Federal Court that said that Treaty 8 Indians did not have to pay any kind of taxes on or off reserve because that is what they believed they had been promised even though the historical record belied that interpretation. The judgment was reversed on appeal, leaving Indians feeling cheated and mainstreamers only slightly less outraged.

The Supreme Court was at it again in *Mikisew Cree First Nation v. Canada (Minister of Canadian Heritage)*, a rather small matter about the location of a winter road off, but just adjacent to, a reserve. Two doctrines promising great future trouble were expounded here by Justice Binnie, the loquacious author of *Marshall I*, whose airy and sweeping language triggered the rocks-and-trees idea. Binnie suggested that Treaties, far from being final and definitive documents of resolution, were in fact mere "frameworks" for future accommodation. Nothing can have been further from the minds of the drafters, but that is for now the law and will so remain until it has caused such trouble as to be changed.

The rise of reconciliation

Even more disturbing was the very first sentence of Binnie's judgment (unanimously supported by the Court): "The fundamental objective of the modern law of aboriginal and treaty rights is the reconciliation of aboriginal peoples and non-aboriginal peoples in their respective claims, interests and ambitions" (para. 1).[30] The idea of "reconciliation" has been a steadily growing part of the vocabulary of the courts since the first days of the

---

occupancy or use of definite tracts of land for hunting, fishing or the exploitation of resources. These apply to nomadic and semi-nomadic groups ..." The practice must be viewed from an aboriginal perspective to translate into a modern common-law right.

30 On a language note, it is interesting to consider the descriptor, "non-aboriginal," as the way to denote all other Canadians. The approach gives aboriginality primacy as to the *indicia* of humanity, a curious concept. Certainly, the main commonality of those who would be better described as "other Canadians" is surely not that they are "non-aboriginal." This usage is another measure of how political correctness has captured this field of thought.

modern cycle of Indian law. But it has gradually morphed from the concept of reconciling legal systems—a proper job for courts—to the reconciliation of the parties to actions.

There is a very serious problem with this approach. The purpose of judging the law in any field is not and cannot sensibly be one of "reconciliation" in the sense of "reconciling ... peoples." That may be a matter of policy or of administration, but not for the courts. They are neither intended nor equipped for this purpose.[31] The purpose of judging the law is to provide order and certainty in social relationships, and to provide for resolution in the case of serious disagreement. That is true of criminal law, labor law, civil law, torts, family law, administrative law, constitutional law ,and everything else. "Reconciliation" of parties is something very different. It requires that all parties agree to, or at least voluntarily acquiesce in, a solution. Any party, acting alone and with determination, can deny that reconciliation and therefore deny resolution and closure.

Unanimous consent is a wonderful thing but a most infrequent rule in human affairs. The reason is obvious: the rule opens an extraordinary opportunity for blackmail and the tyranny of a minority, even a minority of one, to frustrate the common good or purpose. The law is designed to get around this difficulty by (ideally) ensuring that every party is heard, that their positions and rights are balanced, and that a resolution is reached. (The resolution may of course be a trade-off, with each party getting something, but that is very different from "reconciliation".) Each of these elements is essential, including "resolution," by imposed judgment if required.

This harsh reality is a main reason that we prefer to leave most human interactions to the voluntary market rather than the coercive realm of law and government. Even when we abandon voluntary arrangements for the coercive ones of the public sector, we try to keep most things a matter for policy and governments, rather than law and the courts. There is very good reason for this approach: it admits of flexibility, easier change with changed circumstance, better accommodation to particular circumstances and so on. But in some areas we cannot avoid the machinery of the courts and in those areas the purpose of law is not reconciliation of the litigants.

---

31 A close reading of earlier jurisprudence suggests that the earlier usage of "reconciliation" was a strictly legal concept, that is, how to make the evolving law on matters aboriginal fit within the mainstream system of statute and common law. That is a different and proper pursuit. It appears to have been superseded by a judicial desire to engage in "social engineering."

In Indian law, the Court has clearly taken unto itself a role never intended, that of the social engineer. Justice Binnie's words lay bare the unacceptable philosophy underpinning judgments in this area. And of course short of revolution or separation, there is nothing that any of us can do about that. The Court is supreme in Indian law. Parliament cannot over-ride. The Court should contemplate this problem in its future work.

The current state of Indian law is very unsatisfactory to most of society, including Indians, because the overarching characteristic is one of uncertainty as to powers and responsibilities in major parts of our country. *Haida*, mentioned as a British Columbian case but in fact applying to all of Canada under Indian claim and not subject to treaty—that is, much of Quebec and the Atlantic as well—established the principle that Indian collectives must be consulted in respect of activities claimed (not proven as owned) by them, and "traditional territories"—the usual description of lands claimed—can be very large. In British Columbia, this includes almost all of the province. *Mikisew* clearly established that Indians must be consulted about activities on unalienated Crown lands in Treaty areas. '

A current case in the Ontario courts, *Platinex Inc. v. Kitchenuhmaykoosib Inninuwug First Nation* (in progress), is establishing that the same duties extend further within Treaty lands if a local Band is seeking a Treaty Land Entitlement—that is, an application for a Reserve expansion. The court has established that this application gives the Band additional rights everywhere in its "traditional territories" where, in theory, new Reserve lands might be granted.[32]

The net impact of these cases is to create a regime of co-management over much of the land mass of Canada. The possibilities are only beginning to be explored by a creative aboriginal bar. Last year, a judge of the Federal Court granted the Musqueam Band of Vancouver an injunction stopping a sale of major federal government buildings in downtown Vancouver to a private landlord. The Musqueam, Squamish, and a couple of other Bands may become co-managers or co-owners of all Crown real estate in Metro Vancouver under this view. The trial judgment has been recently reversed

32 It is worth noting in passing that the Band takes the position that the Reserve was sized on a per-capita basis when settled in 1929, and this should be adjusted upwards to meet the expanded population at the present time. It is obvious that acceptance of this proposition as a general rule would lead to endless litigation or total renegotiation with most of the 600 Bands in Canada on a regular basis as a result of population changes, a truly daunting prospect.

upon appeal, in part because the federal sale documents retained a right of repurchase if such were required to satisfy claims. Uncertainty continues.[33]

So ends this brief summary of law. It only hints at the underlying complexity and no one should enter this field without the services of an experienced lawyer. The purpose of the above recital is only to illustrate the enormous extent to which the lives and prospects and opportunities of Indian people are governed by the courts. This is of course in addition to the micromanagement of personal affairs imposed by the Indian Act itself. It is worth noting explicitly: people in mainstream society would think such a high importance of litigation and directive law in their lives to be absolutely outrageous and yet we seem to accept it as normal for Indians.[34]

Politics and administration

On the treaty negotiation side, much progress is continually claimed but as of this writing only two new treaties have been (almost) concluded in the British Columbia since Nisga'a. These are the Tsawwassen and the Maa-nulth. Several[35] are said to be in the final stages of negotiation but

---

33 Most students of the topic would agree that most of Vancouver is subject to a strong Indian title claim. This includes private lands as a matter of law (*Delgamuukw*, paras. 172–176), though to date these have been left "off the table" in public discourse, presumably in order not to contribute to the unease of the public. The author has not studied implications for other urban areas but certainly if the Vancouver Bands make a lot of money out of their position, there will be calls for equitable treatment by every Band having a rich urban area in its traditional territory, calling past treaties manifestly unfair in the circumstances. Just such a claim is currently being pursued, with some direct action, by a Six Nation group in southern Ontario.

34 For the reader who might wish to delve into this legal area more deeply, I would suggest as additional reading "Measuring a Work in Progress: 20 Years of Section 35" by John Borrows of the University of Victoria. Borrows traces the evolution of the Supreme Court's thinking on aboriginal rights and reconciliation since the Constitution Act, 1982, and connects this with ideas of Canadian citizenship, which topic will be further studied in chapter 4 of this book.

35 As of November 2008, eight "First Nations" were in Stage-5 negotiations to finalize a treaty and had signed agreements in principle: In-SHUCK-ch Nation,

preliminary ratification exercises by several Bands have not gone well. In addition, the costs of negotiation continue to mount, at the time of this writing estimated at something like $1 billion, all in but not counting Nisga'a, a $100 million exercise on its own.[36] And, finally, numerous interim agreements are being entered into that allow limited resource development in disputed territories.

As an overview, what we have in British Columbia is a very dysfunctional way of achieving reconciliation or dispute resolution. There are three main parties and their goals and motives are not in harmony. For the federal government, this is a distant problem that will be very costly one day and thus there is no hurry getting there. For the provincial government, the situation is an enormously frustrating impediment to the certainty required for economic development but the rules set out by the courts and the costs of reaching agreement are politically difficult. For the Indian leadership, one cannot fail to note that the longer things are strung out, the better the offers become, and interim cash flow can often be arranged. And, most perniciously, for those charged with negotiations, this process provides a very good living with no urgency for resolutions and much incentive for continuation.

While the human problems have been similar in the rest of the country, the legal and historic developments have been less frequent, though some are very important. After Oka, the urge for governments to make concession increased. The Charlottetown Accord was to provide for a third order of Indian government as a part of the concessionary movement. The Pilot Sales project for Fraser River salmon has been mentioned and the creation of Nunavut noted.

Lheidli T'enneh Band, Maa-nulth First Nations, Sechelt Indian Band, Sliammon Indian Band, Tsawwassen First Nation, Yale First Nation, and Yekooche Nation (British Columbia Treaty Commission, 2008). The Maa-nulth and Tsawassen Nations have actual treaties ratified by British Columbia and awaiting action by Canada.

36 The negotiating terms of reference state that the governments will lend the money necessary to pay the costs of the Indian negotiators and that these loans will be reimbursed from settlement proceeds. No one seriously believes this: last minute compensatory adjustments will be made as was done in the Nisga'a case.

Royal Commission on Aboriginal Peoples

The Royal Commission on Aboriginal Peoples (RCAP) was a part of that package, in the process turning into the longest and priciest Royal Commission to date. The Commission recalled, amplified, and proselytized the "parallel society" concept that bedevils us today, romanticizing the "two-row wampum" image as a basis for the future.[37] Strangely, there is not much more to say about the influence of the Commission than that. Its advice has virtually disappeared, ignored even by the government that established it. The RCAP went almost exclusively down a one-way road of the reserve system and a constrained and cloistered Indian culture, virtually ignoring not only the potential opportunity but even the actual fact of massive Indian migration to the cities and to the mainstream society.

Of course, it is not possible to spend almost $60 million without leaving some sort of legacy, and that of RCAP may be divided into three parts. The least important was its report (RCAP, 1996b), virtually ignored by governments except when invoked by reference to support the theory of the parallel society. And it does remain a powerful iconic text for many in the Indian System. It is the definitive statement of the cultural anthropologists' thesis that cultural differences between indigenous and "settler" culture should trump all other dimensions of the relationship. Much more material is the second part, a large body of research, of considerable value to scholars but with little impact on the public. The third and most important is a community of Indian and white[38] academics and activists who received funding from, or were politicized by, the RCAP process. Many of this group remain highly influential in policy making or communications, and the general perspective of the RCAP remains the governing one in the policy field, restrained by the reality pressures on the politicians who tend to be less theoretical and more cautious.

---

37 "The two rows of purple are two vessels, travelling down the same river together. One, a birch bark canoe, is for the Indian people, their laws, their customs, their ways. The other, a ship, is for the whiter people, their laws, their customs and their ways. We shall travel the river side by side, but in our own boat. Neither of us will try to steer the other's vessel" (RCAP, 1996a: "Looking Forward, Looking Back"). The quotation is an extract from a Dutch-Mohawk treaty of 1613.

38 While there are today millions of Canadians who are neither aboriginal nor white, few from these other ethnic groups has become identified with these questions, either as scholars or activists.

Administration—a first look

In the real world, Indian budgets rose exponentially and the effectiveness of oversight by taxpayers seems to have declined dramatically if the repetitive complaints of the Auditor General are any measure. A dreary litany of some 67 of the Auditor General's reports stretching back for 20 years can be found on the internet by the masochistically inclined.[39] It is fair to say that the Auditor General has repeatedly, persistently, and consistently criticized Indian and Northern Affairs Canada (INAC)[40] for a pervasive failure of accountability. Enormous quantities of public money are spent without any assurance that they are buying what they are supposed to buy, and often there is not even clarity on the goal of the expenditure. There seems always to be a plethora of studies commissioned, working plans drafted, grand plans devised, meetings convened, internal reviews conducted, and so on. Results are less obvious.

A 2003 study of housing found over $4 billion over ten years for Reserve housing had lacked clear definitions of objects or outcome—except for the press stories that continue on a regular basis. A 2004 study on education found that the INAC has poorly defined responsibilities in the area, does not know whether funds are being used for the intended purposes, has no assurance that only eligible students are being funded, and is not providing an adequate picture of its performance to Parliament. And so it goes on. The annual fuss is little noted by the media and less by the public. That, one assumes, is how things work at Indian Affairs.

But to be fair to the Department, they are following their theory of devolution of responsibility. Even the Auditor General seems sometimes prepared to "see no evil" in Indian country. In a statement to the Parliamentary Committee examining the Accountability Act in 2006, the Auditor General simply ducked responsibility: "We do not believe it is our responsibility to

---

39 See the web site of the Office of the Auditor General of Canada, <http://www.oag-bvg.gc.ca/internet/English/rp_fs_e_44.html>. See also Clemens, Hayes, Mullins, Veldhuis and Glover, 2005; Clemens, Lammam, Palacios, and Veldhuis, 2007; Clemens, Mullins, Veldhius, and Glover, 2004, where egregrious examples from the Auditor-General's reports have been gathered and tabluated.

40 Indian and Northern Affairs Canada (INAC) is the current name and acronym for what was earlier known as the Department of Indian Affairs and Northern Development; its acronym, DIAND, is still much used.

routinely audit recipients of grants and contributions. As previously noted, this is the responsibility of the managers of those programs. Therefore, I would expect that we would rarely exercise this option" (Standing Senate Committee on Legal and Constitutional Affairs, 2006); "this option" was the proposed new powers to audit Indian governments, a power eventually stripped from the Bill by the opposition parties. This, on the face of it, is shocking. The job of the Auditor-General is value for the taxpayers' money. To fail to follow that trail as far as is necessary is to fail in the job. It is not sufficient to blame intermediaries.

As the twenty-first century began, then, the authority of the Indian System grew apace, and the federal government, democratically charged to control such affairs, simply tried to keep things quiet by smothering any emerging question with money, though not, alas, with effective results. Indian political organizations at all levels—Band, provincial and national (but not local/urban)—grew and prospered by way of public funds, despite occasional setbacks as when a federal Indian Affairs Minister, Hon. Robert Nault, most exceptionally cut his budgetary contribution to the Assembly of First Nations (AFN) for a couple of years.

The provincial organizations in Saskatchewan and especially Manitoba were given very large funding for program administration, with poor oversight and equivalent results over a ten-year period. Finally, in January of this year (2008) a news item appeared stating that the three top officers of the INAC's Manitoba region (handling $800 million *per annum*) were escorted out of the department's offices and placed on paid leave during investigation (Friesen, 2008, January 18: A6). A local MP, Pat Martin, said of the "Manitoba Framework Agreement"—a supposed pattern setter for devolution to regional Indian organizations set up over ten years ago—that it had produced little beyond consultants' reports: "I think there's been a reluctance to have an honest appraisal of the administration because it's such a god-awful rat's nest of formal and informal relationships and it exposes how fundamentally wrong the whole system is" (Friesen, 2008, January 18: A6).

In any event, "self-government" became the nostrum of the day. The problems of Indians, it was argued, arose from the fact of governance by others. In fact, the actual location of Indian governmental authority has been a convenient mystery for a generation, "convenient" because a clear assignment of authority would carry with it a clear acceptance of responsibility. And that is nowhere to be found in this field. To be clear: the "convenience" is general. That is why it works so well for everyone. Ottawa can say that it provides lots of money; it is up to the Chiefs to spend it and the provinces to assist with social services. The provinces can note, with reason, that the Constitution assigns Indians to Ottawa and Ottawa gives the provinces little in the way of funding in this area. The Chiefs can point to the Indian Act and claim that, in the end, Ottawa is in charge of everything. Whichever side is speaking, the fingers always point at someone else.

But surely the financial accounts will tell the story? Perhaps they might, but they are not available. For the past 20 years, Ottawa has taken the position following a legal case that Indian government accounts are private and are not to be revealed even to Parliament, which votes the money.[41] Thus the "inside stories" of Band administration have been hidden. Ottawa chose not to appeal this very vexing ruling, perhaps because it sat well with a normal bureaucratic penchant for secrecy.

The closure of information made life a good deal easier for Ottawa. Details can be embarrassing if the public gets to know them. It is disturbing to speculate how much better things might have worked in Band administration, and how much earlier good things would have been rewarded and mistakes corrected, had there been transparency here. This is a sad but illuminating example of how the Indian System works. The status quo actually functions quite well—for the System.

Indian and Northern Affairs Canada now claims to have notified those receiving funding of its intention to amend agreements to include audit clauses. These clauses are supposed to clarify and strengthen INAC's ability to conduct audits of funding agreements to ensure that Bands have appropriate management, financial, and administrative controls in place, encourage the sharing of best practices, and ensure that contributions are used for the provision of intended programs and services. This is standard departmental language and, until accounts are public, we will simply not know.

To illustrate the perverse incentives for the administrators of Indian governments, recall that every problem resolved is a few System jobs gone, worrisome to those who hold such jobs. Solving the problem of poverty would change the balance; prosperous Indians wouldn't need aid. Educated Indians might make trouble, might move off the Reserve, and then what

41 *Montana Band of Indians v. Canada (Minister of Indian & Northern Affairs)* 51 D.L.R. (4d) 306, [1988] 5 W.W.R. 151, [1989] 1 F. C. 143, 59 Alta., L. R. (2d) 353, 18 F.T.R. 15 (Federal Court Trial Division). The case dealt with an access to information request but also comments on monies raised by the First Nation itself and those which arise from departmental funding. The net result was to close access to Band accounts.

would be left? And surely detailed evidence of expenditure patterns available to taxpayers would cause more trouble than just about anything else imaginable.

This is not to suggest that any of the elites in the System actually wish poverty or illiteracy or substance abuse or any of the other problems common (though by no means universal) in the Reserve system. That would be wrong and unfair. But it is to say that the status quo confers position and responsibility on elites that would disappear along with the problems, were they solved. The Reserve itself is the core of the System. It is also a root cause of adverse social outcomes.

In most social questions, where results are profoundly unsatisfactory and governmental influence is important, there are the built-in checks and balances of media and political questioning and the vote of the taxpayers, which sooner or later force corrective action. Indian policy has been largely insulated from these salutary influences. Why should this be?

Information and measurement are central to identifying and quantifying problems. Statistics as to matters Indian are lacking compared to most of society (notwithstanding the bewildering array of forms that Indian governments are required to file). Indian life on reserves or even in the cities is little known to most of us. On the reserves, there is a problem of access for outsiders, including the media. In the cities, there is a lack of interest and a blurring of Indian outcomes into the general, undifferentiated life of downtown ghettos where most of the problems lie.

As a major example of this problem of information and measurement, consider the Nisga'a government, the much-heralded pattern for the self-government that was to be the key to all things good. What is actually happening there? It is impossible for an outsider to know. The official reports are anodyne. The anecdotes emerging are discouraging: tales of bad education, failed "economic development," nepotism, and continued finger pointing at Ottawa in respect of questions that are now clearly within the sole (and well-financed) authority of the Nisga'a Nation.

But these are only anecdotes. Is this crucial experiment working or not? After seven years of experience, no in-depth, independent report has been commissioned. And yet governments continue to use this idea as the answer. It would be good to have proof of the successes or not of such an important experiment and it is quite shocking that not only governmental, but also media and academic, researchers have not attempted such studies.

It is taken for granted that organizations and spokespersons for problem areas exist in most parts of our society. Surely we can rely on this kind of balance wheel? But the poorest and least educated are always inarticulate. The difficulty is enhanced for Indians because the spokespersons that the media interview are almost invariably members of the System, with all that implies, including an orthodoxy of view. It has been suggested that members of the media should cover Indian issues like foreign correspondents, traveling, investigating, and reporting to Canadians (Blatchford, February 2, 2008). The clear implication is that the usual spokespersons are not to be accepted at face value.

What about the insights available to ordinary people from plain common sense? Clearly there are problems here. What are the reasons? Theories of root causes can assist in the definition and understanding of problems, if those theories are applicable. But when the conventionally advanced theories are not the appropriate ones this approach breaks down. Thus, if unsatisfactory outcomes are attributed to the conventional suspects—racism in white society, victimhood, history, and lacks of funding and of self-government—then that analysis leads in one direction. That is the one that governments have been following, as it happens. But what if the more important reasons are otherwise? If other "root causes" are suggested—constitutional treatment of Indian people differently from others in law, finance and incentives, concentrating governance in an elite, the soft racism of lowered expectations, lack of property rights and a communistic sort of society, disincentives to mobility, disincentives to work and the like—then completely different theories of response might follow. None of these possible explanations are new, but there is a great reluctance to pursue them.

It is difficult to ever-estimate the importance of this truth about human nature. We tend to see things through the lens of our accumulated bias and conventional wisdom. This is conservatism at its most universal application, as it applies as fully to the Left as to the Right. And that is all very well at most times on most things, since we cannot be continually re-assessing all of our benchmarks and intellectual anchors. But when the policies dictated by any given world view persistently lead to failure, it may be time to consider a fundamental re-thinking. In my view, the second list of perspectives is the more applicable one.

As to the remedial influence of taxpayer concern, we have a particularly perverse situation. The directly oppressed of the system, Indians themselves, almost never pay taxes to their own governments. The mainstream taxpayers who actually fund these governments labor under the difficulty of a lack of information (including, as mentioned earlier, the inability of even parliamentarians to know how money is being used). The same mainstream group feels a mixture of a generalized sense of guilt, a suspicion that the question is far more difficult than publicly discussed, and a certain disgraceful indifference, all of which combine into a tendency to "see no evil." So overall, media interest is sporadic, largely confined to the reporting of short-term stories about contaminated water, suicides, or murders, or longer-term stories about poverty or educational statistics, almost never drilling down to the fundamental question of why these events are taking place.

Lacking the balance wheel and support of an informed public, the reaction of politicians to all of this is very understandable. The one thing they can easily do is supply money and transfer power, responsibility, and other public resources, and they do that in spades. The more useful thing they could do is ask the hard questions, but this would pit them immediately against the System, in an area where the public has minimal knowledge and the politicians and bureaucrats have minimal credibility. And hard questions that might seem to imply criticism invariably invite charges of "racism"! Obviously, this is not a useful fight for politicians to engage in unless absolutely forced to it by public opinion.

The usual political response, therefore, is to be appalled at the difficulties, resolute about doing something, generous with money and cooperative with the System, all things that have the signal virtue of buying silence. Whenever a new Minister is appointed, one need only to await the verdict of the head of the Assembly of First Nations. That verdict is almost invariably and fairly quickly: "We can work with this Minister." At that point, you know that reality has been evaded for at least one more governmental cycle. In the following chapter about the realities of today, it will be seen that some writers, especially aboriginal, are beginning to lift the veil of reality. That may finally make a difference.

⸸ ⸸ ⸸

Most of this chapter on history and law has been from the point of view of megapolitics, the big stories that are written about in the newspapers, even if not much noted by most readers. All of this is territory that most of us understand. I now must refer briefly to a viewpoint most of us can only imagine, namely that of the persons subject to this Indian policy. This will introduce the central feature lacking from existing policy, namely the perspective of the individual.

There can be no single account of what it is and has been like to be an Indian in Canada. There are 700,000+ stories. For some, without question, the news is ordinary enough, or even good. For most, equally without question, the news has been bad, at least in terms of such things as life expectancy, health, education, employment, mobility, and other such measurable things. What about less tangible things: happiness, a sense of freedom, culture, personal dignity, and security? These are the real measures of our lives and are deeply personal and specific to each one of us. But all we know of human affairs suggests that the tangibles constitute an irreplaceable base for building the intangibles.

As noted, our media and governments tell us little of ordinary Indians. They speak to the Chiefs. Most of us see little of those in the worst circumstances. Out of sight, out of mind, except for the occasional sad footage of children sniffing gasoline, images of a moldy abandoned house or the latest suicide numbers. So for most Indian people, what has been the result of the megapolitics? Are things even headed in the right direction?

The research of the Royal Commission offered a wealth of insight, holding hope for a better future but showing a pretty miserable present. Various writers have helped. Perhaps the most powerful academic in this area has been Menno Boldt, with his major work, *Surviving as Indians* (Boldt, 1993). Aboriginal writers have given perspective through fiction such as the novels of Thomas King or the plays of Thomson Highway. One might examine *Iroquois on Fire* (George-Kanentiio, 2006) or *Wasáse* (Alfred, 2005). There are many such fine works of fact and fiction but, in the end and mostly unnoticed and undocumented, every story is an individual one.

The megapolitics we have been reviewing do indeed tell a story of some considerable achievement in the legal and political realms. But from the point of view of the individual, has this been satisfactory? The statistics clearly say, "No." Might the money and energy have been expended in more productive ways? Common sense clearly says, "Yes."

To ask these questions is to raise the issue of the individual and the collective and to note, for later consideration, that from the point of view of the outside world, it is the collective that has received all of the attention. But lives are lived by individuals, and only by them. Only by affording Indian individuals freedom to bring their own individual experiences to bear can this tension between the individual and the collective be resolved, and it may be resolved in different ways for different people.

NOTE

The Royal Proclamation of 1763

The Royal Proclamation is a lengthy document to redefine and regularize the government of the lands east of the Mississippi River, provide for settlement by soldiers and others and regulate relationship with the Indians. As to the latter point, the Proclamation begins:

> And whereas it is just and reasonable, and essential to our Interest, and the Security of our Colonies, that the several Nations or Tribes of Indians with whom We are connected, and who live under our Protection, should not be molested or disturbed in the Possession of such Parts of Our Dominions and Territories as, not having been ceded to or purchased by Us, are reserved to them, or any of them, as their Hunting Grounds.—We do therefore ... declare it to be our Royal Will and Pleasure. that no Governor ... do presume, upon any Pretence whatever, to grant Warrants of Survey, or pass any Patents for Lands beyond the Bounds of their respective Governments ... as also ... for the present, and until our further Pleasure be known, to grant Warrants of Survey, or pass Patents for any Lands beyond the Heads or Sources of any of the Rivers which fall into the Atlantic Ocean from the West and North West, or upon any Lands whatever, which, not having been ceded to or purchased by Us as aforesaid, are reserved to the said Indians, or any of them.

And later:

> And We do hereby strictly forbid, on Pain of our Displeasure, all our loving Subjects from making any Purchases or Settlements whatever, or taking Possession of any of the Lands above reserved, without our especial leave and Licence for that Purpose first obtained.

There was a reason for this, as the document continues:

And whereas great Frauds and Abuses have been committed in purchasing Lands of the Indians, to the great Prejudice of our Interests. and to the great Dissatisfaction of the said Indians: In order, therefore, to prevent such Irregularities for the future, and to the end that the Indians may be convinced of our Justice and determined Resolution to remove all reasonable Cause of Discontent, We do, with the Advice of our Privy Council strictly enjoin and require, that no private Person do presume to make any purchase from the said Indians of any Lands reserved to the said Indians, within those parts of our Colonies where, We have thought proper to allow Settlement: but that, if at any Time any of the Said Indians should be inclined to dispose of the said Lands, the same shall be Purchased only for Us, in our Name, at some public Meeting or Assembly of the said Indians, to be held for that Purpose ...

(George III. *Royal Proclamation of 1763* [Royal Proclamation, 1763 (U.K.) R.S.C. 1985 Appendix II, no. 1])

NOTE

What was the intent of the framers of Section 35?

"Section 35" of the *Canadian Charter of Rights and Freedoms* is seen by Indian organizations and by academics as the fundamental charter of Indian rights and self-government. (The shorter s. 25 is more properly characterized as a "shield" against the rest of the Charter and other mainstream laws, rather than a "sword" for taking new territory.) As in all of these questions, what s. 35 eventually means will be what the Supreme Court of Canada says it means—no more and no less. But it is worth recalling what the framers[1] thought it meant.

The current Section 35 reads:

> 35(1) The *existing*[2] aboriginal and treaty rights of the aboriginal peoples of Canada are hereby recognized and affirmed.
>
> (2) In this Act, "aboriginal peoples of Canada" includes the Indian, Inuit and Métis peoples of Canada.
>
> (3) For greater certainty, in subsection (1) "treaty rights" includes rights that now exist by way of land claims or may be so acquired.
>
> (4) Notwithstanding any other provision in this Act, the aboriginal and treaty rights referred to in subsection (1) are guaranteed equally to male and female persons.

It is interesting that the original patriation document proposed to Parliament on October 2, 1980 had no sections 25 and 35, but merely protected "rights" *not* contained in the Charter, "including those that may pertain to native people." It was referred to a Parliamentary committee that was strongly lobbied by

1 That is, Prime Minister Trudeau and the provincial Premiers of the day, with the exception of the Premier of Quebec, who refused to adhere to the Constitution Act, 1982.

2 Emphasis added for reasons to follow.

aboriginal organizations (Romanow, Whyte, and Leeson, 1984). The Committee reported back with a version on January 20, 1981 containing the essential ingredients of ss. 25 and 35.

The subsequent story is told in some detail by Melvin Smith, Q.C., who had been the senior constitutional bureaucrat for British Columbia from the Victoria Conference of the early 1970s through the conclusion of the conferences on aboriginal government following the 1982 amendments (Smith, 2000). Smith commented on the different nature of the Committee additions: "The important point to stress is that this section did not have its origins in, or survive the rigors of, the detailed federal-provincial negotiations to which the rest of the Patriation package was exposed" (2000: 6) This constitution-making by inattention to this topic was to continue throughout the piece. The Supreme Court threw a wrench into Prime Minister Trudeau's timetable in the Spring of that year and he had to submit to a final, major, and acrimonious week of negotiations in November. Smith recalls that all of the debate was about other items: "I attended all of the meetings ... [and] ... the subject of aboriginal rights was not raised during the whole four days" (2000: 6). While the draft at that point contained the essence of s. 35, it was left out of the "final" version of November 18. Romanow, Whyte, and Leeson report that there was serious division among the provinces and among aboriginal organizations and that "[t]he nature of the last minute negotiations—complex, occasionally bitter, and hurried—militated against any careful consideration of aboriginal rights" (Smith, 2000: 7). The prudent view of the day was that the matter should be put off to a future federal-provincial conference. The aboriginal organizations united at that point and demanded the inclusion of s. 35.

In a series of long distance phone calls, the issue was revisited and Premier Lougheed insisted upon the addition of the word "existing" (re aboriginal rights) to ensure, as he thought, that new law could not thereby be created. (Events were to prove him wrong.) A new Section 28 (gender equality) was added and Saskatchewan insisted on the constitutional recognition of aboriginal rights.

Finally the deal was done. Romanow, Whyte, and Leeson: "Thus, the unsettling period of bilateral negotiations over long distance telephone ended. It was a strange way to settle important and complex legal and social questions ..." (Smith, 2000: 8). Smith is more direct: The words came from an exercise "involving only the Premiers and not having the usual deliberation of Ministers and their senior officials" (2000: 9). Anyone understanding the impact of words in a constitution will be chilled by that fact. He adds: "Virtually nothing has been written that suggests there was any serious example of what the words meant. If anyone had suggested (which they did not) that in later years the words would be interpreted to include the constitutional recognition of a third order of government, he would have been laughed out of court" (2000: 9). Bismarck famously said that the public should not know how either sausages or laws are made, and it seems to have applied here.

Section 35 was as yet incomplete and, at a scheduled conference in 1983, subsections (3) and (4) of the existing law were added in a process so chaotic that additions were, in the words of another observer, "as a result of last minute discussions which hardly anyone could have followed, understood and evaluated" (Smith, 2000: 12). Further conferences to entrench self-government followed in 1984, with no success. The very fact that these discussions were thought necessary, however, raises a strong presumption that the subject of self-government was not implicitly resolved by the existing language of s. 35.

In his concluding discussion on the meaning of s. 35, Smith makes the point that the language can mean little or a very great deal, depending upon the attitudes of nine Supreme Court judges on a given day. But, as to the ability of governments to derogate from (or permanently cede) their jurisdictions to Indian governments he says:

> To suggest that Section 35, as amended, allows senior governments to divest their legislative powers permanently through future land claims agreements is to suggest that the 1983 amendment [*i.e.*, *re* land claims incorporating governance powers] had the effect of amending the ***Constitution***'s amending formula. That is impossible because to amend the amending formula requires the approval of *all* provinces. Quebec did not approve the 1983 amendment. (2000: 18)

For additional testimony, I would refer the reader to the Debates of the Senate, April 11, 2000, and the words of Senator Buchanan, Premier of Nova Scotia at the time of the above cited debates. He was discussing the constitutional status of the proposed Nisga'a Treaty and makes it clear that a third order of government based on s. 35 was not in the minds of any of the framers.

There are two central points to take away from this digression. The first is that the framers enacted s. 35 in haste, understood it to mean little, and certainly not to imply a new third order of government. The second is that the language is loose enough that the Supreme Court of Canada has the power either to follow the intent of the framers or to make a great deal of new law indeed. There is much future work for lawyers here, and major cautionary tale for those who would lightly amend constitutions in a hurry.

CHAPTER 3

The existing situation

All of this history and law has had political, economic, and cultural consequences for the Indian people that are quite different from those affecting other Canadians. The differences are not superficial; they run very deep, especially in political terms. The fundamental underlying concept of citizenship and the role of the state is different for Indians, so we must start there.

A different kind of citizen?

The statement above about the legal standing of Indians is so fundamental, so far outside the thought of most Canadians, that it is worth saying again in other words. In terms of citizenship, all other Canadians are people without differentiation of any kind whatsoever—none, not even for persons born elsewhere who have since become citizens. There are minor differences in law as between Canadians related to age (*e.g.* voting rights), religion (guarantees of separate school systems) and gender (which washrooms to use) and some rather more important ones related to the French and English languages but, in theory, that is about it.[1] In general, our laws speak to equality rather than difference. There is no distinction in citizenship—none—based on ethnicity, culture, or heritage except with respect to Indians.

Please note again: this distinction with respect to Indians does not turn on the question of heritable rights (such as property, hunting rights, and so on) although Indians may have such rights in a unique collective way. But

1 It is accepted that significant gender and other differences remain but it is a stated aim of governments to reduce and end them.

all Canadian citizens enjoy heritable rights in one way or another. Rather, it is about a different form of citizenship. The Indian form of citizenship relates far more to the federal government, and ultimately the Crown, than is the case for ordinary Canadians.[2] For most of us, our day-to-day lives are mediated by the private sector mostly, and thereafter by provincial and local governments. Local government exists for Indians too—but "Band government" is exclusively of Indian application. Again, as a general statement, the private sector has much less relevance to Indians and the tribal collective is central.

As well the role of the state is different. It is not simply that Indians are entitled to special benefits from the state in addition to those available to others. Much more importantly, the state has responsibilities to Indians that it does not owe others. It has a "fiduciary duty" to Indians to, in general, look after them. And it has a duty of honorable treatment of Indians (stemming from the "Honor of the Crown"). Surprisingly, honorable treatment is not a duty owed to other Canadians, as is apparent from time to time. The courts have been very clear in imposing these special obligations.

These things may sound theoretical but when bureaucrats craft policy or courts make judgements, they loom very large in practical terms. Bureaucrats in particular create large check lists and systems to ensure compliance with court *dicta*, even almost off-handed *obiter* at times. They create even larger systems to insulate themselves from financial responsibility by off-loading it (to Indian governments who often do not care to accept the responsibility in turn). This is rational in the circumstances but very expensive and destructive of efficiency and accountability.

None of these legal, financial, and structural differences in Indian country are a matter of "choice" by the Indians concerned, except insofar as individuals may opt out. The Indian citizenship and government structure is one that has been, and is imposed, by the mainstream, not chosen by Indians.[3]

On the other hand, another choice is available. Life in the mainstream world is open to Indians. There is no doubt some residual racism to make this difficult in some quarters but this is easily avoidable in our very politically

---

2 It should be noted that, while Indians are subject to an enormous quantity of federal law, they are not exempt from provincial laws except when there is a direct conflict between federal legislation and/or treaty rights. For a detailed analysis of this complex area, see Mrozinski, 2007.

3 The Nisga'a structure is an arguable exception to this statement.

correct society. Large companies, for example, bend over backwards in order to employ aboriginals. Universities pine for Indian applicants and funding is not an issue.

Though people do move back and forth, on balance the ratio between those living on Reserve and off has now been stable for some years after a move "off" in the 1990s. The proportion of Status Indians living off Reserve may again be rising.[4] This relative stability is perhaps not surprising given the incentive pattern. The welfare rate among those living on Reserve exceeds 40%. While many persons on welfare are unemployable (because of age, disability, or health), for employable persons there is, in any event, a lack of work. Actual job uptake is heavily weighted to the Indian System, in its Band, federal, provincial, and justice system manifestations. These financial incentives (welfare, government jobs) for some provide another reason for staying on Reserves, in addition to more natural attractions such as family, familiarity, and culture.

Concepts and realities

These basic differences of citizenship and relationship to the governments suggest and impose important organizational differences, all resulting in different realities on the ground. It cannot be emphasized too strongly: the current estate of the Indian people in Canada did not just "happen," nor is it the result of deliberate planning by bad people. Rather, it is the unintended but predictable outcome of a set of premises and forces that have been put in play by our forebears, modified and augmented by courts, and supported by current federal and provincial governments as well as (in general) the media and academics.

---

4 The 2006 Census reports that "[a]n estimated 40% (of First Nations) lived on the Reserve while the remaining 60% lived off the Reserve in 2006. The off-Reserve proportion was up slightly from 58% in 1996" (Statistics Canada, 2008). This gives the trend. Note however that this survey is based upon self-identifying "First Nations," not "Status."

See Chronology of the Indian land question in British Columbia, p. 237. The post-1985 reinstatements following the passage of Bill 31 that restored Indian status to many who had been excluded under previous law, particularly on the basis of gender, made for an apparent dramatic shift in distribution off Reserve. Recent migration shows a more stable pattern. Both on and off, population has been growing at broadly similar rates for a decade or more.

For those who find the current situation unsatisfactory, that causality should in a way be seen as good news, because what has been brought about by underlying design factors can presumably be changed. But no one should believe that change can be either rapid or easy (or even desired by the alleged beneficiaries; recall the "white paper"). After all, hundreds of thousands of human beings have a great deal invested in the status quo, if only because it is the reliable status quo and we all fear change.

To begin at the level of concepts, there are two primary models in play in thinking about an optimal Indian policy.[5] They relate to that most fundamental element of our existence, identity.

The individual and the collective—an initial look

One theory is the current and prevailing orthodoxy that sees Indians first and foremost as members of a collective. The first thing to be said about any Indian, in this theory, is that he or she is indeed an Indian. Yes, he or she is male or female, young or old, and so on, but "Indian" looms over everything.

To describe the competing theory without elaboration at this point, Indians could be seen, like all other Canadians (at least in theory) as, first and foremost, individuals. Each of us is described by an aphorism of the columnist, Andrew Coyne (speaking of the foundation of a liberal society): "each individual is the unique intersection of all the many groups to which each of us belongs; that such individual is, far from the rootless atom of caricature, the greatest common denominator of social cohesion. Our uniqueness as individuals, the perfect singularity of every human consciousness, is in fact what we have in common" (Coyne, 2006, December 7). According to the second theory, to be an Indian is an additional fact of one's life. According to the first, this status is one's life.

The relative merits of the approaches will not be argued in this chapter save to note two things. Like all life choices, the decision should insofar as is possible be left to individuals reacting to balanced and neutral government incentives, which is not currently the case. Next, note that many Status Indians have in fact chosen the second road, "going to town", notwithstanding the incentive package on Reserve. But governments and the Indian System are firmly focused on the first concept, and close to denial on the second.

---

5 The Trudeauvian perspective of the "white paper" was that conjoining the very words, "optimal Indian policy," was intrinsically oxymoronic, that singling out any persons in this way—having a "Chinese" policy, say—would be a necessarily bad thing.

The prevailing orthodoxy is reinforced in history, the Royal Proclamation, in the Constitution (s. 91(24) and ss. 25 and 35 of the Charter amendments), the recommendations of the Royal Commission, in law (above all, the Indian Act), and in jurisprudence. The courts have been crystal clear: "Indianness" exists and is a collective attribute. Indian rights exist and are explicitly collective, not individual, though they may be exercised by individuals. Indian title exists and lodges in the collective, not in individuals, and decision-making may only be dealt with by the collective. The essence of "Indiannness" cannot exist without the collective. This is separate and apart from the idea of Indian culture.[6]

For the concept of a collective to have meaning and durability, it must be served, elaborated, and buttressed by structures, rules, and organization. Moreover, these elements must be separate and distinct from the mainstream—otherwise what would be the effective difference in being an Indian, point one, and how would the overwhelming assimilative attraction of the mainstream be kept at bay, point two? This observation leads directly and logically to the need and justification for a parallel society. I now turn to an examination of the challenges and opportunities facing the proponents of this road.

Features of a parallel society

Any viable society requires at least some of the following elements:

- shared sense of exclusivity or difference from others
- shared goals or purposes
- shared values
- founding myths
- language
- decision-making rules and enforcement authority (all governments in the end being based on coercion)
- finance
- administrative institutions
- leadership—and "followership."
- Net positive payoff for members (as compared to other available options)

Some of these are matters of choice and some are matters of fact.

6 It should be mentioned here that Indian culture is, like all culture, capable of being shared by all of humanity, though particular artefacts may be exclusive to the collective. Exclusive access to the culture cannot be a part of "Indianness," though certainly adhering to such culture is a part of the concept.

Language

Language, perhaps the most powerful single binding element for a potentially distinct society, is no longer a determining factor in this case and in the twenty-first century, notwithstanding some heroic efforts to the contrary. There never was a single common "Indian" language and very few people today make routine use of any of the various tribal tongues. English and French (in parts of Quebec) are now the usual means of communication.

According to the census for 2006, "about 29% of First Nations people who responded ... said they could speak an Aboriginal language well enough to carry on a conversation" (Statistics Canada, 2008). As might be expected the number was higher on Reserve (51%) than off (12%). However, "[o]nly 1% of First Nations people spoke only an Aboriginal language, although this percentage rose to 5% among seniors aged 65 to 74, and 10% among those aged 75 and over" (Statistics Canada, 2008). Among young people under 14, the ability to carry on a conversation was claimed by 21%, about the same as in 2001.

Shared goals and values

A case can be made for a shared sense of exclusivity, of goals and purposes, values and founding myths. But even here, difficulties arise due to small numbers split up among diverse histories and geographies. However at least one shared goal can be adduced for many, namely "surviving as distinct groups." This can be a powerful motive as noted around the world and over the ages.

Authority

As to legal underpinnings, support for the decision-making rules and enforcement structures of the current version of the parallel society stems almost entirely from the law of the mainstream society (though the power of social pressure should not be underestimated). The best-known exception in Canada at the moment is really only one step removed from statute law, namely the Nisga'a Nation, whose governmental power flows from the Constitution as a result of treaty entrenchment.[7]

---

7 Currently under legal challenge in *Sga'Nisim Sim'Augit (Chief Mountain) v. Canada*, Supreme Court of British Columbia. There are other exceptions based on traditional custom rather than the law of the mainstream society, such as the continued vitality of the Gitxsan Hereditary Chiefs organization, which relies on voluntary support rather than Canadian law. Their very different approach will be later described.

This general situation of reliance on the mainstream is obviously an unsatisfactory situation for those wishing a truly parallel society, which would require *de facto* sovereignty, but there are political difficulties in changing this by (say) expanding the Nisga'a experiment. One "political difficulty" is with the mainstream sentiment that holds that all Canadians are equal, and reluctantly accepted the Nisga'a Treaty as a one-off, distant, and isolated case in northern British Columbia. This difficulty may be declining as treaties are more discussed but I know of no polling evidence of this to date.

A more profound political difficulty is that too much distinction in citizenship leads directly to a reduction in feelings of support and responsibility held by other citizens in the mainstream (discussed by Cairns, Kymlicka, and Taylor; see chapter 4, "Principles"). Yet such feelings are the necessary support for the political will to assist with the economic and other well-being of a "parallel society" that is really only a set of very small and fragmented distinct communities embedded in the Canadian land mass.

Finance

The same problem arises in the matter of finance. With the possible exception of a few oil-rich bands in Alberta and a handful of real-estate-wealthy urban bands, there is no Indian community in Canada today capable of a modern standard of living without mainstream financial aid. Even the wealthy bands gladly accept the federal transfers. Stop the external cheques and you massively destabilize the status quo. Yet those reliant on other people's money, which may be varied or made conditional at any time, can hardly be said to be independent.

The standard cure, advanced by the Royal Commission on Aboriginal Peoples (RCAP) and others, is "economic development" to allow financial independence. Extreme scepticism is advised. The Chief federal negotiator for the Nisga'a Treaty public stated he did not expect financial independence for 15 years and, in fact, federal and provincial payments to the Nisga'a Nation have been growing rather than shrinking. To be sure, there are a few working examples of success such as the Osoyoos Band in southern British Columbia, but in general the actual land base of non-urban tribes is not likely to yield sufficient cash flow to allow the membership to live on either resource rents or local employment. A few urban bands—the Squamish or Musqueam of Vancouver, for example —may make enough from real-estate development to provide a work-free environment for members, but even that is a distant prospect.

The Membertou First Nation located in Cape Breton next to Sydney is an oasis of progress in an otherwise depressed area of Nova Scotia that seems to have achieved a solid "take off" with an initial assist from gaming revenues.[8] There are other such examples but the general statement of economic insufficiency holds true on the great majority of Reserves and the good news of some should not all us to turn away from the problems.

There are two theoretical cures for the general problem of finance of a parallel society. The first is for the members to work in the mainstream society and finance their own internal social project. This is an entirely feasible route (given determination and education) but certainly leads to ever closer integration, which is in opposition to the idea of a parallel society. However, it is the nigh-universal practice of other Canadians who have distinctive projects, be they cultural, religious, political, or whatever.

The second route would be the recognition of a much greater—very much greater—land base, capital endowment, or both for the Indian people. There being a fixed quantity of Canadian land, that option would directly reduce the land base available to the mainstream. An exercise of exactly this sort is currently underway in British Columbia in the treaty process, and is not proving to be easy. The sole example to date—the aforementioned Nisga'a Treaty—does not provide lands and cash nearly adequate for self-sufficiency based on current resource exploitation from the lands or on a "coupon clipping" basis from the cash. The two alternatives to self-sufficiency—Nisga'a people working in the mainstream world to finance themselves and large and growing transfers from mainstream taxpayers to the Nisga'a government—are in fact both being employed but hardly constitute a parallel society in any true sense of the word.

In theory, one could settle an immense capital endowment on Status Indians to provide a guaranteed cash flow sufficient for a modern middle-class lifestyle (say, to choose one target). Using a 4% yield on long-term government bonds as a proxy for a guarantee, a capital funding endowment of $1 million per person would do nicely, even after tax. Unfortunately, some-

8 Analyzed at length by Jacquelyn Thayer Scott in *Self Determination: The Other Path for Native Americans* (Scott, 2006). The analysis discusses governance extensively as the key to the remarkable progress and uses some of the insights of Stephen Cornell (1999) as well as the "Nation Building Model" of Cornell and Kalt (1998). It is a genuine success story that also contains some structural challenges for the future. See "A leading American view on tribal governance," p. 103.

thing costing in excess of $600 billion is not likely to be feasible.[9] There are other schemes—casinos, "urban reserves," timber-cutting permits, fishing set-asides, and the like—that essentially transfer cash to tribes by the free grant of special licenses or the ability to offer tax free environments, neither of which are "real world" or very dignified alternatives.

A special and prevalent example of positional schemes is the recent tendency to "tollgating," using a "veto" to extract cash, sinecure employment, or other valuable considerations as a price for allowing the mainstream to get on with its business. This is particularly relevant to resource development in British Columbia, as a result of the *Haida* decision by the SCC, which requires government to consult with Indians and seek to satisfy objections or overcome vetoes on any lands reasonably claimed as subject to Indian title. The Supreme Court having national jurisdiction, *Haida* now applies to Indian claims anywhere in Canada. Another "tollgating" scheme has recently been established growing out of the continuing Caledonia dispute in Ontario, where a group calling itself the Haudenosenee Development Institute is demanding fees from developers within the original Haldimand land grant, on pain of unspecified but dark alternatives.

As a bargaining tactic, "tollgating" is superbly successful. It is often simpler for a developer to pay the fee than to argue. However, as a pattern of economic behavior, it is an extremely costly way of achieving results: costly in terms of delayed or distorted development; costly, surely, to the dignity of those using the tactics. The costs here are mostly silent, invisible, and unquantifiable. How do you track a potential investor who simply moves on? The hidden costs are also arguably huge, but those paying them—all citizens of Canada—are almost totally unaware that the issue even exists. There is, therefore, almost no pressure to bring greater thought to this issue.

Closely allied to "tollgating" is "direct action." The famous names include Oka, Ipperwash, Gustafsen Lake, and Caledonia.[10] There have been

---

9 Lest this seem a large number, it should be pointed out that the current expenditures on Indians by the federal government, about $10 billion per year, would require an endowment of about $250 billion for permanent funding, on the same basis of calculation.

10 The massive Clayoquot logging protests of 1993, which resulted in the largest mass arrests in Canadian history were in fact more the actions of environmentalists than of Indians, but certainly had downstream advantages for local tribes who took over a much reduced but still major logging precinct.

many less well-known local actions or blockades not reported nationally but very effective where they take place. These exercises to date have probably increased Indian political power on balance but it is a dangerous game and public sympathy can shift. It is "dangerous" because, aside from the sympathy of the courts, public goodwill is essential to continued and growing public financial support, and a sense of guilt will only go so far.

The most important impacts of direct action are totally invisible and out of the headlines. They are the decisions taken and not taken simply out of fear of Indian manifestations. Politicians fear the publicity and, therefore, yield this point or that or more usually, fail to do this or that. Investors have a far easier time of it. They simply avoid any such problems, there being many places to put money in the world.[11]

So, like governance, the finance aspect of independence is difficult. The genuine (that is, non-subsidized) returns from economic development are really trivial in the scheme of things and Indian finance for the foreseeable future will have to depend upon some mix of mainstream-government transfers from taxpayers and earned income by the recipients.

Administrative institutions

Administrative institutions are the main current manifestation of the "parallel society." Indian administrative units are essentially based on the Indian Act's "Band" model, with Chief and Council governing band territory and band members living thereon. They also have the ability to confer benefits like educational support on members living off Reserve. About half of band governments are elected under the Indian Act's rules and the balance are "custom" and can vary considerably, even including acceding to governance by inheritance.[12] This structure is overlaid on memories of the much older

---

11 The above should not be read as a denial of the merits of Indian grievances that may be cited as the proximate cause of any given direct action. All too often, resolution of the cases in point has been disgracefully dragged out or avoided by the authorities. "Resolution" in this sense extends not just to failure to reach a settlement but also to a failure to say "no," if that is the government view, or even, in too many cases, to communicate meaningfully. There is a huge feeling of lack of empowerment on both sides and the result is gridlock, harming everyone.

12 This is a general statement. The Nisga'a Nation again is an exception. There are also other special rules in effect as at Westbank and Sechelt, both in British Columbia.

tribal and clan organization that applied before the imposition of the Indian Act. Of course, the idea of "clan" has by no means disappeared and many Bands or "Nations" are in fact small collections of large extended families, which can produce both good and bad dynamics.

The obvious problem with this arrangement when one wishes to expand governance jurisdiction is the issue of size and capacity. The average on-reserve population in Canada is about 700, of whom perhaps half are children. This is not a large enough group to administer with any economy of scale nor is it a large pool from which to draw leaders.

The Royal Commission on Aboriginal Peoples (RCAP) recognized this problem in designing its ambitious ideas of self-government and settled on the idea of extended "nations," recognizing about 60. This would bring the average population living on Indian territory (covering a number of Reserves) up to about 7,000, geographically dispersed. This is still a rather small number, especially when sovereignty aspirations extend to municipal services, all of the social services, law enforcement, and so on. And, of course, many existing Bands would resist administrative consolidation into larger "nations" in any event. In addition, most of the existing or potential administrative units are not large enough to exercise much in the way of electoral clout, even if Indians chose to vote in mainstream elections, which many do not. This is a drawback in dealing with intensely political federal politicians and bureaucracies.

The national response to this has been the formation of the Assembly of First Nations (AFN), an organization, now well-financed (mostly by government), whose electoral base is the Chiefs of Canada. The Chiefs are jealous of their own prerogatives and tend to keep the AFN Grand Chief on a short leash, though he (only a "he" so far) is in fact the main public face of Canadian Indians.[13] It is important to note that the AFN is a voice for the Chiefs or certain of them, not a governor of the Chiefs. Power is carefully guarded in each Band. In other words, except for publicity purposes and intellectual leadership (two very important dimensions it should be said), the AFN is not powerful.

In fact, if one really wanted to create a parallel society in Canada, empowerment of the AFN, in particular through the democratic legitimacy of direct election of the Grand Chief, would be an obvious first step. It is notable how many politicians who are strongly opposed to the notion of

13 There are other national organizations purporting to represent Métis and urban Indians, as well as an Inuit council, but these are beyond the scope of this book.

a parallel society advance this idea from a narrow thought of "democracy." But centralization is not always a good thing. And if one really cares about "democracy" in the context of Indian policy, surely the proper place to start is with existing local structures.

Provincial groupings of Indians have forged closer ties, Manitoba, Saskatchewan and British Columbia being good examples, though British Columbia has a schism between the "Summit" (about 60%) and the Union of BC Indian Chiefs (about 40%). Perhaps because these provincial groups are smaller in size and geographical reach than the AFN, they have been able to build more influential organizations, to the point of actually taking over the administration of some INAC programs in their territory. But the strong point of these groups was designed to be, and remains, political.

More recent and arguably more successful administrative institutions are being proposed and in some cases actually established around specific functions. There is a First Nations Statistical Agency and an Indian Tax Advisory Board, educational boards, an experiment (disastrous in terms both of cost and delivery) with a provincial health-delivery program in Manitoba, and proposals for health boards elsewhere. Bands already administer welfare, and there are various controversial proposals to raise the responsibility to a multi-Band or provincial level to increase professionalism and avoid the petty politics that is inevitably a part of local cash handouts by elected Councils. For this latter reason the technique holds promise. The reason for this—particularly as a device to separate administration from politics—is illustrated by some research from south of the border.

There are proposals for a national Indian housing authority and, for those who worry about accountability, a special and distinct Auditor General for Indian finance. Economic development agencies abound. There is an Indian finance authority to assist Bands in raising money, given the inability to hypothecate real property assets. The number of these parallel authorities is immense and and responsibilities broad. But, are they solutions, and to what problems?

From the above short list it will be noted that most of the agencies are operating in fields normally assigned to provincial governments. Welfare, education, health, housing, economic development, municipal finance authorities, and so on are all the purview of large government departments in every province. They all work tolerably well and are reasonably accountable. That often cannot be said of the Indian parallel agencies working with on-Reserve people. So why do the provincial ministries not simply get on with fulfilling their responsibilities toward Indian Canadians as they do with all others (including hundreds of thousands of off-Reserve Indians and non-Indian aboriginals)? Exactly this solution has been proposed by many reformers. There are two main reasons in opposition, one shameful and the other understandable, if perverse.

The shameful explanation is that both levels of government are in the way. Most provincial governments do not want to have the problems associated with Indians. They especially do not want to pay for these problems and the federal government (in general—not always) is unprepared to foot the bill. Ottawa takes the general position that people living off Reserve are provincial responsibilities. But, providing beyond the minimum for a large and very costly clientele that is considerably less able to provide a self-financing tax base is unattractive to provincial treasurers.[14] The provinces also can argue that the Reserve system itself aggravates the problems of off-Reserve employment because on-Reserve educational quality is generally low and the system also enables some parents to cycle between living conditions on and off Reserve, which in turn damages their children's ability to learn. Surely, there is a way around this? After all, as an abstract proposition there is no doubt that it would be cost-effective and delivery-effective for Ottawa to turn its social-service dollars and responsibilities in this field over to the provinces.

The second, understandable, if perverse, explanation is this. Many Indian leaders do not want this kind of arrangement. This is often characterized as the need to maintain a special relationship with the Crown, relegating the Crown Provincial to a distinctly junior status for this purpose. But the real reason is the maintenance of the differences that support and define Indianness, and social services are very high on that list of differences. It matters from where you get your income, and if it is from the Chiefs, that develops a different view of citizenship than if social services flow from the provincial government.

It must also be noted that social services are the focus of a very large fraction of the Indian System, a fraction that would simply cease to exist with provincial takeover of the responsibilities. Turf protection is important to all organizations; no less so here. There are other, nobler, arguments that should not be overlooked. There is no doubt that clients of governmental services feel more secure if the service is coming from someone

14 The lower tax base is due to lower incomes and employment rates. According to Richards, the employment rate for Indians living off Reserve in western Canada in 2005 was 50% (2006: 66).

they trust and the cultural connection with the delivering agency may be important. And a case can be made that Indian problems are special and might well be not understood or even simply lost in the giant provincial bureaucracies.

So, the greatest effort, by far, that has been pursued in meeting the criteria for a viable parallel society has been in administration and in the development of the System in its many faces.

Leadership

Of the two remaining desiderata for a functioning parallel society, one of them, leadership, is fairly well developed. In fact, a disproportionate fraction of the available best[15] of the human resources of Canadian Indians goes into leadership of the parallel society. This is unavoidable, as there is a minimum size to any service agency no matter how small or large the clientele, and economies of scale are simply not available in serving the small numbers involved. There can be no doubt that, since the 1970s, the calibre of Indian leadership has grown immensely.

What might be called "followership" is a different matter. While leaders are important, in the end any society is only as strong as its membership, and the civic awareness and involvement in tribal matters of Canadian Indians does not appear to have developed as quickly as the leadership has done, at least if one may judge by such proxies as educational achievement and voter turnout.

Net positive payoff

A viable parallel society must provide a net positive payoff to its members in exchange for membership and support as compared to other options. Lacking this, of course, members drift away. The jury is out on this question. There is no doubt that during the 1980s and 1990s, a great many Status Indians "went to town"—left the Reserve system. Any assessment of migration must take into account the fact that there is a constant movement to and from Reserves, so this statement is about average numbers at any given time. In recent years, off-Reserve trend seems to have continued, with the fraction of Status Indians on-Reserve trending toward 50% by one measure (Canada, DIAND, 2006), or 48% by another (Statistics Canada, 2008) or as

15 Persons who have "gone to town" and found success in the mainstream are generally not "available" in this context.

low as 40%, if we use another Statscan measure that is less relevant.[16] (These various numbers illustrate the statistical dangers avoidable only by precise words.) In any event, the trend lines suggest that the off-Reserve world may on balance have a slight advantage in the eyes of those persons sufficiently mobile to choose either.

What is the Reserve world really like?

What is the Indian world, especially the Reserve world, really like? It is hard for an outsider to say, for any cultural community. Certainly, the dispassionate and objective history attempted in the first two chapters of this book does not pretend to describe properly the human dimensions of the estate of Canadian Indians. Because policy and politics are shaped by human beings, it is necessary to try to understand that dimension. The "Beginnings" statement set out some of the statistical realities but the more emotional realities of actual people should be canvassed too.

For first-hand testimony on Reserve realities, I refer the reader to a recent and remarkable book by Calvin Helin, *Dances with Dependency* (2006). This self-published work has become a major success as a Canadian best seller and is well worth the reader's attention. Helin's particular advantage in describing what it is like to be an Indian comes from the fact he is "Status" himself (having had to win that back through the machinery of Bill C-31) and has both the knowledge of an insider and the ability to speak without fear of charges of racism. His words are tough. I will cite some here, and return to his views in a later section on governance: "Imagine a situation where tragically high youth suicide rates, gross unemployment figures, frequent banana-republic style corruption, and persistent abuse—both substance and physical—prevail, and you might begin to understand what life is like on most Aboriginal reserves" (Helin, 2006: 25). He writes of an "Industry" surrounding matters Indian (whereas, for reasons explained, I prefer "System"), and we share in addition a deep respect for the insights of Paul Tennant and John Richards, both well cited.

In his historical section, he quotes Brian Lee Crowley on the difference between the traditional face-to-face Indian society where simple cooperation was a survival characteristic to the extended and anonymous cooperation of the modern world:

16 First Nations people living on reserve, 2006 Census data (Statistics Canada, 2008). However, the definition of "First Nation" used in this data covers only 68% of Status Indians, who are the focus of this book.

> What transformed Western society, making it so different culturally from many traditional societies, was that, under pressures such as scarcity, urbanization, the growth of technological diversity, and the emergence of the concept of individuality, acceptance of a shared, concrete social project began to break down. People could no longer achieve social solidarity and mutual cooperation merely on the grounds that all could see that their material survival and spiritual salvation depended on their playing a pre-determined role or function. (1995: 77)

Note especially "the concept of individuality," the essence of the post-Enlightenment Western world and consider the tensions this idea (inescapable, today) raises with traditional ways.

After a look at history, Helin turns again to today and the statistics that "tell of a situation so horrific that ordinary Canadians could not imagine the suffering of Aboriginal children on a daily basis. They clearly paint a picture of reserves across Canada that are, in many respects, the inner city ghettos of America" (2006: 107). He develops a concept of "learned helplessness," a condition that arises when people feel things completely out of the control of any action they might take, especially if basic survival needs are met though the uncontrollable actions of others. He is harsh on the federal government, which has engendered a

> culture of expectancy ... [and has] ... through its incompetence and related shortcomings, made it impossible for Aboriginal people to compete in the open marketplace ... in this day and age, it might be asked what sane, practical person would put the fate of his or her family in the hands of any government, let alone a massive central government located in some distant city? Would you put the now depleted East Coast cod stocks or the West Coast salmon in these hands? (Helin, 2006: 119)

He disparages the culture of entitlement based upon past wrongs and attacks "patronage payments that take precedence for those persons or families that support the newly elected Chiefs and Councils" (2006: 123). And on welfare:

> There can be no question that providing an artificial revenue source to Aboriginal communities has hastened the disintegration of the social and cultural fabric of communities. The dignity, respect and

> self-satisfaction received from working together have been replaced by a system that has turned Aboriginal people into spectators of their own painfully slow demise. (2006: 124)

On the matter of governance, see "Big Bear's Treaty" (p. 105) for the withering words of Jean Allard, who has been in the trenches of Métis and Indian politics for decades. Helin's further comments are no less so. He describes:

> a form of wilful blindness on the part of indigenous leaders, and which has become their total formula for governing. If there is a community problem, it is simply the fault of the federal government ... One of the most alarming results of being entirely focussed on the federal government for such a long period of time is that Aboriginal people tend to mold their behavior, activities and community institutions on the model of the federal bureaucracies with which they are so intimately engaged. (2006: 134)

For Helin, this is central: "Notwithstanding the often polarized views, the effective reform of Aboriginal political institutions is absolutely critical for advancing the immediate and long-term interests of Aboriginal peoples" (2006: 141). He quotes Taiaiake Alfred (see chapter 4 on philosophers) as saying "there is almost complete lack of accountability under the system of government established by the Indian Act, and the system makes the band governments answerable to Ottawa—where they are answerable at all—rather than to their own people. That's inherent corruption" (2006: 142). What aboriginal youth see is "a system where Chiefs play a political game for the sole purpose of keeping the gravy rain of benefits and perks flowing to their families and their supporters" (2006: 151). And the formal audited statements that Bands are required to produce are, he says, so vague as to deliver no accountability.

Why do others not blow the whistle?

> Aboriginal people are also reluctant to speak publicly about these issues because they do not wish to provide grist for the political right in Canada who many feel are racist, and have no real interest in making the situation better (though often there is a sizeable but silent contingent that support the publication of such issues in what might be considered right-of-centre publications, because they are regarded as only telling the truth and trying to make things better for ordinary

> Aboriginal folks). Generally, non-Aboriginal observers have been reluctant to raise this issue as well because, in the current climate of political correctness, they might automatically be labelled as racists. (2006: 157)

Helin himself has done a great service by taking these risks, and it helps the rest of us to learn.

Reserve and mainstream

Put simply, the vast majority of the members of mainstream Canada have simply no idea what it is like to be an Indian. The median difference is enormous. Mainstream Canada itself, of course, is not monolithic. There are huge variations. There are ranges from poverty to wealth, from illiteracy to the best of educations, from mediocre to excellent health, from Canadian birth and upbringing to immigrant backgrounds. Some of us are urban and some are rural. Some work at good, secure jobs and others have a marginal attachment to the economy. We have a broad range of different family and ethnic backgrounds. Most of us were born here but, according to the 2006 Census, 6,185,950 of us were born outside of Canada, adding to that diversity.

But, though not monolithic, mainstream Canada does share a number of values and outlooks. It is chiefly positive, constructive, and focused on the future. There is a general belief, or at least hope, that the average individual can get ahead, that there are openings to progress, and that we share the benefits of a perhaps not perfect but still very significant social and health safety net, and an educational and economic system that is based on the idea of equality of opportunity, however insufficiently realized. "Equality" in terms of status is a theme that resonates strongly. While geographical and social mobility is not the aspiration of everyone, it is taken for granted as an opportunity.

For the Indian population, there are also ranges in wealth and education and health and so on, but at a much, much lower level. This is incredibly important in human terms, for two reasons. The first reason is that absolute levels of resources matter. They govern what you can do. Fewer resources imply a virtually total preoccupation with survival, rather than progress. There is little left over for hope, or investment in the future. This has a huge impact upon the human spirit and depresses aspirations. The second reason is relative. There is some wisdom in the idea that individual happiness is in part a function of how well each of us is doing relative to others. For Indians, the answer is obvious on most of the indicators of success or achievement available to the ordinary person. This too is dispiriting.

And for some Indians, the default mindset is not positive, constructive, and focused on the future. Rather it is negative, victimized, and focused on the past (in terms of fault and of opportunity and lands and independence lost). One mindset leads to progress; the other leads to despair. One leads to constructive achievement; the other to mere survival and insulation from reality via substance abuse or—the ultimate statement of despair—suicide.

It cannot be emphasized too strongly: these differences are not a matter of culture. Indians are different in cultural terms but not nearly so much so as immigrants from Vietnam or Bangladesh or Honduras. In our modern world, the cultural overlaps in Canadian society, Indians included, are constantly strengthened by the impact of mass consumerism and media.

In fact, cultural overlaps only exacerbate the sense of difference by raising expectations of the lifestyles and merchandise portrayed on television and the inevitable comparison with the reality of one's life. I have this anecdote from a former senior Northern Affairs advisor.

> In the late 1980s, satellite TV was introduced to Pond Inlet, a beautiful Inuit settlement in northern Baffin Island. Suddenly kids who had no contact with motor vehicles other than the water delivery truck and the honey wagon were immersed in Miami Vice. People who never ate salad saw what whites ate down south. The whole community was re-timed to fit the broadcast schedule of the TBS super-station in Chicago, to the point that school had to be put off till noon since the whole community was up most of the night. For the old, it was no problem; the antics of the southerners were both magical and silly, a source of lots of laughter. But for the kids, TV was a demonstration of their fundamental backwardness, their worthlessness. The child suicide rate went from essentially zero to seven times the national average in a year. (personal communication)

All of these words are perhaps still too abstract. Try this thought experiment. Imagine that you have been told all of your life that you are different—that you are an Indian, very often with negative views of others implied in that description—and that you are living in a small sub-society where very few are employed and there are no expectations of employment, and where the normal means of sustenance is other people's money, which you are told the mainstream got by stealing from your ancestors. Imagine that half of the young people drop out before completing high school and have no hope beyond that. Friends have gone to town and gotten into drugs and prostitution and brought the drug habits back to supplement the already widespread use of alcohol. Family breakdown is endemic, with men in particular feeling failure. Suicide remains a tragedy, but not an unusual one. Housing is inadequate and not well maintained when provided, as the normal incentives of property rights are non-existent. Health is poor: junk food is endemic for the body and media junk for the mind.

Imagine being brought up to believe that this is all someone else's fault and that, if justice eventually prevails, there will be lots of money for everyone, a pot of gold at the end of the rainbow. Can I just hold on—can my kids hold on—until then? What can I do to make justice happen?

Imagine believing that because of your race you are looked down upon, and having too few role models to use to refute that thought. Imagine your leaders working with other people's money and, because of that, following rules so detailed and reporting requirements so extensive, that the needs that are met are often not those that really exist and imaginative progress is nigh impossible. To try is to fail. And imagine the leaders are doing well, and you are not.

Imagine a lifelong feeling of hopelessness, observing premature health decline and aging among your peers, and a relatively early death. And imagine that, in all of this, you have no hope apart from impossible dreams of that pot of gold or the momentary glow of a drug, because you own nothing but the clothes on your back and are beholden to a power structure that is totally beyond your control, not just in the unbelievably remote office towers of Indian Affairs in Ottawa, but even in clique or family dominated local government.

This is a harsh portrait, but try to imagine yourself there. Happily there are many exceptions to this portrait, but there is enough truth that we must all be concerned. But, after so many years, so many generations born, living, and dying, so much money, so many people mouthing the right words, why is progress so slow? And to what extent can our problems or solutions be drawn from the notion of the "parallel society."

Other countries have worked with disadvantaged groups based on ethnocultural differences and history. The American experience with whites and blacks is best known to Canadians but the contrast with South Africa may be the most dramatic.

In America, the three defining events in race relations to date were the tragedy of the Civil War, *Brown v. Board of Education* (a case of 1958 dealing with school discrimination, holding that "separate but equal" facilities based on race were unconstitutional) and the "I have a dream" speech of

Martin Luther King in 1963, wherein the central statement among a number of "dreams" was this: "I have a dream that one day this nation will rise up and live out the true meaning of its creed: 'We hold these truths to be self-evident: that all men are created equal'." This was an explicit rejection of the notion of a parallel society, though it left room for the idea of "affirmative action," that too now a declining concept.

In the same year as *Brown* a different view was being elaborated on the other side of the world. In a "Message to the People of South Africa" delivered from the Senate steps on September 3, 1958, Dr. Henrik Verwoerd described his government's policy for a parallel society for blacks. He said, *inter alia*, "The policy of separate development is designed for happiness and stability provided by their home, language, and administration for the Bantu as well as the Whites" (Pelzer, 1966).

Canada attempted to adopt the view of Martin Luther King. In 1969, the Hon. Jean Chretien, then Minister of Indian Affairs, said in a presentation to the First Session of the Twenty-Eighth Parliament of Canada, "[t] he policies proposed [i.e., the "white paper"] recognize the simple reality that the separate legal status of Indians and the policies which have flowed from it have kept the Indian people apart from and behind other Canadians." Mr. Chretien was of course voicing the views of Pierre Trudeau, the Prime Minister, who had spent a considerable portion of his first year in office on this topic.

It is ironic indeed that 50 years after Verwoerd's statement, the separate treatment of races in South African law has ended (in law, if not totally in practice and also excepting some "affirmative action" requirements for blacks) while in Canada Trudeau's policy had been rejected and much of this under the Prime Ministry of Mr. Chretien. Instead, the doctrine of a "parallel society" has evolved to the status of official policy for Canadian governments and most of the Indian leadership. The likelihood is that South Africa was wrong in 1958 and today is right. And Canada?

NOTE

Clarence Louie

Chief Clarence Louie was elected head of a bankrupt and dysfunctional band over 20 years ago. Today, the 450-strong Osoyoos Indian Band employs 1,200 at peak season, owns nine successful companies, and engages in what Louie calls "community capitalism." A columnist for the *Globe and Mail* compared it to a kibbutz (Breathour, 2008, March 14: 53). Notwithstanding the capitalism, the collective is alive and well.

The Chief's fame has expanded, extending to mention in the 2008 federal Budget. Equally famous are his quotations: "I can't stand people who are late ... Indian time doesn't cut it ... Join the real world—go to school or get a job. Get off welfare. Get off your butt ... You call yourself a warrior? Warriors don't sleep till noon" (Breathour, 2008, March 14: 53).

Surprisingly to the anthropologists perhaps, he maintains "there is no such thing as consensus" and there will always be those who disagree: "Eighty percent like what I say. Twenty percent don't. I always say to the twenty percent, 'Get over it. Chances are you're never going to see me again and I'm never going to see you again. Get some counselling'." "Our ancestors worked for a living. So should you" and "You're going to lose your language and culture faster in poverty than you will in economic development" (Breathour, 2008, March 14: 53).

All of this makes good copy but should not be misunderstood. Says the CEO of Vincor, an international wine company that has joint ventures with the Osoyoos Nk'Mip brand, the chief is "not right wing at all. He's a man on a mission for his people" (Breathour, 2008, March 14: 53). Outstanding people can make a difference even under the most difficult of systems.

NOTE

A leading American view on tribal governance

The Harvard Project[1] centred at the Kennedy School of Government has for the past 20 years conducted research into what factors make for success or failure among American tribes. The lead researchers are Stephen Cornell and Joseph P. Kalt. In March, 2002, Cornell spoke to a session of the British Columbia Treaty Commission about the findings of the Harvard Project and their relevance to Canada. The United States in some ways constitutes a natural laboratory because, while there, like here, there is a central government organization responsible for Indians, in fact there has been much more experimentation over the years both in law and in local initiatives.

Like Canada, "Indian country is poor in the United States, in most cases extremely poor … high indices of ill health, other social problems" (Cornell, 2002: 1). But the poverty is not uniform. Some tribes are doing much better. Their goal was to analyze the data to explain why. The common wisdom at the beginning was that success grew from such factors as gambling ("Casino Indians" is a common US term) or location, that is, proximity to wealthy urban areas, of natural resource endowments. Kalt and Cornell soon concluded that those things are useful but not critical. They settled on four central necessities.

The first is what the Harvard Project calls "sovereignty" but was replaced in this talk for Canadian sensitivities with "jurisdiction." This is a not a sufficient condition for sustainable development but it is necessary : "we have yet to find a single case … [of success] … in which some governmental body other than the indigenous Nation itself is making the decisions about governmental structure, about natural resource use, about internal civil affairs, about development strategies and so on." But Cornell makes clear that the power to decide must include the power to lose: "When decision-making power moves into indigenous hands, they absorb the consequences when they screw up" (Cornell, 2002: 2).

1 See the overview at <http://www.ksg.harvard.edu/hpaied/overview.htm>.

The second necessity is governing institutions of a certain sort. The successful ones absolutely require: [1] stability in the rules of the game; and (probably by necessary implication) [2] separating politics from day to day business and program management; [3] effective and non-political dispute resolution; and [4] a bureaucracy that can get things done. The most casual observer of the Canadian scene will find conditions [1]. [2], and [3] almost totally lacking on Reserves and the fourth, rare. Our imposed system of Band governance virtually guarantees that.

The third factor is that culture matters. This is a fuzzier concept but comes down to the observation that governing institutions have to have the support of the culture or they will fail. And finally, strategic thinking matters: the long-term view.

Cornell's tentative advice based on similarities between Canada and the United States is to take nation building seriously, invest in building capacity, recognize the need to have governance in harmony with culture, provide resources, and tolerate mistakes.

He has specific advice for tribal members: "Change internal attitudes towards First Nation governments." In the United States, he sees "a whole generation of young people on many reservations to whom government is solely about the distribution of resources. Elections are solely about who is likely to give me the most resources. Tribal governments are more about distributing goodies than about building a Nation and reshaping a future" (2002: 6). For success, this has to change.

Two comments from this author on Cornell's advice. First, for those who think that Indians are ordinary human beings, there is nothing surprising about these prescriptions at all. Stability, due process, accountability, strategic thinking—these things are common to all successful societies. Second, on his concluding comment that British Columbia's Treaty process stands as a golden opportunity to put these principles of nation building into practice, I invite the reader to note that view but also to remain agnostic until reading the analysis of the real incentives of Canadian treaty making set out in chapter 5, which have much more to do with the security of the Indian System than with community success.

NOTE

"Big Bear's Treaty: The Road to Freedom"

Jean Allard is a Manitoba Métis and a former MLA and Parliamentary Secretary to Premier Ed Schreyer. He has been with, but not of, the System as it has evolved, close enough to know where the bodies are buried but avoiding personal burial himself in the stultifying conventional ideas in this field.

His major work has been "Big Bear's Treaty: The Road to Freedom" (Allard, 2002), the thinking in which helped me form the policy of a modified and transitional Guaranteed Annual Income that is a part of chapter 6. It is a fine and relatively brief survey and explanation of the problems and hopes of the Indian people and is well worth reading for that purpose. Here I point out some of Allard's insights into the practices of Indian governance backing up the System as they reinforce points made by Helin.

> Reserves are one-dimensional systems. Elsewhere in Canadian society, multiple voices acts as checks and balances on each other (unions, lobby groups, rights activists e.g.) ... There are no such "other voices" on reserves, leaving the single dimension of politics in which to work out solutions to economic, social, and political problems ... Without the checks and balances ... the results are a foregone conclusion. The field is open to misuse of authority with all its attendant ills—nepotism, fraud, corruption and abuse of human rights ... Ordinary Indians found themselves ... powerless and despondent, living with the resultant social breakdown. There is a corollary to Lord Acton's aphorism: absolute powerlessness destroys absolutely. (Allard, 2002: 133)

As to the System,

> [t]he client is less a person in need than a person who is needed ... less the consumer than the raw material for the servicing system ... his essential function is to meet the needs of the servicers ... In other words, the impoverished Indians living in Third World conditions are essential to

the continued existence of the multitude of consultants, program analysts, researchers, administrators and managers who swell the ranks of the bureaucracy. (Allard, 2002:137)

...

Reserves are, in effect, lawless societies. There are some superficial rules regarding administration, but there are no rules comparable to those for municipalities under provincial municipal acts. Whatever chief and council decide are the rules they want, those are the rules they implement. Ordinary Indians have few means to defend themselves against the arbitrary acts of chief and council. Since they are too often destitute and have very little mobility, they are trapped. (Allard, 2002: 148)

CHAPTER 4

Principles

In mid-2005, Toronto suffered a spasm of murders and other violence among black youths. A group called the Coalition of African Canadian Community Organizations proposed a solution, in effect a parallel society for blacks, that would provide a special Office under the provincial government, separate schools, a black economic development program and so on. The *Globe and Mail* exploded in editorial outrage. "Separating races is not the answer," thundered the header. "Segregating people by race, voluntary or otherwise, is not a solution. It compounds the problems of poverty, exclusion and related pathologies." It quoted with approval the US Supreme Court in *Brown*, 1958: "To separate [black children] from others of similar age and qualifications solely because of their race generates a feeling of inferiority as to their status in the community that may affect their hearts and minds in a way unlikely ever to be undone." And it concluded, "No amount of wishing will make separate equal" (2005, October 12: A22).

There is nothing remarkable about this thinking. Public intellectuals express this general truth often. It is the conventional wisdom of the past 50 years—except for Indians. It is instructive to ask at the beginning of this philosophical exploration: "Why the exception?"The answers are not complimentary to mainstream society.

Return to first principles. The chief distinguishing features of modern Western societies (including Canada) as they have evolved relate to the status of the individual. First, the individual is the fundamental unit, with ultimate sovereignty and with paramountcy over the collective. The collective remains immensely valuable, but merely instrumental.

Second is the idea of equality-in-worth among individuals, sometimes expressed as dignity. These ideals are to be found in the Charter and human rights legislation, for example. While both ideas have long been reflected in some human organization or other, the general application of the combination is relatively new and unique. The modern Western society is characterized by a wide degree of tolerance for other beliefs as long as they do not undermine the fundamental organizing principles.

There are three other, more usual, types of societies in addition to that of the modern West, and they encompass roughly two thirds of the world's population. All require or imply the paramountcy of the collective over the individual. The classification I find useful describes "autocratic," "theocratic," and "communal" societies.

In autocratic societies, the main fact of life is power of the ruler(s). The individual is not denied but is certainly not equal. A small group that holds the power is superior. The most successful imperial and autocratic societies (such as the Roman, Austro-Hungarian, or Ottoman Empires) tended to have been relatively permissive with respect to the existence of theocratic or communal societies within their realm, as long as deference to the imperial power is maintained. The more liberal British Empire followed a similar model. The modern, individualistic society on the other hand cannot be tolerated by an autocrat or an empire, as the fundamental notions lead to a rejection of central power, as it was, for example, in the American revolution.

In theocratic societies, which exist today and also pre-date recorded history, the theoretical supremacy is lodged in the supreme being or force of the religion of the day, with actual management carried out by a priesthood. The collective is supreme in its task of carrying out the work of God and the individual is merely instrumental to God's purposes. But individuals do not lose thereby, under this social theory. At a minimum, they will find salvation and, at a maximum, they may be a part of management.

In communal societies, including the sort described by much theory about Canadian Indians, the collective has paramountcy, as the essential vehicle uniting and preserving the relationship of individuals one with the other, and with their past. The life of the individual draws meaning, security, and realization through this organization, and consensual processes are valued.

Neither theocratic nor communal societies can afford to tolerate the principles of the modern society without risking their own destruction. This is the case because the primacy of the individual directly contradicts the paramountcy of the collective. This reality is a cause of much current unrest in the world. Of course these are but four abstract archetypes. In actual practice, elements of each are mixed. But, they are helpful for analytical purposes.

Some will argue that the modern world requires a modern society. Others will say that a modern society guarantees the debasement of the central moral and ethical values of humanity. For our purposes, it is not necessary to enter this swamp; it is sufficient to note that, for better or worse, Canada is a modern society as here defined while many Canadian Indians live in a latter-day version of a communal society. Further, the view of academics and participants in the System is that a parallel, communal society can be, and must be, maintained in this country. This view also finds constitutional expression in the Charter, ss. 25 and 35. It is no mere theory.

The individual and the collective

Since the beginning of human history, there has been a necessary connection and tension between the individual and the collective, a symbiosis, one might say. The individual is not an abstraction. The individual is each of us. The individual is the smallest action-taking and decision-making unit. The individual can feel pleasure and pain, be inventive and curious, dream dreams, create, and procreate.

The collective can do none of these things and yet—in comparison to the individual—can be immensely powerful and effectively immortal. The individual by himself is almost nothing, the proverbial naked ape. Our memories are short but the collective memory can be immense. Working together, we can multiply our capacity exponentially. Working together involves cooperation and a subordination of some of our freedom but the new freedoms created and the expanded spectrum of options utterly dwarf anything we give up.

An enduring relationship of working together makes up a collective. Sometimes we are conscious of this, as with membership in an association or a trade union, say. But our most important collectives, the family at the small end and "society" at the large, seem so utterly natural as to hardly be a matter of choice. The family is small enough to be comprehensible. We understand the relationships and understand as well that the family collective can become better or worse not simply by our own actions but also by its institutions and rules of conduct. Some families are dysfunctional while others with essentially the same individual endowments are not. Institutions can make a difference.

"Society" is so huge as to be almost incomprehensible. We think regrettably little about it, given its importance, and tend but little to its health. Its very foundations for size and success, most importantly at least a minimal respect for and trust in the "other," tend not only to go uncelebrated but be frequently abused. Society is made up of numerous individuals and associations of individuals interacting. It includes major public goods—knowledge, culture, and institutions—compared to which the hard assets like buildings and bridges are trivial.

"Society," according to one's meaning, can be the entire world or a nation state or some more limited subset like "high society." These subdivisions are exceedingly important because they give meaning and definition to the individual. The world as a whole is so immense as to be overwhelming. We need more comprehensible reference points. So humans over the years have developed a pattern of multiple identities, the meeting place of all of which is "me." To cite again the fine phrase of Coyne, we are "intersections" of multiple identities.

So we all tend to define ourselves as of this or that family, gender, age, ethnicity, religion, political persuasion, occupation, subculture, citizenship, education, neighborhood, health status, income, and so on. At the moment, our world is a multidimensional set of almost seven billion points, "I" am here, "you" are there, "he" or "she" over there and so on.

Put in the abstract like this, the axes of variation seem to be more merely interesting than transcendentally important but it is a fact of human nature that each of us takes a fiercely possessive interest in our own set of coordinates. And of course the "hand that we are dealt" is of immense importance to individual lives. Indeed, one preoccupation of modern society is how to compensate for what seem to be unfair variations in the deal.

Some of the associations that define each of us are loose or transient. Others are tight and enduring. To the extent that the web of interpersonal association becomes sufficiently important, we are prepared formally or informally to sign on to the alliances, contributions, and subordinations that define a collective. The *sine qua non* of a collective is service to its membership and they begin on that basis. That does not mean that the "service" remains necessarily constructive to the membership over time. (It is, however invariably constructive to the leadership.) The end result must have had some constructive justification or the collective would not have formed, though collectives may long outlive their usefulness and die only slowly. "Cities" came about for a genuine purpose that continues to this day. The same may be said of the "nation state" or "trade unions" or religions of various sorts. But specific examples of each category have withered and died when utility ended.

Collectives have structures and rules and they act (through leaders and members, both) to preserve their influence and existence. Beyond that, they have an immense variation. They can be large or small. They can be weak or powerful. They can be open (anyone can enter or leave) or closed. Their governance can be democratic or authoritarian. In a free society, we expressly acknowledge a right to collectives, usually styling this the "freedom of association." And, in a free society one need have little concern about collectives that are weak (for they can do little harm) or open (because anyone can join them or not) or reasonably democratic in their governance. Conversely, one must closely watch collectives that have all three of the attributes of being powerful and closed and authoritarian. ("Powerful" may be only in relation to the members.) Why? Because they have power over the individual and, being closed, the individual can neither take his property and leave, nor recruit new allies. Indian collectives under current law fit this description.

The survival of collectives

Do collectives have free-standing merit, independent of their services? Services both to members and to non-members have to be considered in answering this question. This question is a matter of huge importance, for it goes to the issue as to whether non-members should be indifferent to whether or not various collectives survive.

Consider a nameless religion of declining membership. Were its leaders, observing inadequate ongoing interest among the faithful, to one day sell off the remaining assets, throw in the towel, and disband (or merge with a more vital sect), would the world be any the worse off? Or would this merely be economist Joseph Schumpeter's "creative destruction" applied to the religious scene—a development fit for nostalgia, a little tear, the careful preservation of pictures and books of record, and nothing more? Certainly this sort of thing has happened. There is little public interest.

Consider a nameless Amazon tribe, once with primitive but genuine governance, a distinct language and belief set, that has been gradually but definitively and voluntarily absorbed into the larger culture of Brazil. Suppose too, for the sake of this thought experiment, that the individual outcomes under the new arrangements in terms of health, education, incomes, and apparent happiness have been satisfactory. Should we be dismayed that the collective of the distinct tribe has vanished? Or should we rejoice that the individuals previously isolated in a small, culturally and economically impoverished, tribe have now had their world much expanded? In particular, what should be the reply to the (inevitable) charges of "cultural genocide" when small cultures effectively disappear or are reduced to a state of mere folkloric status? Suppose the individuals are all still alive and happy. What has this to do with "genocide"? Is it possible for outsiders to "kill" a culture? Or can it only die by the desertion of its adherents?

Push the same experiment a bit further. The nameless tribe has been discovered but the possibility remains of "undiscovering" them, hiding their existence, leaving them totally alone. Has one a moral duty to offer them the enormous world beyond the jungle or is the moral duty to deny and foreclose that opportunity in the interests of cultural integrity? And, how would the answer to this question affect the Kashechewans of Canada?[1]

What is the collective?

Obviously these are idealized thought experiments. Some time, somewhere there may be a minor opportunity to "turn back the clock" but, for almost all of the indigenous peoples of the world, that time has long past. Irreversible contact has been made and that certainly means the end of indigenousness in the long run. But, the idealized situations may assist thought about the actual world of the long and turbulent transition period. All in all, the relationship between the individual and the collective is a fascinating field. It is at the root of the cultural wealth of any society (for cultural expression is comprehensible to anyone beyond the speaker only on a basis of at least some shared cultural background), of economic performance, of security, of liberty and freedom, of many international disputes, and of the great religions. In the relatively short span of recorded human history, no consensus on an optimal relationship has emerged (though many societies consider they have discovered such a holy grail). It is a particular conceit of the developed Western world that we have at least bracketed the sweet spot of the arrangement between the individual and the collective, among, say, the diversity of the OECD countries. Perhaps. But a majority of the world has yet to sign on. And, even the Anglo-Saxon Western world is of mixed views. We have the individual-centred theories of J.S. Mill in his "On Liberty" and the more collectivist and traditional views of Burke. Our political parties dine out on these differences to this day.

We have to deal with the obvious fact that it is only the individual that can be the "principal" so that the collective must be "instrumental," that is, serving individual purposes. But the "instrument" can be hugely important,

1 Kashechewan is an isolated community in northern Ontario that is in crisis; it had the option of moving to an urban area. See "Kashechewan," p. 207.

beyond even the collection of living individuals, for it stands—or can at least claim to stand—for the wisdom and aspirations of individuals long dead and those yet to be born.

By analogy, consider the author (the principal) and the language (the instrument). No one would for a moment consider a single author, even the incredible Shakespeare, to be as important as the language. No one would consider any citizen to be as important as the nation. So the instrument, and for social purposes the collective, is of immense importance. But that does not mean that all collectives are of equal value.[2] So, just as we can talk of an "optimally" sized government, so we can talk about an "optimal" collective.

This book will not attempt the ambitious project of describing an "optimal collective" but shown in table 1 are some of the attributes of collectives and the options for variance. A typical civic collective such as the city of Vancouver is open as to membership, coercive as to enforcement, of minor importance to the life of its members, non-exclusive, large in scale, has voluntary entry, high mobility, and democratic governance, is instrumental only, and narrow in span. A typical Indian-governed community is closed as to membership, coercive as to enforcement of laws, of high importance to the life of its members, non-exclusive (one may also belong to a union, for example), small, has initial entry stipulated (by birth or adoption), low mobility, elite governance, is existential in concept ("culture"), and wide in span.

It is clear which type has the greater impact on the lives of individuals and where the membership should therefore have the greater concern for due process, freedoms, and so on. However, such freedoms and due process may be inimical to the integrity of certain collectives.

---

2 We insist upon that useful concept of "equal value" in respect of individuals, because it has been found to suit our collective purposes, notwithstanding persuasive evidence of differential merit. But there is no reason for such deference to the idea of equality as applied to collectives. As a perhaps non-controversial but major example, the twentieth-century experience put paid to any idea of superior merit for Soviet communism.

"Value" in this context must, of course, mean service provided to the membership, summed up in some way. For modern Western societies, this summation would have to be done on the basis of a minimum required level of service to any given member but that is by no means either a historic or worldwide requirement.

Table 1: Indicia for collectives

Attribute	Option spectrum	
Membership	open, voluntary	closed, required
Rule enforcement	voluntary compliance	coercion
Importance to life of member	low	high
Exclusivity	none	total
Scale	small	large
Initial entry	random, voluntary	stipulated (e.g. birth)
Entry and exit (mobility)	easy (high)	difficult (low)
Governance	anarchy — market — democracy — elites	
Purpose	instrumental	existential
Span	narrow	wide

Durability, services and continued attraction

A successful collective would have to include at least the following attributes:

1 durability (defence against internal and external threats)
2 security and other services for members
3 continued attraction (without which a minimum critical mass will in due course be lost through deaths or other forms of abandonment).

The last requirement is particularly important. A collective must seem more attractive to its members than other available options. In some cases, this is minor: a symphony society dies while a group of sports fans grows. More importantly, the class of economic collectives[3] known as trade unions has been gradually in decline in North America, yielding shifts in power balances.

In the specific matter of Indian collectives, we have observed the gradual shift of members off Reserve, significantly weakening the core living on Reserve. But we have also noted a slowing of that trend in the past decade as the vigorously procollective policies of governments have buttressed the attractiveness of Reserves through "economic development" (a concept to be examined later), subsidized employment in administrative activity, welfare, housing, and so on.

3 Some with social and political goals as well.

Permeability and organizing principles

There remain two essential attributes of collectives that need mention. "Permeability" is a word for the degree to which a collective is open or closed in its membership policy. This mostly relates to entry. Few collectives other than criminal organizations and totalitarian states attempt to foreclose members departing.

If one looks at the two polar positions—either fully open or fully closed—obviously neither makes sense in a modern world of individual mobility. Any collective has some things that are "public goods" in the sense of being both non-exclusionary in nature and non-rivalrous in use. Some government services—defence, or lighthouses, for example—are there for the taking by all, and are not diminished thereby. The most important aspect of any culture, its language, fits into this category.

But most collective attributes, such extraordinarily important things as real property, natural and economic resources, and, above all, social order, may be degraded as to the position of current members if large numbers of new members are admitted. That is why almost all modern nations have an immigration policy and why many clubs have a controlled membership policy.

But, if full openness would be madness for most organizations of consequence, so may be full closure, if only because the collective would soon collapse through deaths. So for important, durable, collectives there is almost invariably a minimal admissions policy that may be biological (birth) or replacement (maintenance of membership size). Most successful collectives also make provision for the entry of new members who would obviously benefit the existing group, by the importation of talent or diversity or energy.

With the minor exception of adoption into a Band, most Indian collective membership policies are very strict and not permeable at all. In large part, this is a matter of law. The Government of Canada defines who can be an Indian with great precision. But the sentiment also ranges within the Indian community. Bands control their own membership and may be rigidly exclusive, for several reasons.

Indian politicians vary in view on this very basic question. Some local politicians find the current rate of natural increase satisfactory or even a problem (because it requires sharing limited resources). Some national Indian politicians, with a keen sense that the political heft of the System requires numbers, look forward with concern to the forecast long-term decline in the Indian population under existing law.[4]

---

4 See "The Population Implosion?" p. 10.

But, whatever the outcome of this debate, it is clear that Indian collectives have a low permeability. Low permeability is more or less a guarantee of a moribund organization.[5] It would be a brave person, indeed, who would offer a definition of optimal permeability for any organization but that is not necessary for our purposes. It is enough to note that closed systems have problems in this regard.

The other essential attribute of collectives to note is that of "organizing principles." By this, I mean the main common thread(s) that bind the members. These threads may be of territory, of ethnicity, of religion, or of common economic, social, recreational, or other such interests.

Indian and other coercive collectives

In this part, I will focus only on collectives that, by force of law, wield significant coercive powers over their memberships and that, as a matter of fact or of law, are difficult for outsiders to join or insiders to escape. In other words, these collectives have significant control over individuals. This includes some religious organizations and trade unions, though by no means all. It does not include such powerful entities as public corporations (as any shareholder can join or exit with immediate full compensation) or such minor closed entities as clubs. The distinguishing characteristic sought here is the "significant control" mentioned above.

Such collectives may be organized around common interests or beliefs, such as trade unionism or religious organizations. Free trade unionism exists only in the western world, where powers and due process are regulated by law. Sizeable religious organizations in the Western world are no longer afforded much temporal power, though this is not the case elsewhere.[6] I will not comment on these cases. Left for consideration are ter-

5 The nation of Japan, which has very exclusionary immigration polices, has for many years seemed an exception to this rule. It will be interesting to see how long this can continue. But there are two important codicils here. First, Japan has a very large and wealthy population with huge internal human resources. Second, Japan has been very permeable to ideas, which will to some extent provide for internal renewal. This has not been a particular characteristic of the much, much smaller Indian collectives.

6 Iran, e.g., where by constitution a religious leader is the supreme state authority.

ritorially based governments. Because most individuals are *de facto* territorially bound (because of established homes, jobs, friends, and family), the theoretical right of "exit" is less practical—the more so, the larger the unit. National states clearly have more coercive power over individuals than do municipalities.

It is a long-established principle in the Western world that the coercive power of territorially governing collectives can only be wielded by the consent of the governed, such consent delegated from time to time to elected representatives. Significant other protections are built in: the rule of law, due process, protection of minorities, legal equality of all persons within the territory, and political equality of all citizens are the most important. While other parts of the world may be governed by dictators or oligarchies or theocracies, all of which have their proponents, Canadians are overwhelmingly persuaded of the model shared by the developed Western world.

Indian governments in Canada can also, in theory, exercise very significant coercive powers within their territories. These powers are clearly larger than municipal, and reach or exceed the powers of provinces in some areas. They are less than federal in sweep, importantly in the lack of authority of criminal sanction and international standing. Because of the well-known problems of "small governments with large powers" discussed later and the potential inadequacy of normal democratic checks and balances, the ultimate check on the use of Indian government power has always been the Minister, an official of the elected federal government and the custodian of the federal legislation that empowers Indian governments.

The current reigning theory of Indian government is that the ultimate check on its power, the nationally elected Minister, can in these times be safely removed without at the same time ending the federal empowerment of Indian governments. Modern Indian governments formed by treaty (using the Nisga'a Nation as a template) are to be enabled to deploy the administrative, directive, and ultimately coercive powers conferred upon them by federal law and federal money, subject only to internal checks. What is interesting here is that the organizing principle of Indian collectives is different from that of all other governing institutions in Canada. The two main differences are in the areas of citizenship and of the relationship between the individual and the collective.

As to citizenship, in the rest of Canada citizenship in a town or province or the nation is available as a matter of right after some (usually short) period of residence. This is an "open system" that, as a matter of practice, avoids the otherwise difficult issues when residents are not citizens.[7] In the territory of Indian governments, only Indians may be citizens of that government and, indeed, only locally authorized Indians qualify. (There is no automatic right for an Indian to move from Band to Band under current or proposed schemes and, indeed, it is unusual.) So, non-Indian residents in Indian territory do not have citizenship rights. On most Reserves, this is not an issue as there are no (or few) non-Indians resident but, on a few, there are hundreds or even thousands. So this is one issue; the other is much larger.

In most of Canada, the relationship of the individual to the collective government is ordinarily not at all a matter of consequence in daily life. It does not matter whether your MP or the Prime Minister likes you or me; it makes no difference. Yes, we pay taxes and get services but these persons have no discretionary influence over us as individuals. Our jobs have nothing to do with government wishes, even for public servants. Nor do our homes, access to transportation, educational opportunities, or any such things, as individuals. (Of course governments influence the overall climate but that is another matter.) We own and control whatever property we may have and are in general not beholden to the collective authorities. As a result, governments fear the people, rather than vice versa. Further, the people see governments as their servants, albeit with the common reservations of today as to responsiveness, representativeness, and so on.

In the territory of Indian governments, things work differently. As was described above, the legal and financial power deployed by Indian governments comes from an external source in greatest part, rather than from Indian citizens. Thus, rather than the usual check in a democracy of citizens claiming the right to the careful use of their taxes, in Indian country citizens have an incentive to become co-conspirators in extracting money from the external provider. As the Indian government is the chief protagonist in this ongoing exercise, the people need to support it.

In Indian country, it is absolutely not the case that government and politicians are a secondary issue. Since the governments are small and controlled by politicians rather than professional bureaucracies, all of a sudden it is important whether a Counsellor or Chief likes you. What is good in life—income, housing, transportation, access to education—flows in a discretionary manner.

---

7 These difficulties are not inescapable—note Switzerland—but also more common than not—note the issue of "guest workers" in much of Europe and the issue of illegal aliens in the United States.

The bulwark of freedom of private property is not available in a system where the land and most significant assets are owned by the collective. Of course, one part of the option of "exit" is possible. Those who wish to leave the collective can do so, but they cannot take their share of collective property with them. That is a heavy penalty.

So things stand on their head: rather than governments fearing the people, the relationship can run the other way. In this circumstance, the usual check of democratic elections may fail, especially in small societies consisting largely of a number of extended families. The difference between the relationship of citizens and their various Canadian governments and that of Indians and their particular tribal governments is thus very profound and it is a mistake not to understand this when considering issues of "self-government."

These problems are not theoretically insoluble but they are practical facts on the ground. And many of the solutions[8] that would change those facts on the ground are anathema to the Indian System, which relies for its existence on a society where attention to the welfare of the collective from which the System draws its resources is more important than the welfare of the individual. To return to the beginning of this discussion—the nature of the relationship between the individual and the collective—the essential question is: "Who controls whom?" There are many fine points beyond that, including all of the usual checks and balances of modern society. But if the answer to "who controls?" is not "the individual," then on the face of it there is a problem. And that is how the Canadian Indian world is set up by Canada's laws.

What should be changed?

With this analytical background, I now turn to a brief summary of what the major academic thinkers have to say about these issues. As a preliminary observation, it will be noted that almost nothing is said in what follows about the relationship of the Indian individual to the Indian collective.

---

8 For example, importation of advanced democratic practices that do not currently apply into Band affairs, items such as a muscular Freedom of Information regime, human rights legislation and the rule of law including crucially, the separation of administration from political control. Other examples include a significant diversion of funds from Councils to individuals and strengthening private property regimes, both empowering voters vis a vis Indian governments. Further detail will be supplied in Chapter 6.

Almost all of the work talks about the relationship of the Indian collective to the mainstream. Given the intellectual firepower and transparent good will of the thinkers concerned it seems unlikely that this oversight is accidental. There may be a reluctance of mainstream writers (for they are mainly that)[9] to seem to be interfering in the internal affairs of already sufficiently troubled collectives. There might equally be a belief, and for good reason, that close examination of this topic would reveal such controversies as to divert attention from the main theme of academic thought, which has been redressing mainstream perception and treatment of an oppressed people. In any event, benign neglect is the result.

It will also be noted that with certain exceptions (especially the work of Alan Cairns and John Richards) the writings focus almost exclusively on the parallel society—Reserves, Indians governments, Indian organizations—rather than the more than 40% of individuals who have left the Reserves. Again, this is understandable from the perspective of the writers because urban Indians just don't "fit" their theories, which are generally inapplicable once individuals are beyond the control of the parallel society and the federal money to fund various schemes is absent. But, these are people we should care about too, to the extent special assistance is required—and it is.

There is a huge literature in this field, ranging from thinkers like Taiaiake Alfred who aim at virtual sovereignty for Indians to those like Tom Flanagan who see very minimalist accommodation as being best for the mainstream and for Indians as well.

Taiaiake Alfred

The best introduction to the work of Taiaiake Alfred is the introductory chapter to his latest book, *Wasáse: Indigenous Pathways of Action and Freedom* (2005a). It is a call to return to the ways of the original people, requiring essentially the repudiation not only of the System but of the materialist views of modern society. He debates the paths of armed resistance and non-violent contention. He clearly comes down for the latter and calls for a fundamental spiritual revolution. However, he clearly notes that non-violence does not mean pacifism but rather activism in the negotiation of a

9 Writers such as Taiaiake Alfred and Jean Allard, who are aboriginal and will be canvassed, are exceptions. By contrast, the writings of the leaders of the Assembly of First Nations (AFN) and other Indian politicians can be found on their web sites but tend to be the self-serving perspectives common to all political organizations worldwide.

co-existence with the "settler society." The existing structure has "accommodated themselves to colonialism, not defeated it" (2005b). His work, which is clearly and honestly argued, is the fullest call to a parallel society.

In private correspondence in August of 2008, I asked Taiaiake Alfred a question on his work, after noting that my analysis relies heavily on the interplay and symbiotic relationship of the individual and the collective: "At times what I read of your introduction amounts to a celebration of the collective as the primary goal for preservation, but then there is the constant theme of the self-realization of the individual. Which do you see as the end and which as the means?" His reply, used with permission, was:

> With respect to your question: in indigenous ways of thinking, the distinction between the individual and the collective doesn't exist, thus there is no concern with conflict of balancing of that relationship. It's basically the difference between "individuality" (constructing a political identity of autonomous responsibility) and "individualism" (ideologies of individual freedom), the latter being the Euro-American way and the former being the Indigenous. There is some similarity in this thinking to traditional collectivist European thought, but a real difference too in that the Indigenous way precludes a transcendence of the individual by a universalizing state. That is why I am now focusing on a philosophy I'm calling, anarcho-indigenism, because the theoretical anarchism seems to be the only European body of thought that shares Indigenous non-hegemonic and anti-institutional principles.

Tom Flanagan

Tom Flanagan, by contrast, represents the position at the other pole. The work of both scholars is based upon deep thought and careful research. Alfred's position, passionately held, I think is unlikely as to accomplishment; it asks too many people to do too much beyond their ordinary lives. Flanagan's position is one instinctively held by many egalitarian Canadians but its accomplishment too is unlikely as it would require breaking not only the "Iron Triangle" of the law, the media, and the System but of re-doing the Constitution as well. It is a simple fact that ss. 25 and 35 exist.[10]

---

10 It would be wonderful to hear a debate between the two men. The positions are so far apart that such appears unlikely. As it happens, however, we have had a debate between Flanagan and Alan Cairns that is worth mention. It appeared

Flanagan's major work on Indian policy, *First Nations, Second Thoughts* (2000), is indispensable reading for even a casual student of the field. It is a root-and-branch assault on what he terms "the aboriginal orthodoxy." (Notwithstanding the "aboriginal" word, his book is almost entirely about Status Indians.) The organization of the book sets up eight propositions of the "orthodoxy" and offers a contrary view for each. Thus, for Flanagan, the fact that the ancestors of aboriginals were here before the rest of us is of no logical or moral import. This squarely opposes the single most important argument of what I call the System. He says that European civilization was thousands of years ahead of aboriginals at contact. Aboriginal organization was not consistent with what they now call "sovereignty," though the American concept of "domestic dependent nations" (articulated in the early nineteenth century by Justice John Marshall) would be acceptable. But the usual concept of "nation" does not apply: "Aboriginal government is fraught with difficulties stemming from small size, an overly ambitious agenda, and dependence on transfer payments. In practice, aboriginal government produces wasteful, destructive, familistic factionalism" (2000: 7).

Aboriginal property rights are being handled the wrong way. They should be individual or familial; this was often the case before contact and is much better suited to today. The treaties mean what they say and should not be stretched. And the goal of the Royal Commission on Aboriginal Peoples (RCAP) of an economically self-sufficient aboriginal society is a chimera.

On the particularly important matter of Indian governments, Flanagan argues that the small size, broad scope, and excessive reliance on kinship constitute the necessary ingredients for a big problem. He refers to the "rentier" society, where "[t]he purpose of political action is to get more favors from those in power" (2000: 104). This is as applicable to the relationship of the Band member to the Council as it is to that of the Council to Ottawa. The cure or prospect?

> There is no shortage of visionary reform proposals, but there is a countervailing abundance of fiscal constraints and political veto points.

---

in the journal, *Inroads*, in the Spring of 2001 (Cairns and Flanagan, 2001). I will not attempt to describe the exchange here as there are too many enjoyable subtleties and professorial sharp elbows to survive any summary. But those who think that the Indian issue should just go away in the modern world in the interests of the Indians and everyone else, and those who say "It ain't going to happen" will both find cause to cheer.

> Aboriginal communities will continue to be small, impoverished, supported by fiscal transfers, and mostly governed by elected Chiefs and Councils trying to carry out an extraordinarily wide range of functions. The contest for advantage of extended kin groups will continue to be the motor of internal politics. (2000: 106)

On proposed theories of economic development, "[t]he RCAP's emphasis on ownership of land and resources reflects deeper fallacies in the new aboriginal orthodoxy—its twin beliefs that the land produces wealth and that aboriginal people were deprived of wealth because colonial settlers took their land. In fact, only human ingenuity and effort produce wealth" (2000: 184). Yes, "[o]wnership of resources will produce some royalty flow, which allows the recipients to purchase consumer goods as long as the flow lasts; but unless the rentiers acquire the skills and attitudes—the human capital—needed in a modern economy, the royalties will quickly be dissipated" (2000: 184).

So, pour in more money? "My prediction, then, is that implementation of RCAP's economic vision would actually increase unemployment welfare dependency, and human misery in aboriginal communities. Of course, with that much money sloshing around, some people would do very well" (2000: 187). This prophecy does not lack contemporary evidence.

His summation: there are three main problems (highly compressed here). "First, the aboriginal orthodoxy is at variance with liberal democracy because it makes race the constitutive factor of the political order" (2000: 194). "The second problem is that the aboriginal orthodoxy wrongly encourages aboriginal people to see others—so-called EuroCanadians—as having caused their misfortune and, therefore, holding the key to their improvement. Most aboriginal advocates define 'doing better' as succeeding not by their own efforts, but by getting something from the oppressors" (2000: 195). "The third problem is that the aboriginal orthodoxy encourages aboriginal people to withdraw into themselves." This is wrong because "[i]n order to become self-supporting and get beyond the social pathologies that are ruining their communities, aboriginal people need to acquire the skills and attitudes that bring success in a liberal society, political democracy and market economy. Call it assimilation, call it integration, call it adaptation, call it whatever you want: it has to happen" (2000: 195).

Flanagan's book is descriptive and historical and devotes only two final pages to cures, which in general can be summarized as more accountability of Indian governments, breaking up the highly concentrated power of Chiefs and Councils, and introducing a regime of individual property rights. His final paragraph begins: "Aboriginal self-government will be a failure if it means nothing more than transferring the powers of the Department of Indian Affairs to band councils" (2000: 198). Most would agree with that statement.

Curiously, despite its scholarship and the power of its logic and intellectual influence, Flanagan's book has had little more impact on actual outcomes than has the report of the RCAP (though it is far more readable!). I think perhaps it is too hard-edged for Canadians, too "in your face." We look for a "win/win" rather than a "win/lose," even if the "lose" is really for the benefit of the loser. In fact, the "aboriginal orthodoxy" sails on little wounded. The problems are real, the analysis trenchant, but the support for the orthodoxy from the courts and the media, the indifference or sense of guilt of the citizenry and the caution of the political class have combined to defeat this powerful attack.

Much other work has been done by legal scholars like Kent McNeil and James Tulley who seek to push the constitutional possibilities for Indian independence to the very theoretical limits of ss. 25 and 35. To focus on any of them necessarily implies a choice but I believe that the two I will briefly describe are respected all across the spectrum as mainstream writers with a deep sympathy for aboriginal[11] causes and an extremely broad knowledge.

Alan Cairns and Charles Taylor

Alan Cairns has been a leading scholar in this field from a philosophical and constitutional point of view for four decades. While his work has evolved with his thinking and with the times, the central core has remained the idea of "Citizens Plus" that he developed in the 1960s with the team that wrote the *Hawthorn Report* (Hawthorn, 1966/67). As Cairns put it in his like-named *Citizens Plus: Aboriginal Peoples and the Canadian State* (2000), the idea was "an earlier attempt to accommodate the apartness of Aboriginal peoples from, and their togetherness with, the non-Aboriginal majority. The "plus" dimension spoke to Aboriginality; the "citizens" addressed togetherness in a way intended to underline our moral obligations to each other" (2000: 5). In other words, Indians (though he believes this may be generalized to the Inuit and the Métis) are Canadian citizens but also something more. "So too are we all," one might respond but philosophers in this field are nigh unanimous

11 Because their work is broad, "aboriginal" is the correct descriptor, not the more limited term, "Indian." Indigenous peoples generally (that is, outside Canada as well) fall within their philosophical range.

in maintaining that the "something more" possessed or deserved by aboriginals is of a different order of importance. The justification for this is generally said to be that their ancestors were in Canada when the Europeans arrived and that the "national" rights passed on to successors. Immigrants may come to Canada as individuals and, no matter what their culture, adopt Canada as their "nation." This outcome is not the philosophers' case with respect to the descendants of Indians who were here as "nations" previous to contact.[12] The framers of the Constitution Act, 1982, agreed that there should be a constitutional distinction in favor of "aboriginals" if not necessarily with the precise reasoning, and that is the law. As previously noted, the Constitution Act, 1867 had already singled out "Indians."

According to the law, aboriginals are entitled to a bundle of rights (varying dramatically by the class of aboriginal) that flow from their connection, by either biology or legal definition,[13] to the descendents of those here at contact; and that are in addition to their rights as Canadians. The size of this "bundle" continues to be defined in the courts and in negotiations and the ownership is collective. Until any specific right finds its way through the courts or treaty documentation, the general position of writers in the area is that the bundle of aboriginality is large and legitimate, though how much of the entitlement flows from inheritance and how much from a right to compensation for oppression is usually left vague.

Cairns shares these views, and like many other scholars finds a justifying and explanatory analogy in third-world decolonization. He says that Canada itself was a colonizing power *vis-à-vis* the aboriginal inhabitants of this land.[14] The indigenous are the "fourth world" and, for the most part and

---

12 The same claim is often made in favor of the descendants of the French settlers at the time of conquest by the British, though of course the constitutional arrangements made with respect to this "nation" have been different, yielding certain protections for the French language and a province with a French-speaking majority.

13 —for some "Indians" have no Indian blood but are Indians by law, whereas most "aboriginals" have some degree of Indian ancestry.

14 As earlier noted, the detailed oppression was only allowed by the existence of s. 91(24). Would things have been different without that? Some scholars point to the case of New Zealand's Maoris and Australian aborigines (where there was no such constitutional remit) to argue that the colonization process was inherent in the settler society. I argue that things would have been very

particularly in Canada, their "decolonization" cannot follow the third-world route of national independence. That is simply not practical. At the same time and for the same practical reasons, this no doubt accurate academic characterization of Indian policy as a Canadian manifestation of "colonization," to be rolled back by the same worldwide forces, seems disconnected from a modern age where neither today's citizens or governments remotely see things in this way.

The problem then becomes how to do the right thing within the constraints of reality. Cairns most recent and succinct (a mere 59 pages, plus notes) paper on this topic would be my first recommended additional reading for any lay person. *First Nations and the Canadian State* (2005) covers most of the background one needs to know, with the exception of the currently important treaty process, especially in British Columbia but also in northern Canada and Quebec.

The high value of *First Nations and the Canadian State* lies not simply in its elegance, though it has that, but in its practicality. Cairns is deeply sympathetic to the plight of Canadian aboriginals. (He does not insist upon the tight focus on Indians of this book.) But that said, he is prepared to discuss the inconvenient realities that, as he notes, "verge on taboo status" because they call into question the grander ambitions of sovereigntists and the System. These realities include, "first, the fact that an urban route to the future complements the more visible reserve-based self-government route; second, intermarriage; and third, the large number of individuals of Aboriginal ancestry who do not identify as Aboriginal" (2005: 11)

One reads between the lines. My understanding on the first topic is that Cairns agrees with those who see the urban environment as the future of aboriginals, like most other Canadians. He is explicitly critical of the failure by essentially everyone—academics, governments and the System—to pay attention to this issue, without venturing an explanation. The reason in my view is clear. When aboriginal people move to the city, they are out of the control of the collective and the collective is the indispensable expertise and responsibility and power base of the above usual suspects. Without the collective, aboriginals are just people like anyone else and specialized power over them disappears.

---

different. The American example does not help us in that because, while there was no s. 91(24), the Supreme Court in defining status of "domestic dependent nations" conferred total legislative power *re* Indians on the Congress, so in the end the legal framework was similar.

Intermarriage (that is, marriage or cohabitation between Status and non-Status persons) is seldom discussed but will eventually be (as matters demographic so often are) definitive. To quote Cairns again:

> Off-reserve figures for the five-year period ending 31 December 1995 hover slightly below 58%, while the on-reserve figure is somewhat less than 23% (Four Directions Consulting Group, 1997: 20). When two out-marriages in a row result in a loss of legal status for the children, out-marriage rates threaten the long run survival of the legal status population. By mid-century, the legal status population will begin to decline. A number of small bands near urban centres will legally disappear in coming decades. (2005: 13)

These are explosive facts. Many writers on aboriginal issues make much of the growing population but it is only Status Indians that have the strong legal position and that population will be in decline. It will be a major and controversial issue of public policy as to what (if anything) to do about this.

Non-identifying aboriginals offer another controversy. These are people with aboriginal ancestry who do not, in response to Census questions, identify as aboriginal. Cairns notes that this fraction is a full one third of those with aboriginal ancestry and expresses astonishment that RCAP's observation was a single cryptic footnote. He speculates on the reason:

> The most plausible reason for the commission's otherwise inexplicable unwillingness to analyze and report on the non-identifying Aboriginal ancestry population—a reason mentioned by various informants—is that this very large group could be portrayed as an example of successful assimilation, and thus employed as counter-evidence to the dominant and preferred nationalist discourse. (2005: 15)

In other words, many aboriginals appear to be doing just fine, without the assistance of (or having escaped) the System. Is it morally correct—I will not put such strong words in Cairns' mouth—to ignore this evidence of what many might call a good thing?

As another unpleasant reality, he describes "[s]mall populations and other practical concerns" with gentle words but devastating numbers: "By way of illustration, only 5.6% of Indian bands, 35 out of 627, have on-reserve populations of more than 2,000; nearly two-thirds of Indian bands have on-reserve populations of less than 500. One hundred and four bands have an on-reserve population of less than one hundred. (Canada. DIAND 2002, xv.)" (2005: 16). The limited capacity, for which he provides evidence, are as obvious as they are undiscussed. Quasi-provincial "self-government" is perhaps practical for compact Prince Edward Island (135,000 persons) but, by the results, clearly not for far-flung Nunavut (30,000), notwithstanding a billion-dollar annual subsidy. Yet, this idea remains the goal of the System and governments for much smaller Indian groups. The above observations are "inconvenient truths" in the currently popular phrase, but truths none the less.

In this brief summary, I skip over the interesting sections on constitutional alienation, "voice" (that is, the adequacy of representation through existing political structures such as Parliament) and mixed Indian responses to the Charter (a wholly logical position for those sovereigntists who would support a genuinely different Indian society) to arrive at the bottom line, what Cairns thinks should be done. At this stage, he invokes and builds upon the ideas of another of Canada's famous thinkers, Charles Taylor, and his two approaches to this issue. "Taylor I" is the classifier of Canadian diversity as either "first level" or "deep."

"First level" diversity describes the differences, be they cultural, background, or outlook, of citizens who nevertheless belong directly to Canada. This includes immigrants who have chosen to come here and adhere to our basics. "Deep diversity" is a term reserved for those whose membership in Canada is indirect, by way of an established collective, in Taylor's view, Quebecois and aboriginals. This does not necessarily imply a larger cultural distance: indeed, many new immigrants have a much greater cultural distance from the Canadian mainstream than French Canadians or aboriginals. But, " 'Deepness' according to Taylor, resides in identity, in the sense of nationhood and the desire to continue as a separate people into the future ... In its simplest form, for Taylor first level diversity Canadians share a common patriotism but not a common culture. Deep diversity communities increasingly share a common culture but not a common patriotism" (Cairns, 2005: 33). That is Taylor I. The reader may be sceptical, as am I, as to the durability of such deep diversity in this modern world but the idea articulates well the philosophical foundation of the RCAP and of the System (to the extent the System has a philosophy beyond self-interest).

"Taylor II" is more clearly founded in the practical, as distinct from intellectual, world. In an essay, Why Democracy Needs Patriotism, "Taylor II argues that 'strong identification on the part of their citizens' is a necessity in democratic societies" and that democratic states "need 'a high mobilization of their members [which] occurs around common identities.' Finally, 'a high degree of mutual commitment' is necessary to sustain redistributive policies to reduce the alienation of minorities and the disadvantaged'" (Cairns, 2005: 33).

This echoes the point that has long been made by Cairns himself that, if the mainstream does not see a shared commitment to Canadian citizenship by Indians, there is a danger it will lose sympathy for them. In my translation to the cruder language of the street: "You want us to help you? We want something back." Human nature is what it is and good will has value. Even the powerful courts cannot move the hand that writes the cheques.

Cairns describes the link between Indian nationalism and "Taylor I," with examples from various exponents, discusses the "nation to nation" relationship and then makes the intriguing point that "[t]reaty federalism, in which treaties rather than citizenship are the bonding mechanism, in effect proposes to internationalize the domestic system and has only a weak answer to the question as to what is to be the source of cohesion" (2005: 36). To be precise on this point, the "treaty federalism" to which he refers springs from the theories of James Tully (1999) but his comment is also apt for the modern treaty process, the major focus of governmental policy today, on which Cairns is relatively silent for unspecified reasons.

Where does all of this leave us? Cairns writes: "At the extremes, Taylor I and Taylor II are not only incompatible with each other, they are unworkable in the Canadian setting" (2005: 37). But the details of reconciling the ideas are murky, essentially a call for generosity of spirit and compromise on each side. Cairns finally offers a seven-point set of recommendations but, alas, not only do they deal largely with process and urgings, but in the end, "[t]he likelihood of a comprehensive implementation of the policy thrust of this postscript being implemented is minimal" (Cairns, 2005: 59). Even for the premier scholar in this field, not only are there no easy answers, there are no complicated ones either. We will simply have to see how the forces involved play out.

Cairns recognizes the Indian as an individual in his insistence upon citizenship and an individual relationship with the Canadian state in any viable long-term future. There is, however, very little discussion of the relationship between Indians and the collective, except for some cautionary thoughts about what I refer to as "small governments with large powers." And, in common with almost all of the literature, there is no discussion of whether in fact the Indian collective is a useful main focus for the living of a life for all Indians, or whether this might in fact be a matter of genuine choice for many or most. This is simply taken for granted and to question it is, of course, the ultimate heresy for the System. But looking through Cairns' immense sympathy for aboriginal people to his insistence on the data about the actual choices made by Indians in real life (including "going to town" and comfortable integration with the mainstream), and to practicality and realpolitik, he surely poses that question.

More theoretically, but also of importance, the question of whether indigenous collectives have any free-standing value beyond their services to members (a status again assumed by virtually all authors) also should be examined, above all by the membership. There is no hurry in this—history will sort it out as it has with other collectives around the world and over the millennia. But it is a helpful thought experiment.

Will Kymlicka

The relationship between the individual and the collective is directly and thoroughly addressed by Will Kymlicka, especially in *Multicultural Citizenship* (1995). For the lay reader, the Introduction (1995: 1–9) provides an uncommonly lucid and readable outline of the major issues and the means of addressing them.

Kymlicka points out that the word "multicultural" (notwithstanding the title of his book) can be confusing and that better words are "polyethnic" and "multinational" states. Polyethnicity typically arises from immigration and the intent is integration into the mainstream, even if still retaining distinguishing cultural characteristics. This phenomenon need not further concern us here, except to note, as is usual in political matters, that there are grey areas where the one division fades into the other. "Multinational" is a different matter. This relates to historic groups that wish to retain a significant separate identity, even if necessarily within the arms of the mother state. This is reminiscent of Taylor's "deep diversity," and Kymlicka also offers aboriginals[15] and French Canadians as examples.

Kymlicka's canvas is the whole world and my attempt will be limited to a brief and necessarily incomplete description of his application to Canadian Indians. He sees three forms of "group differentiated rights": rights of self-government, polyethnicity, and special representation (in mainstream decision-making bodies). The second does not concern us.

---

15 Words again: Kymlycka calls the word "Indian" a legal fiction for two reasons, only one of which I accept. It is quite right that the word conflates a multiplicity of Indian nations. But the distinction from non-Indian aboriginals is not a legal fiction but a legal fact, a matter of such life-changing consequence that it is the focus of this book.

Speaking of self-government, he acknowledges the usefulness of federalism but explicitly rejects it as a solution for indigenous peoples in North America because of the difficulty of drawing "national boundaries" wherein the indigenes would be a majority. Hence, special forms of self government must be developed.[16] The idea of special representation rights, that is, reserved seats in Parliament, is a complex one for later treatment. Kymlicka sees them as promising. Canada has always seen them as unnecessarily divisive[17] but of course it is not an open-and-shut question.

Kymlicka then turns his attention to the core question of his (and of this) book, namely the relationship between the individual and the collective: "A liberal democracy's most basic commitment is to the freedom and equality of individual citizens" ... "How then can liberals accept demands for group-differentiated rights by ethnic and national minorities?" (1995: 34). He returns usefully again to the meaning of possibly misleading words: "collective rights" spans a broad area, from trade unions to the right to bring class actions and the right to clean air. Though he does not make this point, such collective rights are "open access"—that is, available to all—and thus uncontroversial. The collective rights sought by national groups are by definition "closed," only open to members by birth with minor exceptions, and thus controversial if they impinge negatively upon the mainstream society, either as to finances or values, or upon the internal rights of individuals within the closed societies.

He acknowledges the traditional aversion of liberal societies to group rights and attempts to meet that by defining two classes of them. The first is "external protections," those being by and large acceptable in his view. The second is "internal restrictions," more dangerous and possibly not acceptable.

External protections are designed to protect the minority from the decisions of the larger society. Some of them—a provincial government's rights of jurisdiction vis-à-vis Ottawa, say, or (lesser, non-constitutionalized) municipal rights vis-à-vis provincial capitals—are usually accepted by the

---

16 I note here a point I will develop later: the more general idea of "subsidiarity," which like federalism is a well-accepted approach in western democracies, can admit of much more flexible and smaller boundaries. This concept is not sufficiently explored and could provide a fertile ground for young researchers.

17 Serious proposals have been made in this regard, including by the RCAP (for a third aboriginal Chamber of Parliament), other commissions and parliamentary inquiries, various academics, and even a former Government of New Brunswick.

mainstream as belonging to all Canadians in their respective locations, though people are not always logical as can be seen, for example, in the strong opposition to Quebec using its constitutional powers to privilege the French language in various ways. But external protections become more controversial when they extend to *de facto* immunity from most of the Charter for Indian governments (via s. 25) or to a considerable immunity from taxation. Yet these things have long been a part of our law. Modern treaty making or self-government powers are aimed at giving group protection from a much broader range of federal and provincial law (see, for example, the description of the Nisga'a Treaty in a previous chapter.).

Internal restrictions are group powers to be wielded, not against the mainstream, but against members of the group, as to their basic civil, political, or economic rights. Such restrictions (early removal from the educational process for Amish and Hutterite children, for example) Kymlicka rightly sees as problematic but maintains they exist more in theory than in practice and sometimes the trade-offs have merit. For example, for him the inalienable nature of indigenous land holdings can only be established *de facto* by collective ownership. This is a restriction upon freedom of property but a necessary evil in pursuit of a greater good. A key paragraph framing the debate is this:

> This distinction between internal restrictions and external protections is often ignored by both proponents and critics of group-differentiated rights. Thus we find liberal critics who assume that all forms of group-differentiated citizenship are "affected by an inherent deficiency in that they place the group over and above the individual." While this is a relevant objection to internal restrictions, it is not valid for external protections which do not place the group "over and above the individual." (1995: 44, quoting Tomuschat, 1983)

This puts the issue. Now, consider a small government with large powers. Those powers are meant for "external protection" (so they cannot be wielded by outsiders against the wishes of the group) and yet these same powers will be largely used for or against insiders, individual members. It is one thing to say that this reality exists for all governments but what if the democratic control of the small government is not functioning well? And, in addition, in Canada we also constrain all governments by constitutional mechanisms such as the Charter and Rights Tribunals. Why should small Indian governments be exempt? The alleged disjunction between "external," good, and "internal," bad is not a persuasive defence because of such large practical questions concerning the potential illiberal internal use of powers afforded for the purpose of protecting the collective from the outside world.

In addition, the problems intended to be addressed by group rights (self-government and protection from the mainstream majority in selected areas) may in my view often be addressed by a thorough application of the ideas of subsidiarity (the idea that decision-making authority in any given head of power should be available to the lowest level of government that can marshall the resources to deal with it), which presents no philosophical problems whatsoever, even if differential uptake by local authorities leads to *de facto* asymmetry. In a familiar example, all provinces might be offered a role in this or that federal power—immigration, say, where Ottawa has paramountcy—but only Quebec might choose to take it up. There are then no grounds for complaint. The application of this concept (of *de facto* asymmetry) to Indian policy needs much more study.

Kymlycka knows well and describes the traditional debate as to the "proper primacy" question, that is, which is more important, the individual or the collective, and whether the collective has free-standing value beyond its value to its individual members. However, he rejects this debate as inapplicable here, since group rights are "based upon the idea that justice between groups requires that members of different groups be accorded different rights" (1995: 47). In other words, the important issues of group rights are not really between the individual and the collective but rather between group and group.

That is as may be but it only takes the problem to one remove. What exactly is "justice between groups" and should it not be viewed through the larger lens of justice to individuals? In that case, we are left with a practical rather than philosophical question, perhaps more suited to politics than constitutions, without disparaging the need for minimal constitutional standards. And moreover, in the group-to-group model the issue of inter-group power inevitably arises because group equality cannot be claimed in the same way as we recognize individual equality. That is simply a political reality.

In such circumstances, dominant groups will in the end invariably insist upon the recognition of their interests. That is a reality as well and is, of course, the reason that minority groups seek constitutional protection. But, again in the end, constitutions are reshaped as the tools of dominant majorities if they perceive the situation to be sufficiently unsatisfactory. That is why "win/win" and cooperative solutions are always better, though "win/lose" pressures and demands upon the majority may prevail in the short run.

Doubtless Kymlycka understands this, which is why he seeks to influence the majority view. But, if that does not work …? Then, as he notes with some sadness at several points, the dominant interest prevails and "justice may be subordinated to stability" (1995: 57). But that will always be the case. Security issues always trump hope for justice in a society that highly values order. (Which Canada does: recall the easy public acceptance of the draconian imposition of the War Measures Act by the federal government in 1970.) Progress demands that we demonstrate the ability to have both order and justice at the same time.

We turn now explicitly to the relationship between individual freedom and culture. Kymlicka argues, and I accept, that individual freedom (measured by what I call the "option spectrum") is vastly increased by association with a societal culture.[18] That is common ground. I would go on to argue—and Kymlicka does not specifically address this but takes the opposite view by the equal deference he seems willing to afford most cultures—that some cultures serve the purpose of the individual better than others. He notes in passing that "[t]he sort of solidarity essential for a welfare state requires that citizens have a strong sense of common identity and common membership, so that they will make sacrifices for each other" (1995: 77). This directly recalls Cairns' worry that should mainstream and Indian citizenship become too disconnected, the bond for mainstream support may atrophy. He goes on to say that, "Given the enormous significance of social institutions in our lives, *any culture which is not a societal culture will be reduced to ever-decreasing marginalization*" (1995: 80, emphasis added). This bodes ill for those who cannot meet the hurdle set by his definition of a "societal culture" (footnote 17) and that arguably applies to all Canadian Indian tribes.

He quotes Ronald Dworkin (1985) with apparent approval as follows: "Cultures are not valuable in and of themselves, but because it is only through having access to a societal culture that people have access to a range of meaningful options" (1995: 83). That is exactly the position of this book but one must then ask, if cultures have no value in and of themselves, why protect any given version? This is obviously an explosive question for the System,

---

18 By "societal culture," he means not small things such as teenage gangs but rather to "a culture … across the full range of human activities, including social, educational, educational, religious, recreational and economic life, encompassing both public and private spheres. These cultures tend to be territorially concentrated, and based on a shared language" (1995: 16). This is a very high hurdle for any of Canada's small Indian nations to surmount.

which avers that the Canadian state (not Indians alone) must protect Indian cultures. As Kymlicka notes: "We do not feel obliged to keep uncompetitive industries afloat in perpetuity, so long as we help employees to find employment elsewhere, so why feel obliged to protect minority cultures, so long as we help their members to find another culture" (1995: 84)?

His answer takes a while to emerge and leads us through various philosophers and a look at communitarianism (an approach Kymlicka rejects, though it could arguably be one label for the approach of the System) but, in the end, he says that a culture is not just (like employment, say) a part of one's life; it is one's life. With this, I agree. But how much of the Canadian Indian culture is distinct from the mainstream? Recall the expansive definition: "a culture ... across the full range of human activities, including social, educational, religious, recreational and economic life, encompassing both public and private spheres. These cultures tend to be territorially concentrated, and based on a shared language." By this definition, Indian and mainstream cultures have a very large overlap, urban more than rural, and rural in turn more than isolated Reserves. But if in many cases the cultures do mostly overlap, what are we really talking about?

Kymlicka recognizes this and notes:

> After all, societal cultures are not permanent and immutable. (If they were, group-specific rights would not be needed to protect them.) And given the coercive attempt to assimilate many national minorities—particularly indigenous peoples—it would not be surprising if there is very little left of some cultures ... [And so] ... would it not be better for the members of the national minority to integrate into the mainstream, rather than struggle in vain too preserve something that is already lost? (1995: 100)

Another of the explosive questions that he is so honestly prepared to address; however, we "... must leave this option open." But then crucially, "... the decision about whether to integrate must be up to the members of the minority themselves" (1995: 100). Not up to the mainstream. And interestingly, not up to the collective but rather the "members." I cannot comment on the rest of the wide Kymlickian world but in the case of Canadian Indians I fully agree with this position and will later propose measures to make that choice between separation and integration a meaningful one for individuals rather than the collective, with the comfortable ability to go either way.

But, of course, this is not the usual choice facing real people. These are polar positions. In fact, these things need not be "either/or." A culture need not be a box. It can also be a huge field with indistinct or porous boundaries for exploration. It is quite possible to have something of many worlds. All that one loses in partaking of that cultural smorgasbord is purity but we are all mongrels in that sense. The truth is, with the exception of a few academics and sovereigntists who genuinely believe in a parallel Indian society, cultural walls are erected by the System, for the System, not for ordinary members.

Kymlicka moves next to the issue of "benign neglect" as the proper state view of cultures. This idea holds that

> a system of universal rights already accommodates cultural differences, by allowing each person freedom to associate with others ... [Moreover] ... giving political recognition or support to particular cultural practices or associations is unnecessary and unfair. It is unnecessary, because a valuable way of life will have no difficulty attracting adherents. And it is unfair, because it subsidizes some people's choices at the expense of others. (1995: 107)

He rejects this proposition as both mistaken and incoherent, since government decisions (driven by the mainstream) inevitably privilege the mainstream culture. For him, "[g]roup-differentiated rights—such as territorial autonomy, veto powers, guaranteed representation in central institutions, land claims and language rights—can help rectify this disadvantage" (1995: 109). He invokes philosophers such as Dworkin and Rawls, who insist upon the importance of rectifying unchosen inequalities, including cultural, whose effects are "profound and pervasive and present from birth" (Rawls, 1971: 109).

What Kymlicka means by "disadvantage" here is a bit confusing but the "unchosen inequality" is presumably not the judgmental idea of being born into a less-valuable culture but rather into one that is less robust. He uses language as the most important area of cultural oppression, in the sense that public schooling will be in the mainstream language, which unavoidably chooses between cultures. Like other arguments in this section, this one is puzzling in the Canadian context. Minority schooling can easily be had with a voucher system but, in any event for Canadian Indians, the language of the home is overwhelmingly a mainstream language (that is, mostly English, some French).

He goes on to invoke the role of historical agreements such as treaties as a possible basis of group rights but admits that, "[o]ne difficulty with historical agreements is that they are often hard to interpret" (1995: 119). Indeed, historic treaties with Canadian Indians are almost wholly about negative rights, that is, the right to be left alone on their remaining lands, though small compensations ("treaty money," tools, or clothing may be added). In practice, of course the Indians were not left alone. They were made subject to the Indian Act. And in modern times, the enormous expenditures in respect of Canadian Indians are made as a matter of current policy rather than arguments from historic agreement.[19]

In the end, though the arguments are muddy and challengeable, I suspect that most fair-minded people would agree with the general proposition that people should have tools to support their culture of choice to the extent there is not a net negative impact on the society as a whole. Again, as will be argued later, "subsidiarity," including the availability of a general devolution of power and resources to smaller units, has a much more acceptable flavor than "group rights" and may go a long way to achieving the same thing.

On the difficult question of special representation rights in an egalitarian democracy, Kymlicka and Cairns are equally tentative. Both see arguments as to why national minorities may require representation in central institutions that may make decisions important to minority lives; both admit the immense complexity. There are scattered examples around the world, reserved seats for the New Zealand Maori for example, but none seem terribly persuasive

To the extent that "self-government" rights are available, this is in fact an argument for diminished representation at the center for the persons concerned, as, for example, in the famous West Lothian Question in Britain or Trudeau's question as to why MPs from a Quebec with special powers should have votes in those areas in respect of federal activity in other provinces. Politics is in many ways a zero-sum game. There is only so much money and more for the Atlantic means less for British Columbia. So clear issues of group power arise when parliamentarians are seen as group representatives rather than impartial seekers of the common good.

The issue regarding the elevation of impartiality over representativeness is even more intense with the judiciary, a calling the public trusts much more than politicians. And yet the Supreme Court of Canada, not Parliament,

19 This is the long-time view of the federal government. Many Indians claim such expenditures as a matter of right. The courts have not definitively opined as yet.

has the final word on the content of Indian law. We already, wisely or not, require that one third of the SCC bench be from Quebec. Should, say, one out of nine be Indian, as a similar requirement? I would argue against, for reasons of democratic and governance theory that are not central to this book, but that essentially reject the politicization of tribunals.

In addition, as Kymlicka notes, "some liberals will object to group representation on the grounds that institutionalizing group differences, and ascribing political salience to them, would have serious implications for social unity" (1995: 150). I agree. The better answer again may well be subsidiarity. The less influence the federal government (for example) has in anyone's day-to-day life, the less that person needs to worry about their representation there.

We turn next to the knotty question of what a multinational state (if one agrees that this is indeed an apt description of Canada) where the mainstream is based upon liberal principles (as is certainly the case with Canada) should do if one of its constituent nations wishes to treat its members in an illiberal manner? Are we to grant the "nation" autonomy or insist upon liberal values? This is no mere theoretical question, as has been evidenced by the Doukhobor crisis in British Columbia in the 1960s (keeping children out of school) or the very recent storm over *sharia* law in Ontario. I earlier described the fight in Parliament between the parties and with the AFN as to whether the Canadian Bill of Rights should be applicable to Indian governments. At this writing, legislation has just been introduced proposing property rights for Indian women after marital breakdown. And of course the Charter in s. 25 comes down on the side of autonomy (where traditional practices are involved, which may be a very large field) but in the one case in the Charter debates where specific political push actually came to shove, *re* gender equality, liberal principles prevailed yielding s. 28 (which, being more specific in content, will trump s. 25).

The Kymlickian analysis is lengthy and tortuous, and I will substitute my own summary: "It depends." There are weighty arguments on both sides. Some say, how can you recognize a national minority and then not let it practice those very values that defines it, however offensive that may be to liberals? They cite the millet system of the Ottoman Empire, where the Greek and Armenian Orthodox and the Jews were permitted to deal with their nationals as they wished, as long as all bowed to the Empire in matters of imperial importance, taxation, security, and the like. The system worked. But the Ottoman Empire was not founded upon liberal principles, and Muslims therein suppressed heresy (questioning the faith) and apostasy (leaving the faith) as crimes, as many Muslim states still do. Others say, no, the essence of liberalism is freedom of conscience and we will not brook such oppression anywhere within our society, multinational or not.

There is a bit of case law. In *Hofer v. Hofer*, the SCC upheld the right of a Hutterite colony to expel two members for apostasy and allow them no share of the colony's property, even though they had helped to create the wealth by their labor. According to Kymlicka, "[t]he Hutterites defended this practice on the grounds that freedom of religion protects a congregation's ability to live within its religious doctrine, even if this limits individual freedom" (1995: 161). My guess is that this precedent will not turn out to be very helpful. As a practical matter, the strongly felt values of the mainstream society will likely be imposed by the courts. Certainly the politicians felt that way by inserting s. 28 (gender equality) into the Charter against the opposition of some Indian voices who insisted this was an internal matter for a parallel society to resolve. Sexual orientation may have reached that powerful political status by now.[20] The application of the Canadian Human Rights Code was temporarily side-railed as a partisan skirmish in a minority Parliament but the more specific and therefore "hotter button" married property rights will, in my guess, sail through. If it does, will the SCC uphold the new law or set it aside on the basis of s. 25? The court could do either. But even courts need public support.

Perhaps more to the point, Indian governments need public support. The mainstream is too large and they are too small. So what we will see as to this particular issue is an ongoing political negotiation, somewhat mediated by the courts but tending always in a liberal direction (and thus closer to the mainstream).

But that may not be easy. In his final chapter on "The ties that bind," Kymlicka provides two fine quotations about self-government. The first is this: "It seems unlikely that according self government rights to a national minority can serve as an integrative function ... Moreover, there seems no natural stopping point to the demands for increasing self-government" (1995: 182). These are cautionary words indeed. But then, just a few pages later, "Since claims to self-government are here to stay, we have no choice but to accommodate them" (1995: 185). These two statements, contradictory in implication if not logic, may be true. If they are, they certainly signal a

20 However sexual-orientation freedoms were "read in" to s. 15 of the Charter and Indian society is probably protected from the judiciary in this sort of s. 15 case wherever s. 25 applies.

continuing tension, with an equilibrium reached only at that point where "national" claims test the goodwill of the mainstream to the limit. This seems to me an unfortunate future. We should be able to do better. It all comes down to living together. The Western liberal ideal overall is surely for us to celebrate together the things we have in common, leaving the individual to celebrate difference.

There is a very real sense in which a pursuit of symbol and principle can get in the way of accommodation. Of course, I do not mean that such things as principle are unimportant. But the world is a very complex place, and one should find a way of blending principles and symbols for maximum advantage rather than fighting about them. Over the course of history, the fights have normally been about issues between rulers and priesthoods and their own convenient principles and symbols. But there is a lot of room for "live and let live," and that has been a part of the genius of Canada.

At the end of this all, there is a another, very fundamental problem with the application of the Kymlickian analysis to the estate of Canadian Indians. That is because no given tribe is a robust "nation" by his definition of that word "a historical community, more or less institutionally complete, occupying a given territory or homeland, sharing a distinct language and culture" (1995: 11). Whatever may have been the situation at the time of contact, it is a challenge to find today genuine institutional completeness (virtually impossible given small numbers) and distinct languages have fallen into desuetude. This applies not only to Indians but *a fortiori* to other aboriginals. Indeed, it is a sad irony that it is likely that the only reason any weak version of "nation" continues among the larger tribes is because of the historic oppression and isolating effects of the Indian Act and related policies, without which Indianness might well have disappeared by now.

What are we to think of all of this? For me, Cairns' approach is in essence moral and political: "We owe you. How can we work this out in a way that is reasonably satisfactory for everyone?" Kymlicka's approach is more ambitious, something like: "This is what is right; this is what we all ought to recognize and act upon." This philosophical approach implies group rights simply because the groups have been defined (according to one certain logic, among several available) and make demands. There are weaknesses in this philosophy, at least insofar as the position of Canadian Indians is concerned, but whether it is right or wrong is less important than the fact that the current Canadian approach is a mixture of the two. Public opinion (for those who care at all) is essentially driven by Cairns' approach. Court and government opinion and, therefore, the great power of official policy is much more driven by Kymlicka's approach, and that because of academic and nationalist views and words in the Constitution, words that, as argued elsewhere, are having consequences that were not intended by the framers.

What to do? Public opinion will eventually govern in the end in a democracy. However, it may take such a very long time as to be irrelevant in our days. But current policy is a demonstrated failure of epic proportions. We cannot change the Constitution in the short term but governments and courts have a very great deal of flexibility if they adopt new ways of thought. Upon that slender hope, hangs much of the short-term welfare of the Indian people.

The "inherent right to self-government"

Before leaving this chapter I return to a concept briefly mentioned in the section, "On language," namely the so-called "inherent right to self-government." This right is said to by some to lodge in indigenous collectives anywhere in the world or, for our purposes, some or all Canadian aboriginal collectives. The concept is enormously important to the System. If the idea is sustained it must have content and the content must be non-trivial. It is a key to the moral, intellectual, and legal validation of a parallel society.

Note that the right is said to inhere in a collective. No one could reasonably oppose the idea that individuals have an inherent right to govern themselves. This is a part of the natural order, as the individual is both the smallest and the only fully integrated and free-standing decision-making unit. It is also a fundamental part of the Western liberal tradition to which Canada is heir. But in a collective? That is another question. Any collective larger than a single family (which may of course be quite large) is hard to see as a part of the "natural order." Larger constructs are by definition social and cultural entities.

So if there is a right of governance in such a larger entity, from whence comes the empowerment? One can claim it comes from God but that response is not very helpful in terms of modern secular governance. One can claim a provenance of tradition, the British constitution, say, unwritten but sweeping and durable. Each newborn Briton simply accepts the collective right of governance because it is there, pervasive and powerful. But note, that is not to say it is inherent and indeed, had World War II gone the other way, the British constitution would no longer exist. In other words, any larger-than-natural, larger-than-family governance structure must first of all be created and that (like the British constitution) may take a very long time. Thereafter, it must be sustained and defended from enemies within and without. These tasks are not as easy as the era of decolonialization hoped they might be. Failed states around the world attest to that. In other words again, no national government is "inherent." Such a thing either "is" or "is not" or is in transition. So the "inherent right," if it exists, must mean something different.

We can perhaps learn something from the study of other "rights." All of them share two characteristics. The first is that they must be widely agreed to be entitlements, not facts *de novo* but "ought-to-be" things. The second is that, to become anything more than theory, they need to be enforceable. Some of the rights in the Charter would have been laughed at a century ago. Today they are enforceable. They were not then "rights"; they are now. If a desirable entitlement is not currently enforceable that does not mean that it should not be an aspiration; but it is not a "right."

The difficulty with the word "inherent" is that it implies something that is latent, already there, needing only unopposed development or discovery. But that suggests a part of the natural order, which is hard to credit. Certainly a gender right to equality seems far more "inherent" than any claimed inherent right to self-government, but even that gender equality is very, very recent as a right in human history and still far from of worldwide application.

The mere fact that people from similar gene pools have lived in the same area for a long time does not mean a great deal unless there is a will to live together under a common order for common purposes. Moreover, to submit to a "government" that affirmative will must extend over a range of issues and be of a considerable intensity. [21] So, for our theoretical nascent group of proximate, like-gened people, unless there is an existing, dominant governing entity (which of course would not be inherent but rather factual), any "inherency" for a new form of government—if such inherency exists—cannot reside in an unborn collective but rather in its would-be members.

The better phrase it seems to me is "aspirational right" rather than "inherent right" to describe the wishes of those spokespersons or would-be leaders who would establish (or re-invigorate) an order of government. In other words, this is no different from the conditions for any other form of governance. The requirements of creating, sustaining, and defending all exist. Those who claim an aspirational right must meet those tests. There

21 I speak of voluntary association reacting to a force of inherency. Wherever humans of the most modest modernity gather there will be some form of government, possibly as part of a much larger state that has coalesced and expanded in some way. Unity through force is the more common option but that is not what "the inherent right" is said to be about.

is no reason (other than possible motives of either self-interest or charity that must be either demonstrated or felt) why others should assist in this. The British constitution in all its glory is neither here nor there to China, except possibly as an example of one way of doing things. The only question in *realpolitik* for the Chinese (or anyone else) is, who governs the Britons?

The view of the System

It is putting it mildly to say that the above is not the conventional wisdom of the System or of the United Nations. Prof. Bradford W. Morse (1999) gives a sympathetic overview of the conventional wisdom of most Canadian academics. He begins with the common ground that Indian[22] governments certainly existed and exercised power: they "governed this land with care and reverence for thousands of years" (1999: 16) he says, revealing a brief glimpse of the vein of sentimentality that influences many otherwise serious scholars in this field, perhaps seeking somehow to atone personally for a history of white guilt. He goes on to say that this right "has never been relinquished" (1999: 17), which may well be true, certainly according to the System. However "relinquished" and "extinguished" are different words. A greater power may extinguish a right that I held and did not relinquish, but it is still gone. While he does not make that point, the balance of his survey deals with that tension.

Morse notes that, notwithstanding the passage of the Indian Act, a long-following history of treaty making suggests the federal government must have been dealing with entities having a capacity to make such agreements. He then turns to the extended history (roughly from the mid-1970s to the Charlottetown Accord of 1992) of negotiations among Indian organizations, the federal government, and the provinces. The federal government under Trudeau and the early Mulroney took a "contingent right" position, that is, a governance right existed if and only if the content was agreed. This was unsatisfactory to the Indian side and by 1991 Ottawa had moved to suggesting a "general justiciable[23] right to self-government that would have recognized the Aboriginal people possess autonomy over their own affairs within the Canadian federation" (Morse, 1999: 22). He cites the AFN's view at the time:

22 —or "aboriginal": the terms were interchangeable at contact and Métis did not exist, by definition.

23 —that is, a right enforceable by a court.

> Our Creator, Mother Earth, put First Nations on this land to care for and live in harmony with all her creation. We cared for our earth, our brothers and sisters in the animal world, and each other. These responsibilities give us our inherent, continuing right to self-government. This right flows from our original occupation of this land from time immemorial. (1999: 22)

Well, maybe. Many societies that might have been upon nature's earth may have made the same claims and then disappeared. Claims are only claims; facts are facts.

By the time of the Charlottetown Accord, federal and provincial governments had come around to an agreement that an inherent right would be recognized.[24] Note the distinction here: the "contingent" theory has been abandoned and the proposal is "recognition," not "creation." The Accord was intensely controversial in the land. It was put to a referendum and soundly defeated, including in polls on Indian Reserves.

The RCAP opined: "Self-government is the way forward and the main source of hope for Aboriginal people" (1993: 26). Thus did the Commission signal the sterile and narrow street it was following. Had they said that "education" or "jobs" or other attributes of assistance to individuals pointed the way forward, most people would have agreed. This focus on "self-government" is not self-explanatory, but it was clearly the RCAP's view.

The newly elected Liberal government in 1994 proposed a new approach recognizing "the inherent right ... under s. 35" (Irwin, 1994) and the next year began a process of unilaterally imposing limitations on the content of the "right," which began to take legislative form in the Yukon self-government agreements of the mid-1990s (the federal government can act alone in the territories as there is no provincial government to consult) and found more or less final form, to date, in the Nisga'a Treaty. As Morse notes, this policy has been criticized from both sides, by some for going too far, from the aboriginal side for unjustly foreclosing the negotiations.

From the legal side, Morse notes that the Constitution acts of 1867 and 1982 expressly mention only two sovereigns (federal and provincial) but adds somewhat hopefully that "[a]lthough the inherent right of self-government has not been judicially confirmed as an Aboriginal or treaty right, there is no Supreme Court of Canada decision that directly prevents such a finding"

---

24 See The inherent right of self-government as defined in the Charlottetown Accord, p. 150, for the relevant sections of the Accord.

(1999: 35). That seems a bit optimistic. His own footnote allows as to how the SCC's "decision in *Pamejawon*, however, does not give great comfort in that regard" (1999: 35, footnote 6). That is a considerable understatement. What the Court actually said is:

> In so far as they can be made under s. 35(1), claims to self-government are no different from other claims to the enjoyment of aboriginal rights and must, as such, be measured against the same standard.
>
> 25 In *Van der Peet*, *supra*, the test for identifying aboriginal rights was said to be as follows, at para. 46: "... in order to be an aboriginal right an activity must be an element of a practice, custom or tradition integral to the distinctive culture of the aboriginal group claiming the right.
>
> (*R. v. Pamajewon*, [1996] 2 S.C.R. 821)

This is no barn door. (The reference to the concurring judgement or Major and Binnie in *Mitchell v. MNR*, earlier cited, supports this sceptical view.)

Morse takes some comfort from American jurisprudence, "where residual sovereignty of Indian nations has been accepted by the United States Supreme Court for almost two centuries" (1999:35). The difficulty with this comparison is that Indian sovereignty in the United States is wholly dependent upon the goodwill of Congress. There is no constitutional protection. The Congress can (and does) change Indian law as it wishes. In the end, even as hopeful an observer as Morse is led to conclude that "[s]ignificant doubt remains as to whether or not Canadian law, as it stands, acknowledges the inherent right of Aboriginal peoples to determine their own futures and govern their own affairs" (1999: 41). I would add, however, that there is absolutely no doubt about the legal capacity of Indian individuals to govern their futures as anyone else, at least once off the Reserve and free of the racist s. 91(24).

Morse concludes his piece with what I consider a signal piece of wisdom: "far too much energy has been devoted to debating questions of entitlement. More attention is needed to address the practical realities involved in making self-government work" (1999: 42).

The view of the United Nations

The current federal government has been much excoriated for refusing to affix the signature of Canada to the United Nations' *Declaration on the Rights of Indigenous Peoples* (2007). Part of the criticism came from the Opposition, which can be dismissed as the usual partisan fluff given that the Opposition, when in government, did not itself sign. In fact, the position of Canada over the years has been quite consistent and, briefly put, holds that the Draft Declaration has some serious conflicts with the Canadian Constitution and court rulings and, if adopted, would throw the law into chaos.[25]

The words of the System on failure to adhere to the Declaration are more bitter, and understandably so. A golden opportunity for its expansion has, *pro tem*, been frustrated. To underline the importance of such agreements, recall the words of Chief Justice McLachlin of the SCC for a unanimous seven-judge bench in *Health Services and Support [etc.] v. British Columbia*, [2007]: "The Charter should be presumed to provide *at least as great a level of protection as found in the international human rights documents* that Canada has ratified" (emphasis added). As the reader will see from the following, there is an excellent chance that adherence to this United Nations document, then to be read into the Charter by the Court, would have seriously destabilized the evolving pattern of Canadian law.

The concepts of "indigenous peoples" and "inherent rights" are central to the *Declaration* itself. No definition or listing is given. In common parlance, this is signing a blank cheque. In the *Declaration*, indigenous rights are not merely individual; they are collective. No provision whatsoever is made for democratic or even good governance of the collective. Indigenous tyrannies may apply for UN blessing. Article 3 implies potential separation rights for indigenous peoples, though this is carefully obfuscated. Article 4 requires taxation (of the mainstream) without representation. Articles 5, 20, and 33 provide for a parallel society. Article 11 provides for retroactive compensation for things done "in violation of their laws, traditions and customs". Article 18 provides for reserved seats in mainstream decision making bodies. Article 22 is so deliciously politically correct that it really is worth citation: "Particular attention shall be paid to the rights and special needs of indigenous elders, women, youth, children and persons with disabilities in the implementation of this Declaration." Middle-aged male indigenes have a complaint. Article 26 again is worth citing because it is the main concern of the government of Canada: "Indigenous peoples have the right to the lands,

25 The Canadian position in detail, along with a historical summary, may be found in Canada, Indian and Northern Affairs Canada (2006a). While the document does not say so, Canada has little to learn from the United Nations Human Rights Council, many of whose members are unfree. The lessons should in fact flow the other way.

territories and resources which they have traditionally owned, occupied or otherwise used or acquired." Ottawa says this would over-ride established and ongoing processes.

None of this is surprising if you know how the United Nations operates. The reason there is no definition of an "indigenous" person, when that ought to be the very first line of text, is simple. The Asians and Africans absolutely vetoed it. The Chinese claim they have no indigenous peoples and the Indians and Pakistanis say they are all indigenous. The Africans are terrified of tribal schisms. In a like way, giving a definition to "self-determination," "peoples," or "inherent rights" would have been dangerous to many countries. It is true that some of this language is used in the UN International Convention on Civil and Political Rights but there "peoples" are interchangeable with nation states or with liberating colonies. It is not an internal concept in that context.

It is worth recalling that the United Nations is, *inter alia*, an assembly dominated by undemocratic states that have themselves no intention of abiding by rules they dislike but a great propensity to make rules for law-abiding western nations. Adherence to this *Declaration* would immensely complicate a developing pattern of Canadian accommodation and should be resisted. Recall again that our Supreme Court is prone to importing international law to guide us and that this Declaration is not in the usual "aspirational" language but rather the "rights" language of Conventions. Signing this would be a recipe for legal chaos and the bad, not the good, of Canadian Indians.[26]

Conclusion

That concludes the philosophical survey of this book. But after all of this theory, what are we left with? We are left with the facts on the ground: there are Indian governments in Canada. But and the importance of this cannot be over-emphasized—there is nothing "natural" or "inherent" about these governments at all. They are wholly artificial structures on limited territories, built by the mainstream in replacement of whatever arrangements were in place at contact. The territories were all prescribed by the (then) settler

26 On matters international, it is interesting that in the new Tsawwassen Treaty the Crown binds itself to consult in advance with the Tsawwassen Nation in cases where new international Treaty or Tribunal positions to be taken by Canada might affect Tsawwassen (ss. 2-30 and 2-33). There are at least 22 mandatory heads of consultation specified in addition to the usual Court requirements.

society, as was the grouping of persons into Bands. The powers, minimal at the beginning and now much expanded, have all been defined and supported by the law of the mainstream. The financing has been almost totally from the mainstream.

There is nothing "natural" or "inherent" or even durable about these governments. Were the laws of Ottawa and its cheque-writing machine to disappear tomorrow, so would these governments. Had s. 91(24) never existed, neither would these governments. It is an interesting thought experiment as to what (if anything) would be there instead but, whatever it would be would be neither natural nor inherent but rather subject to other kinds of mainstream social forces. In other words, the facts on the ground are the creation of the mainstream society, their continuation to this day has been courtesy of the mainstream society, and they are therefore our responsibility, which cannot be avoided.

⸙ ⸙ ⸙

In the end, the real essence of this chapter is to ask how well the various governance schemes and organizing principles meet the most ancient, durable, and generally accepted guide to action known to religions and ethicists around the world. That would be what is sometimes called "The Golden Rule:" "Do unto others as you would have others do unto you." The mainstream society, to the extent that it interferes in Indian affairs with law and money (and such interference is unavoidable unless one turns a blind eye to human potential and human problems) should ask this about any given structure or plan: Would you want this "done unto you?"

At the end of this entire chapter on philosophy, I return to my basic point of individual choice as the solution. In other words, I am not much impressed by the idea of multinationalism as useful for the purposes of any Canadian, save those who profit by it as a business. But this view has a strong codicil, as far as Indians are concerned. Because of the strong implied contract of well over 100 years of the mainstream treating Indians differently as a matter of public policy, then in equity Indians must continue to have that path open to them for a reasonable future—but again—as an individual choice on a neutral field.

NOTE

Julius Grey on the Accord and the third order

The noted Quebec lawyer and civil libertarian, Julius Grey, had this to say in the *Montreal Gazette* shortly after the defeat of the Charlottetown Accord. He noted *en passant* that *re* the Accord, including its self-government clauses, "if one looks at the electoral map, those regions affected by autonomy voted decisively for the 'No'" (January 6, 1993: op. ed.). In a powerful column, he worried about the oppression of internal minorities by ethnic governments.

He took on some of the sacred cows of the System directly:

> Assimilation is not a dirty word. For the Canadian state it should be an indifferent one, a choice we respect as much as the opposite ... The argument raised by advocates of self-government is that the native nations were here first. That is demagogy. The aboriginals were not here. Their ancestors were ... Collective rights are not inherited. If they were, we could justify special privileges for the French Canadians descended from the settlers whose ancestors were here second; the Anglo-Saxons who came third and so on, down to today's arrivals who would have the fewest rights. (January 6, 1993: op. ed.)

To his last point, it is an arguable objection that French Canadians are in fact privileged in the Constitution; but this is only as to language, not ethnicity.

NOTE

The inherent right of self-government as defined in the Charlottetown Accord

41 The Inherent Right of Self-Government

Note: References to the territories will be added to the legal text with respect to this section, except where clearly inappropriate. Nothing in the amendments would extend the powers of the territorial legislatures.

The Constitution should be amended to recognize that the Aboriginal peoples of Canada have the inherent right of self-government within Canada. This right should be placed in a new section of the Constitution Act, 1982, section 35.1(1).

The recognition of the inherent right of self-government should be interpreted in light of the recognition of Aboriginal governments as one of three orders of government in Canada.

A contextual statement should be inserted in the Constitution, as follows:

The exercise of the right of self-government includes authority of the duly constituted legislative bodies of the Aboriginal peoples, each within its own jurisdiction:

(a) to safeguard and develop their languages, cultures, economies, identities, institutions and traditions; and,
(b) to develop, maintain and strengthen their relationship with their lands, waters and environment so as to determine and control their developments as peoples according to their own values and priorities and ensure the integrity of their societies.

Before making any final determination of an issue arising from the inherent right of self-government, a court or tribunal should take into account the contextual statement referred to above, should enquire into the efforts that have ben made to resolve the issue through negotiations and should be empowered to order the parties to take such steps as are appropriate in the circumstances to effect a negotiated resolution.

42 Delayed Justiciability

The inherent right of self-government should be entrenched in the Constitution. However, its justiciability should be delayed for a five-year period through constitutional language and a political accord. (*)

Delaying the justiciability of the right should be coupled with a constitutional provision which would shield Aboriginal rights.

Delaying the justiciability of the right will not make the right contingent and will not affect existing Aboriginal and treaty rights.

The issue of special courts or tribunals should be on the agenda of the First Ministers' Conference on Aboriginal Constitutional matters referred to in item 53. (*)

(*Charlottetown Accord: Consensus Report on the Constitution*, Charlottetown, August 28, 1992)

CHAPTER 5

Treaties, governance, and other arrangements

New treaty and governance arrangements (such as the First Nations Governance Act proposed by Jean Chretien's administration but abandoned by his successor, Paul Martin) are widely claimed to be the "silver bullets" that will allow the solution of difficulties in this field. As a broad generalization, this is the approach that says, "Empower the collective!" as distinct from the individual. It is also the essence of current policy so we must examine these ideas closely. Treaties first.

The first thing to be said about treaties is that they are a further example of how the attention of governments, federal and provincial, is focused almost uniquely on Reserve Indians and the parallel society.[1] The well being of those who have "gone to town" is only affected by such policies to the extent that the persons concerned might wish to re-enter Reserve life and there is little evidence to date of this occurring on a net basis. This is exemplary of the case that will be made in this chapter that treaties have really become instruments to satisfy the needs of power structures rather than individuals. The roughly 50% of Registered Indians living off Reserve are not much assisted by a treaty for their tribe except perhaps for a "signing fee." They are the "forgotten people" of Indian policy because they have left the System's ambit.

1 Municipal governments, by contrast, without the splendid federal and provincial isolation of distance and large bureaucracies, perforce focus on actual human problems within their boundaries, including urban aboriginals, without the luxury of asking "whose jurisdiction?"

Treaties are broadly misunderstood in at least two other ways. The first is the idea that the completion of a treaty marks a significant step in the progress of individual Reserve Indians. That may be a by-product but, indeed, the reverse also might occur. There is no direct incentive or requirement for such an outcome either way in the process. For a treaty really is something that is directly germane only to the collective, which entity may then use this new estate for good or ill.

To illustrate the point, here is a quotation from an editorial in the *Vancouver Sun* commenting on the "Yes" referendum vote by members of the Tsawwassen First Nation on a draft treaty in 2007. After a generally positive discussion of some pros and cons, the newspaper concluded: "But if the Tsawwassen treaty achieves nothing else except giving band members a fair shot at obtaining the same quality of life enjoyed by other Canadians in the Lower Mainland, it will still be a success" (*Vancouver Sun*, 2007, July 27). This comment shows a profound and common lack of understanding of treaties. In fact members of the Tsawwassen First Nation have always had a "fair shot at obtaining the same quality of life enjoyed by other Canadians in the Lower Mainland." This is a small reserve of about 300 people in the municipality of Delta. Children from the Tsawwassen Reserve go to ordinary public schools and have done so for generations. They have access to and use the same services in health, education, and so on as anyone else in the area. Most particularly, they have the same shot at a very strong and growing job market and economy as anyone else in the area. A child from the Tsawwassen Reserve had the same "fair shot" as any other child in the community, except as they might have been advantaged or burdened by the legal facts and perceptions of Indianness—and treaties underline, rather than remove, the matter of Indianness. To repeat: treaties are for the collective, not for the individual.

If the treaty does anything for individuals, it will be by way of a wealthier collective: more administrative jobs, more low-cost housing, more unearned income, perhaps a costlier celebration of traditional culture, and maybe a boost in group pride. But these things have little to do with individual equality of opportunity. The merits or otherwise of the Tsawwassen treaty[2] have to be assessed on other considerations.

Some of the other modern treaties having to do with more remote areas (e.g. northern Quebec) could arguably be justified as improving the conditions of individuals on the basis that strengthening the collective may

---

2 It has been very controversial because it takes land from the Agricultural Land Reserve, zoning that enjoys a semisacred status in British Columbian politics.

make for the more efficient provision of services to them. This is, however, an empirical question requiring measurement and there is no persuasive history that gives ground for an *a priori* assumption that new service delivery vehicles do this.

As noted above, it could be argued that completion of a treaty gives individuals some sort of sense of a kind of national pride, which could be empowering. On the other hand, a significant fraction of British Columbian Indians (especially those under the banner of the Union of BC Indian Chiefs, though a much larger group including other Bands has, as of this writing, stated similar opposition to the Tsawwassen treaty) have so far taken the position that treaties really represent a diminution in existing Indian sovereignty and therefore a sort of national defeat. The significant "No" vote on most ratification referendums may so indicate as well.

Treaties could in fact be structured to the advantage of individuals, and that thought was a part of the historic treaties, which provided for "treaty money" (an annual payment, usually $5 for ordinary Band members, at a time when $5 meant something).[3] Very occasionally, a treaty could pro-

---

3 I have received a recollection from a guest at an "exceptionally pleasant" Treaty Day in Saskatchewan, 1989:

> I think of treaty days on the Prairies, when all of the endless bickering over bucks stops for a day and departmental staff and community members join together for the immensely symbolic paying of treaty ... The day starts with prayers and speeches, with the invocation of the sacred relationship between the Crown and First Nations, and proceeds to a table, set up outdoors, with DIAND officers scrubbed, in shirt and tie or tailored dress ... jeans and boots, the normal uniforms of our field staff of both sexes simply will not do for an occasion of such joy and solemnity ... and a Mountie in full-dress red serge. There is a strongbox on the table full of brand-new $5 bills and there is a box of ammunition, too. The whole community lines up, joking and gossiping in the bright Prairie sun, behind the Chief. One by one their names are formally checked against the pay list, solemn-eyed young additions to the pay list in tow, and the payment required by treaty is passed to the senior officer present, who passes it over the flag, a Union Jack laid out on the table, to the recipient. Heads of families get ammunition—a box of .22s these days, restraint being what it is—and every third year, the Chief gets a special payment for a new treaty suit. Then everybody goes to the community hall for another speech or two.

vide for settlement "in severalty," which gives individual Band members the option of taking title to their share of land and other settlement proceeds. In the provision for the possibility of private land ownership and access to the BC Land Registry system included in the Nisga'a Treaty, individual interests could be advanced but this will only be triggered, if ever, by legislative acts of the Nisga'a Nation. In addition, the constitutions of the new treaty governments (such constitutions being a normal requirement of modern treaties) can add to individual rights, especially as compared to the old Indian Act. But in fact, to date, these things remain mostly in the realm of possibility rather than practice.

So, the first general assumption in this area—the positive impact of treaties on the welfare of individuals—is theoretically possible but not often seen. The great and obvious impact of a treaty is on the collective and the structure of the parallel society, which have much more complex and largely negative implications for individuals in long run.

A second assumption often made arises from a linguistic confusion. Just as the word "nation" in "First Nation" tends to import an international context in the minds of many, so the word "treaty" also imports the more usual international meaning of that word. Generally, treaties are entered into between sovereign powers. Are there therefore implications of sovereignty with Indian treaties as well?

Many will make this argument, for obvious reasons. First, any acceptance of this claim to sovereignty by a third party increases at least the moral bargaining power of the alleged sovereigns. Second, it confers a kind of dignity and psychological balm to the act of entering into an enduring commitment. Given our national characteristic of niceness, most Canadians do not feel disposed to argue with such claims as sovereignty as long as the deal is made. Agreeing to such a happy gloss is the province of politicians but it is not useful to the analyst. But, is there an Indian claim to sovereignty that exists outside the four corners of the Canadian Constitution, without which there can be no "international sense" in the words "Indian treaty"?

The usual meaning of "sovereignty" is the capacity, in a comprehensive and enduring way, to make others do what you want them to do, within a defined jurisdictional or geographical area and by way of coercion if required; plus the ability to defend that capacity if challenged. That definition makes it clear why an act of conquest ends the sovereignty of the conquered party in international law. In many cases in the United States, the Indian Wars were in fact acts of conquest. In other cases in the United States and almost all cases in Canada, the extension of sovereignty by the (as it then was) settler society was done without war or even the application of much force. It was much more an act of displacement than of conquest but the end result was the same.

There can be no question but that the displacement was massive. No Indians or any other identifiable group within the borders of Canadian territory have been able to assert and defend their sovereignty against Canadian governments at any time since Confederation, and the only major attempts (the Riel rebellions) were forcibly put down. The same fate met smaller pre-Confederation uprisings such as those in British Columbia's Chilcotin territory. Was the displacement complete? Only the Supreme Court could opine for certain, and they have not done so explicitly, though it would be surprising if it decided otherwise as the assumption of omnipresent Crown sovereignty is a foundation of Canadian law.

As previously noted, in *Campbell*, Williamson, J., Supreme Court of British Columbia found that a tiny residual of British sovereignty withheld from Canada was large enough to contain a Nisga'a sovereignty recognized in the Nisga'a Treaty. But even that imaginative conclusion implies the prior extinguishment of Indian sovereignty by Britain and any study of the post-Confederation period confirms that the control of the Crown was absolute, for good or for ill.

As a practical matter of tribal politics or academic hope, some will continue to claim that sovereignty was never extinguished, but the law will almost certainly hold otherwise.[4] Treaties, therefore, are best regarded not as agreements between sovereigns but rather between the state and an internal collective defined under the laws of that state, with the extraordinary status, not available to ordinary agreements, of constitutional protection and the impossibility of change without tripartite agreement.[5]

It should also be noted that treaties are different from "rights," though treaties become entrenched and a part of aboriginal rights (Section 35) upon completion. There are two fundamental differences. The first is that "rights" are invariably and indissolubly collective, though they may be exercised by

4 Though as previously noted, the Nisga'a Treaty and its two successors so far do confer several heads of "internal-to-Canada sovereignty," or quasi-provincial powers.

5 It is an interesting question whether s. 35, which gives this constitutional protection, could itself be repealed by the ordinary process of constitutional amendment or whether that would require Indian assent. Once again, only the Supreme Court could rule on this and the question has not been asked. This will be specifically addressed later.

individuals (e.g. sustenance hunting or fishing). The second is, being pre-existing by definition and not subject to negotiation like treaties, the expansion and delimitation of "rights" is managed by the courts rather than a political process. Rights can be extremely powerful, especially when they arguably gather matters of title within their reach. This fact may bring fear of potential court action as a powerful motivator (to date, motivating governments into concessions) or hopes of great court victories (to date, mostly motivating the Indian side of the table to raise the stakes), thereby acting as a forceful background driver in treaty negotiations.

The real negotiating incentives

The primary reason for negotiating treaties is to suit the convenience of the power structures on each of the three sides (federal, provincial, collective) of the table. There is no necessary connection to the interests of the constituents behind the representatives, that is, ordinary citizens and individual Indians. There may be a connection as argued above but it is not a necessary one, even in the case of the Indian side where a referendum must be held.

For the governments at the table, the essential elements are enhanced legal certainty about land title and management, and political credit that might be useful at the ballot box. For the Indian representatives, the essential elements are continued and enhanced arrangements providing for money and power for Indian governments and the collective, in a package that can survive a referendum and thereafter gain constitutional protection. Without these elements, an agreement will not happen. With them, it will. These few and inadequate things that are necessary are unfortunately also sufficient. The good of individuals is not a necessary condition.

Of course, there may be collateral advantage or damage from treaties as well. Advantages will invariably be claimed. Capital funding will be said to provide long-term solutions. Self-government will be said to do the same. Both claims will be made in the face of substantial experience to the contrary in the past. Disadvantages will invariably be overlooked. These may include the continuation of unhealthy, remote, and uneconomic lifestyles, the usual consequences of "coupon clipping" entitlements, and the ideal of the parallel society, which is invariably furthered by treaty agreements.

Skilled negotiators seeking to gain approval in the referendum will build in matters of immediate tangible interest like cash payments (such as a "signing bonus, hugely attractive to cash-short people) and exclusive wildlife access. To the Indian constituent, the attractiveness will depend upon their individual "discount rate." How much is a bird in the hand worth? How long will it take to obtain something better? As innumerable union agreements demonstrate, a "signing bonus" is a powerful inducement to rapid settlement after drawn-out talks.

For the mainstream voter, these things matter little. The treaties are hard to understand and the money and land is (usually) not material in any given case, though cumulatively of great importance. So there will be little opposition, unless matters of principle are stirred up or the settlements include particularly treasured public lands. Examples of principle would be the contradiction of the idea that "all Canadians are equal" posed by the Nisga'a Treaty or the threat to agricultural land by the Tsawwassen treaty. As to public lands, in Vancouver a claim to the University golf course has caused tensions and Stanley Park (for which a good claim exists) would bring real trouble. In general though, the public has vague feelings of guilt it would like to have assuaged and, if treaties help this, good. But even if members of the public feel opposed to any given treaty, they have no veto on the agreement and (so far) this has not been a major electoral issue.

The Indian constituents have a better lever, through their votes in the referendum. But it is limited. The claim of negotiators, "It must be this or nothing; it's the best we can do," is powerful.[6] People become discouraged over time, and thus more agreeable or realistic or even fatalistic.

In summary then, given these incentives of *realpolitik*, the essential feature of modern treaties[7] has been a trade of some land, some cash, and some ongoing governmental power recognized (or ceded, depending upon your perspective) by the federal and provincial sides in exchange for a delimitation of claims or protests and threats of court action given up by the Indian side. These agreements are made by elites and therefore can be taken as being satisfactory to elites, meeting their needs, primarily for power and security (on both sides) but also the need to meet minimal tests of political acceptability by their respective constituencies.

That is all that one can be sure of, given the process. It may be that a given treaty helps the members of a particular collective, but that would

---

6 Though it does not always work. The people of the Lheidli T'enneh in the Prince George area rejected the first attempt, though the various establishments are seeking a second referendum.

7 That is, since the first James Bay agreement of 1975; there was a second in 1987.

be an additional advantage, not an essential. Or, a treaty may disadvantage Indians. The same may be said about advantage or disadvantage to society generally. Such an advantage or disadvantage will be an add on, not a fundamental. That is the way our political process works, particularly in negotiations as opaque and guilt-ridden as these.

Most people would say this is not good enough. Surely, we should also require benchmarks to ensure that treaties actually do good for ordinary Indians and the mainstream? This is especially the case since the treaty process is almost certain to continue, for better or worse (since it serves the interests of the politicians on all sides of the table). So, for that part of Canada not covered by treaties (most of the Atlantic, some of Quebec, some of Ontario and most of British Columbia), there is much unresolved business.

Nor is that all. It is about as certain as these things can be that one day a significant movement will grow among Indians holding—and correctly so—that there is an enormous difference between settlements afforded in the historic treaties compared to the modern ones. This may or may not be true in economic terms, even taking into account inflation—a major study would have to be done to determine that. But the economic settlements look so large today that parties to the historic agreements feel cheated, and that feeds into mainstream guilt as well.

On the non-economic side—governance—there is simply no doubt that modern treaties are far more advantageous to the Chiefs and Councils. There will eventually be calls for re-opening historic agreements across the country on an "equal treatment" basis. Expect years of some chaos and much uncertainty in this field and the actual re-negotiation of existing treaties. It will not be an easy debate. Thus it is all the more important that we have principles to guide us, and those developed so far are inadequate.

Better incentives

In *Principles for Treaty Making*, I set out a series of qualities desirable in treaty settlements: reconciliation, finality, clarity, equity, disentanglement, equality in law, governance, management of assets, individual empowerment, and transparency.[8]

---

8 A recapitulation of the discussion in *Principles of Treaty Making* follows; for details, see Gibson, 2000: 9–19.

Reconciliation

Reconciliation of the parties is an important object though not, as noted before, as a duty of the courts. The job of the courts is to interpret the laws and adjudicate disputes. Reconciliation is, and should be, a political and relationship process. And reconciliation is not always possible. It is one of those rare objectives that are sufficient, but not necessary.

It is very important to stress: Reconciliation occurs not only between individuals and groups. The most important reconciliation is with reality, absent which the life of anyone is bound to be unhappy. In many cases, we may not like reality but recognizing it is the indispensable starting point to improving it.

The essential foundations of interpersonal reconciliation, not only here but everywhere in our diverse society, are understanding, which is a matter of knowledge and respect, a matter of attitude. Both of these are easily acquired if the effort is made. Alone, they will not solve problems but, without them, the problems will certainly endure. Thus, treaties should be framed so as to be understandable to and respectful of the parties.

Finality

The goal of finality is both elusive and controversial. For the mainstream, this is an obvious wish. The Indian question is a problem they do not need. It is costly and unproductive. Let us put it behind us. For the Indian System, finality is fatal. The System is founded upon a continuation and elaboration of an "Indian Question."

No modern treaty has attained the virtue of finality, though such is the frequent and dishonest claim of governments. All of them establish extensive and ongoing mechanisms for consultation, veto, finance, and so on, which serve to preserve and justify the System. In theory, this need not be so. With a truly self-sufficient parallel society, ongoing relationships could be limited to state-to-state diplomacy. But the Indian parallel society, which is constantly being constructed, brick by brick, is not self-sufficient. It is instead absolutely dependent and symbiotic upon the mainstream society. Finality in such a relationship is impossible.

Historic treaties sought finality and, indeed, achieved that goal for a century. Alas, the achievement was at the expense of fairness and decency and could not last. Future finality, if any, will require a foundation of absolute propriety.

The courts have not been friendly to finality. In *Mikisew*, Justice Binnie for the Court wrote: "In summary, the 1899 negotiations were the first step in a long journey that is unlikely to end any time soon" (para. 56). That would almost certainly have been a surprise to the Crown signatories of Treaty 8, who would have thought this was indeed a final agreement with complete Crown discretion over ceded lands, but support by the Supreme Court for ongoing powers for the collectivity is the new legal reality in Canada. Thus "finality" is not easy in law and must be very specific if there is to be a lasting effect. Any "weasel words" (the kind that so often facilitate agreement) will on the historical evidence be interpreted in favor of continuity rather than finality.

The concept of finality also gives rise to what I call the "forever problem," because treaties immediately become a part of the Constitution with all of the rigidity that implies. Human beings are rightly suspicious of arrangements that are to persist "forever." This applies on all sides of the treaty table. Accordingly, "caution" and "boilerplate" become the watchwords rather than openness, generosity of spirit, and experimentation. It would not be surprising if such constraints were to stand in the way of reasonable or generous or experimental agreements, which parties might be more prepared to enter into on a trial basis. This lack of experimentation has indeed been the case.[9]

In short, then, one of the major advantages claimed for treaties—getting everything behind all of us through a full, fair, and final settlement—"finality," in a word—is very difficult to achieve. Rather—and this is very important—the only finality of modern treaties is to prolong parallel societies, contestation, and legal uncertainties for the foreseeable future. Notwithstanding, governments have used the claim of "finality" to justify treaties. They should not be allowed to get away with this untruth.

It is worth noting that the Residential Schools settlement, whatever other merits or demerits it might have had, is indeed one of finality. The difference is that that settlement was made with individuals rather than collectives. Individuals can get on with their lives. But collectives cannot get on without their members' lives. Unless they have dependent members and an ongoing purpose, which includes an everlasting relationship with the membership, they are nothing. This in turn, inclines them against finality.

---

9 There is another factor that constrains imagination and experimentation in the current negotiating process. The government negotiators at both levels have fixed mandates, though these mandates are not publicly disclosed. What this means is that the alleged negotiators are little more than very highly paid messengers. Messengers have their usefulness, especially if they are insightful and honest in their reporting to their superiors, but it has proven so far to be an immensely frustrating way of doing business.

Clarity

This requirement may seem obvious but experience has shown that clarity may be traded off to reach agreement by way of papering over hard issues. The appearance of agreement through clever words when agreement does not in fact exist is a favor to no one (except those with short-term political interests) and stores up grief to be amplified to the detriment of future leaders and generations.

There is a respectable school of argument holding that benign neglect or "constitutional abeyance" can be useful in finessing intractable problems that may be otherwise solved by the simple passage of time. But this theory does not apply in cases where the neglect or finessing is actively misleading and productive of false or impossible expectations that grow larger and stronger with time. For example, it is no favor to Indian children to give them the expectation of events such as a rich treaty settlement or even merely guaranteed welfare, for such forecasts will tend to reduce incentives to acquiring an education.

Differences on the hard or awkward issues need not be papered over in shaping settlements. They can be acknowledged. An example of this is to be found in the opening paragraphs of the Westbank First Nation Self-Government Agreement, 2003, in which the parties expressly agree to the existence of an "inherent right to self-government" but also expressly disagree in unspecified ways on the content. The example would be a happier one still if the parties had been prepared to state their actual positions.

Lack of clarity can serve another function, namely a guarantee of the continued entanglement of the parties. The less clear matters may be, the greater the need for committees, negotiators, conciliators, lawyers, consultants, and the many paid positions endemic in the System. Lack of clarity is in this sense a "win/win" for the children of the negotiators but a "lose/lose" for the children of everyone else.

Equity

All are agreed that equity is a desirable quality in treaty settlements but this elastic word means different things to different people. The one certainty is that most Indians are likely to think the settlements too small and most mainstreamers will think them too large. That is a given, and perhaps an indicator of some sort of rough justice in any given case.

From the Indian side of the table, if you believe your ancestors used to own it all and you have to settle for only a piece today, that hurts. From the mainstream side of the table, for those who believe that the lands and resources that the Indians occupied and exploited came only from Mother Nature whereas the immense increase in values have come about from the productivity of the large and growing populations of today, there is a different perspective.

There are at least two other ways of looking at the issue of equity. One would be by way of a court directive but there has been none in this area. The courts have instead (quite properly) preferred to give incentives to negotiation (in which the balance of power has normally favored the Indian side of the table for reasons elaborated below) rather than assigning values. The other approach is more productive. This takes as a start the idea that Canadians are universally determined that there are minimum standards of living, health, and social services in this country for every single citizen. This implies an expenditure of *x* dollars on Indians, *x* at the moment being something like $10 billion per annum, about $13,000 per Registered Indian or $25,000 per Reserve Indian.

Of course, much of this money never reaches or comes close to individuals. It is caught up by elements of the System. The other thing that should be said, to those to whom this sum looks large, is that it is in effect a combination of what would be the expenses at the provincial and municipal levels for other Canadians for health, education, and social services. On the other side of the equation, federal expenditures like OAP are not included in the $10 billion; nor are many other federal, provincial, and municipal expenditures on services such as roads and other infrastructure, hospitals, policing, defence, and revenue collection that benefit all Canadians, including Indians living off Reserve. The greatest problem, of course, is that the expenditures, whatever they may be, are not producing satisfactory outcomes for individual Indians in areas such as health and education.

Returning to the equity issue, by this financial line of argument, any diminution that might be brought about in currently routine expenditures on Indians as a result of treaty settlements could be capitalized into a lump sum to which the Treasury would be financially indifferent. For example, if the fruits of a capital settlement were to reduce annual Crown expenditures by $5,000 per Reserve Indian, the Treasury should be prepared to pay $125,000 cash in a settlement for that permanent reduction, assuming a federal bond rate of 4%.[10]

10 Capital lump sums are extremely sensitive to interest rates. For example, long-term bond assumptions of 3.3% or 5% would yield capital sums of $100,000 and $150,000, respectively.

This idea is worth exploration but in practice so far there are four difficulties. The first is that while there is provision for a reduction of federal expenditures as the own-source revenue of the collective grows, the treaties to date (e.g. Nisga'a) explicitly exclude the fruits of the lump-sum settlement from this own-source calculation. This effectively cancels that part of any "offset" calculations.

The other offset claim against the cost of treaty settlements is that the ensuing economic development will significantly augment the own-source revenue of the collective. There is to date no evidence of this, whereas most of the economic development schemes financed by Indians Affairs have either not been profitable or else poorly publicized. (The occasional success story, such as the Osoyoos Band or the Ngamis "Polaris" gravel project on Vancouver Island, receives major publicity, but they are quite rare.)

The third difficulty is political. If Indians continue to leave reserves that is one thing but, if the Reserves begin to grow again (from natural birth or legal definition or 'in-migration'), then it will be argued that the deal based on the old numbers was unfair. The fourth difficulty, also political, large capital sums attract attention and questions from media and taxpayers. That is currently unwelcome for all parties in the world of Indian policy.

In theory, the eventual phasing out of the tax exemptions that form part of the template for modern treaties[11] could enhance own-source revenue, mostly by way of Indian governments taxing their own people for on-Reserve services to the people. (Phasing out of the exemption will make little difference to tax revenues from Indians living off Reserve accruing to the federal and provincial governments.) The reality of this theoretical extra revenue remains to be seen. A reading of the Nisga'a Treaty, again the main modern template, reveals numerous tax-avoidance devices (public trusts, public corporations, and so on).

That does not mean that the removal of tax exemptions as a part of treaties is meaningless. Indeed, it is essential if the treaties are to be seen to be equitable from the mainstream side of the table, which is why governments have been so insistent on the inclusion of the provision. And, many Indians strongly resist the loss of exemptions as an important stage in the erosion of "Indianness" as conferred by the Indian Act, which of course it is.

11 As previously noted, tax exemption of Indians is statutory, not constitutional. It could also be eliminated by amendment of the Indian Act, unless the courts ruled otherwise.

In the end and under the heading of "equity," the "offset" argument is not nothing but also not convincing. The more certain way of regarding lump-sum cash and new land settlements is simply as compensation. That is so even though the federal and provincial governments vigorously and consistently maintain that "compensation" is not a factor. At first blush this stand is curious. What does it matter what the settlement is called as long as it is reached? But a bit of thought uncovers immense difficulties, rightly foreseen by governments. The source of their concern is, of course, the difficulty in calculating fair compensation were the matter to be approached from that point of view. Compensation relates to lost opportunity or to damages. What would be considered the initial value of that which was taken? What inflation rates would be used (e.g. for land values, consumer price index, and so on)? How would the contribution of Indians and the mainstream respectively to the change in values be assessed? What would be the damages for herding on Reserves? For impact on culture? That this would be a hornet's nest is clear and the potential for bitterness and misunderstanding all too obvious. Avoiding this legal swamp is the course of wisdom but the notion of compensation remains the easiest for laymen to understand and is the political (as opposed to the legal) justification for land and cash settlements.

Disentanglement

The best way for everyone to get on with their lives is to cut the strings binding Indians to government back to the minimum applying to all Canadians in the mainstream. But treaties to date do not do this. For example, the Nisga'a Treaty provides for up to 50 *future sets of negotiations or consultations.* To a certain extent this is unavoidable. For example, when a senior government provides funding for a social program, ongoing negotiations, expected program standards, and auditing are required. This is true whether the recipient of the funds is a native government or a municipality or a voluntary agency.

But some of the greatest problems are totally avoidable, particularly with respect to resource administration. Provisions for "co-management" of timber, wildlife, and fishery resources are simply a recipe for continuing disagreement and bureaucracy (see *Halfway River First Nation v. British Columbia (Minister of Forests)*). This is one of those areas where the Indian System (on all three sides of the table and including System members on corporate payrolls) is set on building in its own continuing importance rather than working itself out of business. Simply put, continuing entanglement means continuing fees and continuing masking of responsibility.

An ever greater problem is the provision in the Nisga'a Treaty that the government of British Columbia must consult Nisga'a government on any future legislation that might affect the subject matter of the treaty; the provision is too broad, to the point of being ridiculous. No municipality, even the largest, has such an understanding, nor should much smaller Indian governments. Indeed, the provinces and the federal government are not required to consult one with the other, even when their legislation might affect the other, as it not infrequently does. This provision is simply unreasonable and yet has been included and strengthened in later treaties in northern Quebec.

As to "co-management," to the greatest extent possible treaties should allow each government to do its routine business without reference to another. At a very minimum, co-management is a guarantee of increased time, cost, and bureaucracy. At its worst, co-management and consultative requirements (including those mandated by the courts) are effective vehicles for "tollgating," a thoroughly illegitimate and widely practiced activity.

It does not really matter whether this or that block of wildlife or timber resource is managed by an Indian or a provincial government. Indeed, there are arguments in favor of Indian management because it results in a form of "privatization" of the resource, provided that the land is held in fee simple and subject to provincial law (of which more later). But co-management is bad. "No man can serve two masters," goes the ancient and wise proverb. Equally, no man or resource should be subject to two masters on the same issue. The maximum practical disentanglement is a good rule.

Equality in law

For constitutional reasons, equality in law can never be complete. Indians will always have special rights, continuing beyond that happy day when their special burdens are ended. And yet, in modern societies there is near universal agreement that the differential treatment in law of identifiable groups is not just wrong, but wrong, wrong, wrong. Even a country like India, historically based in a pervasive caste system, has outlawed that system. The only exception in the Western world, and even this is controversial, is the occasional application of "affirmative action" for specifically disadvantaged groups for a (theoretically) limited time sufficient to overcome the disadvantage. Persons permanently and significantly disabled in physical or mental terms also merit special support.

How do we square the ongoing legal distinctions in respect of Indians with this great principle? How do we justify the expansion and entrenchment of those distinctions by way of treaties? The apologists for doing so invariably rest their case on the idea that Indians are different because they (or rather some of their ancestors since the bloodlines are very rarely pure) were "here" (that is, on the North American land mass) first. Every reader will have to decide whether this is a satisfactory response and, indeed, whether the claimed extra rights are a blessing or a curse.

As a practical matter, we are going to have more treaties. They suit the elites on all sides, and they seem to suit the courts although no court as yet has ruled on whether the treaty process is fair to individual Indians (of which more later). Further treaties being inevitable, they should aim at achieving the other goals like equity with a minimal enhancement of the legal distinctions among Canadian citizens. Rather treaties should have as an explicit object the conversion of such distinctions, where possible and by agreement, into cash or into the some kind of property rights (the control and ownership of land and capital, for example) available to all Canadians, so as to gradually reduce legal distinctions among Canadians.

This simple goal is truly revolutionary. The existing policy is to expand, codify, and entrench legal differences between Canadians who are members of one group and all other Canadians. The author believes this to be plainly and simply immoral in the broadest sense of the word and the root cause of the unhappy current estate of many Indians in Canada.

Governance

The central issue of "equality in law" comes down to governance. Special rights to large sections of land, special rights to take fish and game? Many societies have these sorts of differential property entitlements and they are mere irritants, usually privileges of the rich, but accepted. But governance is another matter that affects political rights, where the notion of equality is held most fiercely by most Canadians, who at the same time willingly accept that some of us are richer than others, or smarter or stronger or younger or whatever.

A Third Order?

This matter of governance matter is not mere theory; it is a real issue. Senior governments in Canada have committed themselves to a "Third Order of Government," even though it was rejected by Canadian citizens during the referendum on the Charlottetown Accord in 1992 and is directly contradictory to notions of political equality held by an overwhelming majority of Canadians. The then new Liberal government adopted the mystical phrase "inherent right"[12] from Jean Chretien and Paul Martin's "Red Book" (Liberal Party of Canada, 1993) without ever defining (even in the politicians' private thinking, as far as is known) exactly what those words meant. The related "Third Order" (of government) is also the bedrock concept of the Royal Commission on Aboriginal Peoples. To this point, no appellate court has endorsed this idea.

There are three theories underpinning the demand for a "Third Order." One, earlier mentioned, is that Indians are different from other Canadians: somehow more so than men are from women, old from young, Scots from Chinese, gay from straight, Left from Right, religious from atheist, hermit from Hutterite. Ordinary governments in Canada manage to span these differences quite nicely. Indeed, that is a central part of their job. But, it is claimed, Indians are so extraordinarily different as to require a Third Order. This first justification is patent nonsense. Indians are ordinary human beings like all of us.

The second theory is that the historic structure of Indian governance in place at the time of contact should in some way be reinstituted today. Exactly why is never explained. But governance structures need to suit circumstances and have, in all societies around the world, changed almost beyond recognition over the past few centuries, mostly for the better. Surely, the test for governance today should be grounded in utility rather than historical sentiment.

The third theory is that the Third Order is required as the indispensable condition for the preservation of aboriginal culture and identity. Indeed, some go so far as to state that a refusal to buttress a parallel society by the introduction of a Third Order of government amounts to "cultural genocide." This is an extremely serious charge, "genocide" being an international and grave crime.

It is also a misuse of words: "genocide" refers solely and explicitly to human life. A culture is not the same as a life. Rather, it is an amalgam of history, ideas, works, symbols, and beliefs shared by a group of people. The only persons who can give life to a culture are its adherents and they are the only persons who can kill it. A culture dies by way of abandonment, at least in modern times. Around the world, there have been many attempts

12 The two words "inherent right" are a usual short form for the idea of an inherent right of self-government. As elaborated elsewhere, this surely exists for individuals but any such collective right is highly dependent upon political, social, demographic, and economic realities. It cannot simply be proclaimed.

to suppress cultures and, in the Canada of a hundred years and less ago, there were shameful attempts to suppress Indian culture by, for example, the outlawing of potlatch celebrations or forbidding the use of Indian languages among students in residential schools. Canada today is quite the reverse. The country goes out of its way to support cultures, almost promiscuously. No cultural niche is too small to escape the embrace of the Department of National Heritage and no "Third Order" of government (of Ukrainians or Tamils or whomever) is required for this purpose. No such legal discrimination has been required to preserve the Amish in the United States nor the culture of the Jewish people around the world in the face of much persecution.[13]

Perhaps it is thought by the proponents of this theory that aboriginal cultures are less robust things, but is the preservation of any culture by extraordinary means—especially means such as different legal status and a parallel society that are of questionable effectiveness and at the same time do violence to Canadian norms—a proper object of government? I would argue that beyond such minimal things as the archiving of existing and historic culture and the instruction of young persons in that heritage, the preservation of any culture is the responsibility of its adherents and the role of government is simply to be neutral.

When the smoke spreading from the three theories adduced in support of a Third Order clears away, the true, immediate, and practical advantage of the idea is seen to accrue to the Indian System, wherein are found the vast majority of the few Canadians seeing sense in such an idea. A Third Order identifies elites, preserves them, and gives them status and pay. But is this solution good enough for the society that has to support it?[14]

The usual counter-argument from the System to this practical objection is: "If the mainstream hadn't taken all of our land and resources, we would have the money." To which the mainstream might reply: "Those lands and resources yielded mere sustenance and you still have that, and far more

13 Israel, the state, is a political rather than cultural construct.

14 Otherwise—that is, without the necessity of taxpayer support—it would be a different story, and no business of the taxpayer as long as demands of the Charter are met by any parallel society such as the Hutterites on the prairies, or indeed major, if less all-embracing, organizational arrangements such as trade unions and large corporations. But the maintenance of a Third Order of Indian government is quite impossible without the laws and money of the mainstream society.

besides. We have added the extra value." To this, the System would say: "But we were oppressed or we would have progressed as well." And so, the arguments will continue with points on each side. It really does not matter in practical terms. The mainstream and Canadian Indians are so intertwined in every way (including culturally) that the views of the mainstream are going to be important. A significant marker of this basic fact is Section 28 of the Charter, which reads: "Notwithstanding *anything* in this Charter, the rights and freedoms referred to in it are guaranteed equally to male and female persons" (emphasis added). This provision expressly and intentionally added to the Charter, in part at the insistence of Indian women at the time, trumps the "Indianness" protections of ss. 25 and 35, no matter what historical practices may have been.

An even more more important question is whether the Third Order is good for the very people it is ostensibly designed to serve? That is the core question. As I have argued elsewhere (Gibson, 1999b), it is much more likely to be a bad thing. You do people no favor by drawing a circle around them and calling them different in some fundamental way. There is no greater evidence of this point than that the existing governments established under the Indian Act are already a "Third Order" in all important respects except constitutional entrenchment. To be sure, on paper the Minister still holds enormous powers. However, the reality is that, while providing massive funding, the federal government has at the same time so far withdrawn from interference in the internal affairs of most Bands, that their governments are already to all intents and purposes "Third Order" entities.[15] The results, to put it mildly, have not been universally positive in terms of democracy, the social, health, and educational well-being of the populations, freedom from corruption and improper use of power, accountability, or economic development. It is hard to understand why one would wish to constitutionalize such an experience.

Imagine living in a municipality where it really mattered who the Mayor and Council were and whether they liked you or not. Imagine that the politicians have an absolute veto over whether you have a house or not, and on what terms, whether your plumbing gets fixed, if you have access to the transportation pool, whether your child will be subsidized for college, or whether you can get a government job when those are the only jobs

15 It is true that at any given time a number of Band governments are under external administration by order of the Minister but this occurs only in the most egregious circumstances.

available. Imagine that the Mayor and Council can really, personally, run the educational and welfare systems should they choose to do so, displacing the professionals and forbidding measurement of outcomes. Imagine this same group controlling all business licences and zoning (and having paramountcy over all federal and provincial laws in these areas), with no appeal. Imagine, most frighteningly, that most of the money in your community flows through the hands of the politicians. Imagine the system to be set up to minimize contacts with other levels of government by ordinary citizens, and that elections are decided by a few handfuls of people, often voting along family lines or to support the "ins" against the "outs."

This is what can happen when small governments wield large powers, with few checks and balances and no independent bureaucracy. That is a fact of life today on many Reserves. It has nothing whatsoever to do with ethnicity or culture or Indianness. People are people all around the world. Power corrupts. That is why free societies seek always to control power in designing governance systems. We should not be so blind as to ignore the possibility that pervasive, treaty-conferred power for small governments might not corrupt its aboriginal recipients as surely as if they were non-aboriginal. The powers contemplated—and in the Nisga'a treaty already implemented, with other examples in the pipeline—are enormous relative to the scale of the communities. The members of those communities deserve the protections the rest of us take for granted, with an active media, rights tribunals, ombudsmen, an Official Opposition, and so on, and these they do not have.

It is a very different and more respectable argument to say that government services to people will be more effective if delivered in a culturally sensitive way, but this does not require a Third Order. It is one thing, for example, to have many public servants who speak Chinese delivering services to the tens of thousands of Chinese people in the Vancouver suburb of Richmond but quite another (and quite unthinkable) to call for a Chinese Order of government although many Chinese in Richmond are arguably less integrated into Canadian culture than Canadian Indians, since it is possible there to live, read papers and watch television and movies, work, die, and be buried exclusively in a Chinese language.

The model treaties before us today would not only invest these kinds of Third-Order powers in small government; they would cast them in constitutional concrete. Perhaps we should wait and see how existing experiments work instead?

Based on the above, I conclude that, for Indian communities, governments of the municipal type used successfully for the governance of small communities all over Canada are far more appropriate than the Third Order kind. They are geographically based rather than ethnocultural but can be designed to be (by appropriate boundaries) *de facto* overwhelmingly Indian in make-up and control. There is plenty of room for experimentation with powers, even up to and including the level of the Nisga'a treaty, as long as the governmental structure is of a delegated nature, that is, instituted by legislation passed by existing levels of government, and subject to oversight and modification by the parties in the light of actual experience. These expanded powers can provide all that is required in terms of preservation of culture and identity. To many in the System, this kind of solution would be unacceptable, because the very fact of delegation fails to acknowledge an Indian sovereignty. That is indeed the case but, if one accepts my view of the law holding that Indian political sovereignty has long since disappeared, this concern is of emotional consequence only. Of course I do not deny that emotion is terribly important in politics, and can doom us to mistakes made over and over again.

If it can be sustained, a non-constitutional, experimental approach to differing kinds of local government would also give us room to deal with one of the most vexing issues in Indian governance, which is what to do about the political rights of non-Indians living in territory under the authority of an Indian government?[16] The simple approach is to allow everyone to vote, on the practical basis that the Indian vote will always prevail with boundaries drawn for that purpose. The new Territorial government of Nunavut is an example of this approach, though a very costly and unpromising one.

Another solution is that of the Nisga'a treaty: no votes for non-members. Similar (though unconstitutionalized) situations are developing in Sechelt and Westbank, British Columbia, where in each case the non-Indian vote would swamp the Band membership. These are not unlike arrangements in shopping malls or apartment buildings, where the tenants must accept the rules of the landlords. These cases are experiments and should be monitored carefully as such. But they are unusual experiments, as they deny usual rights (especially, the right to vote, a Charter right) that cannot ordinarily be taken away by private contract.

16 It should be noted that non-Indian residents live on Indian land only by sufferance—leasehold or other arrangement—and those arrangements themselves, which the non-Indians *de facto* accept by entry, can stipulate how the question of political representation is resolved.

Yet another theoretical approach is to negotiate a trade-off between powers and representation. The fewer the powers wielded by an Indian government, the less representation needed by non-Indian residents. Were the powers cut back to simple management of assets by Indians, no representation at all for non-Indians could be argued.

In the end, the essential issue for new treaties comes down to this: Is there to be constitutionalized Third Order or delegated governance? The latter is the strong recommendation of this book. Let me be clear: this is not a *de facto* rejection of the "parallel society" option, which I say in good conscience must be maintained. Rather it is a recognition of the reality that we are all learning here and it is better not to cast governance arrangements in constitutional concrete while that learning is underway. Everyone will have to decide how much delay they can stand while this stand-off is resolved, but sound constitutional arrangements are worth a long wait. It has been a long time already. The Indian side of the table wisely tries to take the long view. So should the rest of us. We can get by with interim arrangements and litigation in the meantime, until views on all sides come to coincide.

Management of assets

Modern treaties commonly settle significant assets of cash and land and resources in favor of the signatory band or tribe. To date, they have been so structured as to make the ownership and management of assets communal rather than private. This stems from a view in the courts and elsewhere that Indian title and rights are fundamentally communal, not individual. This is based on a reading of history that history does not support (Anderson et al., 2006). The general mythology is that hunter-gatherer societies harvest a resource that is so episodic and geographically dispersed that individual property rights are impossible and survival requires communal understandings. But that is a generalization that can change with place (e.g. a defensible small weir location for fishing) or technology (traplines, now well established in practice and law) or other developments quite ancient, such as agriculturally based tribes. In any event, the facts matter little. The courts are quite determined that assets are communal and governments have found this a convenience as well. It is much easier to make a deal with a Chief and Council than a dozen families or a few hundred individuals.

This is no small matter, because in many cases "the deal" will be about virtually the entire asset base of the community, anomalous in a modern world where private (rather than communal) property is understood as the best guarantee of political freedoms. That guarantee does not exist on Indian land.[17] It should.

That said, the future status of Indian property is not a judgement to be made by outsiders, notwithstanding that the current communal status is a construct of mainstream law rather than natural or historic law. As a practical matter—unless some Indian individual or group wishes to challenge this in court—this is a call to be made by the collective owners of Indian property and nobody else. But at a major decision point like a treaty negotiation, other choices should be open, and specifically assessed and chosen by the community involved, rather than having the communal model simply imposed as a part of the usual template in the negotiation process. And even given continuing communal status, the details are important. For example, research in the United States by the Harvard Project (Cornell, 2002) has demonstrated superior outcomes when tribal assets are administered by agencies that are Indian but non-political, at arms length from the tribal councils.

Individual empowerment

The issue of individual empowerment raises two more fundamental questions. First, what ought to be the role of the individual Indian, possibly in the negotiation and certainly in the ratification of the treaty, and what, if anything, should be done to recognize potentially strong disagreements by a minority of individuals in a situation where property in communal? Second, what provision for the rights of individual Indians, if any, should be built into treaties *re* ongoing governance?

Ratification rules

This is a potentially explosive question. Treaties, by their nature and by the law of Canada, deal with unsettled Indian rights and title and, as noted, these things are in their nature communal. How do you deal fairly in communal assets when there is disagreement within the community? For example, say a proposed treaty comprises the typical elements of a bit of cash for individuals, a lot of cash for the Band, an area of land, various rights to take wildlife, and an ongoing governance structure.[18] Suppose next that, as is

17 The weaker "Certificate of Possession" tenure is available on some Reserves, but allows neither free transfer nor mortgaging.

18 All of this is in addition to the continuity of regular governmental funding for the Band, always assumed in negotiations. Many Canadians think that treaties

typical, about half of the membership lives away from the lands. Then, add to the theoretical mix the not unlikely element of vigorous disagreement as to whether the settlement bundle is sufficient.

The first question that arises is, what is an adequate ratification process? There is general agreement that the process must involve a referendum, on the Indian side.[19] But what majority in the referendum held by the Indian collective is sufficient? The courts have never opined on this matter. Is 50% good enough for a "forever" settlement? Or should it be 60%? Two thirds? Adequate international examples exist for all of these thresholds. And, what must be the voting turnout? Would 30% be good enough? 50%? 90%? A 50% turnout and a 50% majority gives 25% of the voters in favor of the most important deal most will ever make in their lives, which will be constitutionalized and last effectively forever. Is that good enough? This is not like a Parliament where a law will pass with 50% support but can also be amended or overturned by a future Parliament if it does not work out. To say it again,

---

change this pattern of routine and continuing payments. That is not the case. The Nisga'a Treaty settled about 2,000 square kilometers and about $200 million on the collective and simultaneously increased the routine annual funding by about 10%.

19 Governments have never been prepared to contemplate a referendum on the mainstream side, even with respect to a treaty template or pattern. They say it is inappropriate to have a vote on minority rights. That statement is indeed true, but not applicable. The treaty issue has nothing to do with minority rights, including the collective rights of Indians, which are fully protected by the courts; they are negotiated deals. There is nothing *a priori* improper about a referendum for the mainstream. But governments fear the results of such a process, with reason, given their customarily poor representation of mainstream views during negotiations and their goals, which are to foster the elite and its power.

The government of British Columbia did, in fact, hold a referendum on a set of treaty principles, such as an end to tax exemptions, the preservations of parklands, and municipal-style government, all of which achieved overwhelming majorities. The integrity of the results was impaired by a campaign for abstention mounted by opponents. In perhaps a more accurate reading, an Ipsos-Reid poll around the same time found a three-fifths majority for the propositions on taxation and municipal governance (that is, delegated rather than by a Third Order). In any event, the government has ignored the results ever since.

a treaty is a commitment embedded in the Constitution "forever." So, even if the total agreement is over two thirds, say, is that good enough? Should 80% be allowed to destroy the way of life of the other 20%? Condominium demolition in British Columbia requires the consent of 100% of all owners (not just of those who choose to vote) or 95% with a court order.

Next, exactly who should be voting? A "nation" or grouping of Bands? A single legal Band, being a fraction of a much larger tribal grouping? A "wilp" (or House) or other subunit of a Band as demanded in Chief Mountain's constitutional challenge to the Nisga'a Treaty? Should a vote by a member who has long lived off the lands be as heavily weighed as that of a life-long resident?

And, most basically and controversial, should anyone who feels seriously aggrieved by the treaty settlement and ongoing arrangements have the option to take his or her share of the settlement "in severalty" as some older treaties allowed, as their own private property from then on?[20] While the "in severalty" solution is controversial, its adoption would much reduce the morally required majority, as dissidents would have an option of exit.

Quite apart from those who may feel aggrieved, however, there is the situation of the roughly 50% (of average Band membership) who do not live on the lands. The structure of modern treaties to date affords almost all of the advantages of the settlement to those who live on Reserve. This is the case because the funds are controlled by politicians who themselves live on or near the Reserves and whose mandate (as they naturally see it) is to spend most of the money for those living on Reserve. This phenomenon is not much constrained by routine electoral considerations if those living off Reserve do not vote and indeed may be exacerbated by the constitutions adopted under modern treaties. In the Nisga'a case, for example, the ongoing voting weight (after ratification) per capita of off-Reserve people is roughly 10% of an on Reserve person. The "in severalty" solution provides a way of addressing such inequities.

The reason the "in severalty" option is controversial is clear: significant use of this "opting-out clause" would markedly reduce the size of the continuing Indian governments and perhaps the size of their territories (though not the number of Status Indians). On the other hand, it is also possible that the agreed withdrawal of objectors would result in greater harmony in the remaining collective with the future exclusion of dissidents.

---

20 Presumably such persons would also lose Band privileges, though they would continue as Registered Indians under existing law.

Those who are concerned as to whether individual Indians would properly manage and husband a sudden settlement that might involve considerable cash make that argument against severalty. The idea is rather insulting, even if in some cases realistic, but at the option of the negotiators this concern can be countered by such ideas as conversion of the settlement to an annuity for life for the departing Band member and a survivorship settlement or trust for offspring.

Those objecting to the "in severalty" option can try to overcome objections to a universally binding vote by a "signing bonus," which really amounts to a small amount of severalty for every Band member, along with a promise of perpetual income support, a powerful, have-one's-cake-and-eat-it-too argument. But of course, a "signing bonus" from another point of view is really a bribe to vote a certain way. We would never allow that in ordinary elections but it is common in labor-management disputes. A signing bonus was used in the referendum on the Tsawwassen Treaty.

There is no easy answer here, let alone one that can or should be imposed by the mainstream society, as long as society continues to agree with the courts that the settlements are indeed communal. Under that logic, the decision must be made by the community. That said, mainstream negotiators have made settlement invariably conditional upon specified ratification procedures. This is only sensible in order to, among other things, reduce the possibility of subsequent legal challenge. But the adequacy of the specified procedures has never been tested in court.

It could be—and it would be the advice of the author—that such required procedures should include the demonstration of an adequate internal process for dealing with the essential questions of approval thresholds and severalty, so that question is at least considered in every treaty. Different Bands have already had different ideas as to what ratification threshold is adequate in the treaties considered thus far.

Entrenching individual rights?

The other aspect of individual empowerment relates to clauses to protect individual rights. This too is not an easy issue. Even the Charter was structured to protect the Indian collective from the application of Charter rules inconsistent with Section 25. Modern treaties invariably say that the Charter applies, but as previously noted, s. 25 can act as a shield from the rest of the Sections (except s. 28, gender equality).

That is not the only exclusion. In 1977, the Canadian Human Rights Act included a Section 67 that expressly excluded the operation of the law as against Indian governments. This was supposed to be transitional but has not yet been addressed. When Bill C-44 was introduced by the minority government in 2007, attempting to phase out this exemption, it met with furious opposition from the Assembly of First Nations (AFN). Opposition parties, seeing a way to frustrate the government, used their Committee power to kill the Bill.[21] Proposed amendments to Bill C-44 tabled by the AFN June 12, 2007 would have the effect of seriously weakening the application of the law. One mechanism would include an interpretive provision requiring due regard to "First Nations Legal Traditions and customary law" to be inserted in recognition of "the fact that First Nations have this unique history to balance individual and collective rights and interests." From the point of view of the parallel society, this is a perfectly reasonable requirement. From the point of view of usual human rights law, this is a "barn door" exemptions. Some of the old traditions and customary law of any of the world's societies simply do not meet modern standards. All have dark corners in their pasts.

In the end, a modified Bill was adopted in June 2008, with Indian governments winning a further three-year transition period. The difficulty in requiring over 30 years to achieve such an obvious thing as a Human Rights Code for Indians vis-à-vis their governments is illustrative of the general inertia in this area. Alas, there is nothing surprising in this resistance. All governments, Indian like any other, tend to resist such things as rights and Freedom-of-Information legislation as a bothersome curb on their authority and actions.

Included in this matter of entrenching individual rights is the really basic question of private property. Private property provides a major bulwark against the power of the state and, thus, is central to the empowerment of the individual, which in turn has historically been necessary for both a functioning democracy and for economic development. Collective ownership of property, by contrast, has historically been associated with stagnation at best and, more normally, with inefficiency and corruption.

---

21 This was a fine example of political hypocrisy, as these opposition parties took exactly the opposite stand when the government of the day refused to adhere to the proposed UN Convention on the Rights of Indigenous Peoples. The only consistency shown by the opposition parties was opposition to the government, another example of how even Indian rights are considered a fit subject for political games.

The question of ways and means of securing private ownership, at least of household land, has become the subject of a major debate in Indian policy. Should such private property rights be a required element for modern treaties? If the Charter's rules on gender equality trumps Indianness, what about property?[22] But then the puzzle—how to square this with collective ownership of most assets?

Transparency

Transparency is important not only for good government but also for continued support of Indian governments by taxpayers. A lack of transparency (and, therefore, of accountability) in Indian affairs generally is the single greatest reason that the national disgrace of governance and social outcomes has been left in the shadows for so long.

The template provided by the Nisga'a Treaty gives no reason for optimism in this regard. Indeed s. 2-44 of the treaty (now constitutionalized) provides that "information that Nisga'a government provides to Canada or British Columbia in confidence is deemed to be information received in confidence from another government." That is, this information is protected from Freedom-of-Information laws and from Parliament. This is not right. The accounts of all taxpayer-funded organizations should be open, currently and in detail, as a condition of funding. The fact that federal and provincial governments are unduly secretive and practice delay with respect to their own information does not give excuse to expand the evil. Timely information is not only necessary for the taxpayer; it is essential if a well-functioning democracy is to have any chance to work inside a treaty government. Moreover—I repeat the case made before—the Nisga'a Treaty is held out as an example of the right way to settle Indian claims and yet we simply do not know how it is working after seven years and cannot trust any of the three governments involved to tell us of problems. They all have too much "face" or self-interest on the line. Indeed, there is probably no single prescription that would have more impact on intelligent, mainstream Indian policy than full and strong sunshine on the realities of the situation today and as it evolves. This is highly desirable and highly unlikely because the idea suits none of the negotiating elites.

---

22 Few recall that Prime Minister Trudeau also attempted to insert a property-rights clause in the Charter. The New Democratic Party then forming the government of Saskatchewan led fierce opposition and the idea was traded off.

Communal land, private land, or cash

What type of asset should be used for settlement purposes? The usual approach is that land is to be a major component. That suits the federal government very well because lands are almost all contributed by the provinces.[23] But there are several problems with land. The first is availability, especially in urban areas. Since all parties seem to have agreed (though not in a binding sense) that privately owned land is "off the table" for political reasons,[24] that leaves urban Bands somewhat out in the cold if no government land is available. This cuts two ways, of course. Where urban land is available, it is immensely more valuable, which seriously short-changes rural Bands.

---

23 In 1993, the Government of British Columbia signed a Memorandum of Understanding (MOU) with the federal government that accepted provincial responsibility for around 50% of settlement costs. This was apparently done with no real idea of how much land would be involved and notwithstanding that Term 13 (see below) of the Terms of Union and a confirming federal Order in Council in 1924 stipulated that the province's obligations in this regard were already fully discharged. It was an extraordinary error in negotiation that the province should now at least use, by threatening to withdraw the MOU, to lever more federal cash for urban aboriginals.

> Term 13. The charge of the Indians, and the trusteeship and management of the lands reserved for their use and benefit, shall be assumed by the Dominion Government and a policy as liberal as that hitherto pursued by the British Columbia Government shall be continued by the Dominion Government after the Union.
>
> To carry out such policy, tracts of land of such extent as it has hitherto been the practice of the British Columbia Government to appropriate for that purpose, shall from time to time be conveyed by the Local Government to the Dominion Government in trust for the use and benefit of the Indians on application of the Dominion Government; and in case of disagreement between the two Governments respecting the quantity of such tracts of land to be so granted, the matter shall be referred for the decision of the Secretary of State for the Colonies.

24 The inclusion of private property would immediately awaken the sleeping giant of public opinion and the *Tsilhqot'in Nation (William)* case may assist with this. As noted in that earlier discussion, Delgamuuukw, paras. 172–176 make it quite clear that, from a legal point of view, private property is not off the table.

The next problem with land is that it is subject to a huge "fudge factor." The Government of British Columbia in the Nisga'a Treaty probably overvalued the land actually ceded, to help sell it to the Nisga'a voters and gain credits for generosity in the urban south where none of the voters really knew or worried where the Nisga'a land was. By contrast, the Government of British Columbia in 2007 appears to have seriously undervalued the land to be ceded in the Tsawwassen Treaty, in an area where the public cares about the lands concerned.[25]

Private land

The greatest problem with land, if transformed into Reserve or "Indian" land, is that it takes more of the country into the parallel society, free and clear of the taxes and regulations of ordinary lands (though provisions are normally made for environmental standards). The separate status of this land is an undesirable and unnecessary thing. Far better to convey settlement lands as private land with the same entitlements and status available to all owners in any province. Of course, if the new owners wished to put some caveats on title (such as non-transferability without communal consent), they would be free to do so. Zoning authority could lie with the new owners, a very important "plus" compared to usual private lands.

There are two main reasons to recommend conveying settlement lands as private land. First, the distinction in law between Indians and ordinary Canadians is not thereby increased by treaty settlements, which is a good and proper goal; and second, the quantum of land that can responsibly be transferred as private land rather than "Indian lands" is much, much higher. In the opinion of this author, it is appropriate to err on the side of generosity using the private-land rule, which merely changes ownership, but at the same time to resist most calls for the expansion of lands excluded from ordinary provincial jurisdiction as "Indian lands."[26]

---

25 Even with these fudges, however, the average settlement under the Tsawwassen Treaty appears to be in the area of $250,000 per capita as compared to about $100,000 for the Nisga'a, both numbers using government valuations. Actual value for the Tsawwassen is probably in excess of $700,000 per capita (see page 185). And as usual, the Treaties do not diminish previous annual subsidies, which continue unabated.

26 *Nota bene* that, per *Tsilhqot'in Nation (William)*, previously cited, land acquired as a result of court declarations of Indian Title may well be "Indian lands," not

There will be an objection that such settlement lands would then be subject to normal provincial taxation. The response is, "Yes, that is true, and that would be part of the trade-off for the greater amount of settlement land." But it is also true that the landowners will continue to benefit from ordinary Canadian services in return. Beneficiaries have a responsibility also to be seen as eventual contributors and a lack of such symmetry will do nothing but reduce public support for treaties.

Cash is best

In the larger scheme of things, however, the focus of settlements should be cash, not land. Of course, cash can always subsequently be used to buy land (in fee simple). Beyond that simple truth, there are four reasons to prefer cash.

1. No fudging

It is impossible to "fudge" cash. The valuation is transparent and honest. Politicians on all sides hate that idea because it reduces their room for spin but it is a sound one. The amounts can be debt financed as required. What might be the total amount?

The most recent and valuable treaty settlement is the Tsawwassen First Nation. We need to determine a per-capita amount. Government puts membership at about 270 persons and the Nation says a newer number of something like 330 as members have been tracked down in various parts of North America. I will use the number 300. Governments give the total value of the package as about $70 million. (These are settlement values. All usual subsidies continue, post-treaty.) The non-land portion is about $45 million. It is the land value that is controversial. The local MP, John Cummins, used figures supplied to him by Colliers (a realty firm) and confirmed by a local municipal official to arrive at a land value of about $250 million, an incredible gap in values.

subject to provincial legislation. Moreover, there is no existing federal legislation in respect of Indian lands that are not Reserve, on such vital matters as tenure, expropriation for public purposes, and so on. It is probable, but not certain, that Parliament could unilaterally legislate in this area, but if so, Court oversight on such matters as consultation, minimal impairment, and compensation would surely follow. These factors, if this aspect of *Tsilhqot'in Nation (William)* is upheld, will give Indian negotiators a strong incentive to use courts rather than negotiations to gain title.

The difference appears to be in whether the land should be valued in its Agricultural Land Reserve (ALR) status (a local British Columbian zoning that prohibits the use of much land for any purpose other than farming) or at free-market rates for the 207 hectares (of a total of 407 hectares of new land for the Nation) that is to be released from the ALR.

In my opinion, Cummins' number needs substantial devaluation (because of the costs of servicing and the lower value of very large blocks of land) but the government number needs considerable escalation because of the new higher value of the zoning available as a result of the treaty settlement. Research with a local appraiser on that basis leads me to estimate about $170 million as the new land value, for a total treaty settlement valued at about $215 million. The per-capita number is then about $715,000 per person.

I do not believe that this necessarily sets a new benchmark as the circumstances in Tsawwassen are unique and their negotiators have done extremely well. But British Columbia's Indian leaders are sophisticated and will understand this precedent for what it is.[27] It stands as an extraordinary increase over the Nisga'a settlement's valuation of about $100,000 per capita.

No one can say how this will shake out. The negotiations have not been made easier by escalating expectations. But, if the long-run trend settles at between $400,000 and $500,000 per capita, with an estimated 140,000 Status Indians in the province (and as the Tsawwassen experience shows, numbers escalate when there is money in the air), then that suggests a long-term settlement somewhere between, say, $55 billion and $70 billion.

This cost is irrespective of whether the cash or land option is selected. The non-land amounts would presumably be largely paid by the federal government, which is responsible for cash components under the 1993 Memorandum of Understanding with British Columbia, and payable over a number of years. The numbers are large, but not crushing. Of course, revised claims from elsewhere in Canada will escalate these amounts. Settlements of this nature in British Columbia will not be overlooked by tribes in other parts of the country. Big numbers but, if these are proper debts, as is claimed, they should be recognized and quantified. Auditor General, take note.

---

27 Grand Chief Ed John of the Summit worried about a "me too" clause in a Tsawwassen treaty specifying that, should another tribe negotiate a better deal on "own source revenue," the Tsawwassen can re-open. John feared this would put a *de facto* cap on future deals. Tim Koepke, chief federal negotiator, denied this: "Just because X was done, doesn't mean X-plus-one can't be done" (Hunter, 2007, November 3: A11).

2. Fairer for rural Bands

Cash settlements make it much more possible to treat rural and urban Bands fairly. The dramatic example of the Tsawwassen Treaty is surely to be duplicated or exceeded by the much more numerous and urban Musqueam and Squamish Bands in due course. It is simply not fair that Indians whose ancestors lived in this or that rural part of British Columbia 200 years ago should be disadvantaged as compared to those whose ancestors happened to live in what is today downtown Vancouver, which was likewise only wilderness at the time, and indeed perhaps less valuable than places that are today more remote but boast greater wildlife resources.

3. Settlements "in severalty" more feasible

Cash makes settlements "in severalty" an easily feasible option without the complication of dividing Band lands. This is important for fairness to individuals. It is also a reason that the System fears too much cash—in addition, of course, to public reaction to the large amounts described under point 1.

4. Calculation of "offsets" easier

Cash also makes the calculation of "offsets" (reduction in support from taxpayers as a result of increases in a Band's own-source revenue) much easier. It should be added that there is much flexibility in how cash can be allocated. The range is from handing all the money to the collective (essentially the Nisga'a model) to handing all of the money to individuals, at which point the patrimony of future generations becomes a concern. (This, of course, is a primary argument for inalienable land, rather than cash.) The patrimony question could in effect be addressed by, say, trusts, as matters for negotiation. The American cash settlement with Alaskan aboriginals was a mixture of some to persons and some to collectives, the latter styled as commercial investment enterprises intended to generate employment and wealth building.

⚶ ⚶ ⚶

The above presentation sets out parameters for the comprehensive and responsible resolution of treaties. But such a resolution could take a very long time, perhaps shortened by the gradual accretion of wisdom on all sides, but inevitably lengthened by the natural complicating forces of politics. The courts can either advance and help or delay and hinder this timing. Help would be by way of rules that would give certainty in actually settling questions rather than dictating process. "Process" rules such as requirements for consultation will, beyond a certain point, slow things down. Sudden changes in the balance of power like that brought about by *Delgamuukw* and, possibly, *Tsilhqot'in Nation (William)* will, whatever their other merits, also retard resolution.[28] In the meantime life will go on, which brings us to the interesting topic of "interim arrangements," which in the fullness of time will be far more important than treaties.

Interim arrangements

The phrase "interim arrangements" is generally used for short-term agreements about resource harvesting and that sort of thing but the notion actually applies to relationships of every kind between the mainstream and Indians. This is where the interest arises. The short-term economic agreements are usually pretty prosaic.[29] Economic agent A wants to do work—logging or mining, for example—in territory where title or jurisdiction is claimed by Band B, and they make a deal for some combination of cash, jobs, investment, and joint-venture activity in order for the work to go ahead. Or, the parties fail to make a deal, and nothing further happens except by court order.

While these agreements are of some economic importance, especially to particular companies, their usefulness to Indians is a much more complicated question. In some cases, the money gained will be put to good use, the employment experience will lead to work in the longer term, and the joint venture-activity will be a base for further business activity. In some cases.

In other cases, the money obtained will be siphoned off by elites, the jobs will be filled by nepotistic practices and no real work will be expected, and the main business lesson learned will be that "tollgating" (which amounts to extortion by way of legal threats) is a profitable activity. Most deals will contain elements of both a positive and negative sort. The determining force as to the balance between the two is really the contracting Band

---

28 See "The new Gitxsan initiative" (p. 195), for a description of a surprising, and potentially very important, initiative taken by the Gitxsan Nation.

29 Exceptions include the unilateral cession of major lands by the BC government to the highly sophisticated negotiators of the Musqueam and Squamish Bands with no visible *quid pro quo*.

government. The company, municipality, or other party on the other side of the agreement has little leverage to influence such things.

Sometimes these interim arrangements will be further encouraged by way of government subsidy. This should, in theory, give some leverage to increase the positive aspects of the deals. There are two problems with this theory. First, governments are notoriously incompetent in assessing or seizing business opportunities. Second, governments are today so afraid of adverse publicity in their dealings with Indians that they shy away from imposing conditions that would amount to the taking of responsibility. It is much easier to take the position that responsibility is being delegated to the Band government concerned and that the credit or blame should be totally lodged with that Band. Whether this is a responsible use of the taxpayers' money is in principle for the taxpayer to determine but, alas, even that is effectively impossible, because a fair assessment requires detailed inside knowledge that is almost invariably not available.

Overall, and with the exception of care for the taxpayers' money, there is no reason to oppose interim agreements of this sort in the short run, even though they very clearly reduce incentives[30] to come to overall, "final" arrangements by treaty.

Useful interim arrangements

There are, however, truly useful interim arrangements, some of which can be implemented unilaterally by federal or provincial governments and some of which would need the initiative of Band governments.

Affirmative action for Indians living off Reserve

The first class of arrangement would involve a determination by governments to make mainstream life more attractive for Indians by significant measures of affirmative action.[31] An Indian arriving in Regina from a remote Reserve in northern Saskatchewan faces as many or more problems of adaptation as a Bengali arriving from Bangladesh. Yet, the latter person will find available a wide range of "settlement" services—education, housing, assistance in searching for a job, and so on. The Indian, being just a Canadian,

30 Why sell the cow if you can just milk it forever instead? Especially if, like the other dairy industry, the agreements are subsidized.

31 Such measures, while discriminatory, are explicitly protected in the Charter, s. 15(2), when explicitly directed at disadvantaged groups.

arrives and makes do, often successfully. The majority of urban aboriginals do reasonably well. Some, however, are drawn into the ghetto-like neighborhoods that exist in large western Canadian cities. The cultural comfort of the ghetto may be helpful (or not) but the collateral geographic factors of drugs and other unhealthy practices, prostitution, and poverty are very bad.

Granted, even with the lack of a major settlement assistance program, the average social-indicator outcomes of Indians living off Reserve exceed those of Indians living on Reserve by a considerable margin, but these outcomes will not be acceptable until they reach parity with the mainstream population. Governments should make that an explicit target. This means establishing the necessary programs, along with benchmarks and real-time measurement and disclosure protocols. The obvious areas for programs are housing, health-support services as required (very much including decent food), education, training, and job assistance, all delivered in a culturally sensitive manner.

We would not be re-inventing the wheel here. There are experiments, some long-term, that work. There are experts who know what to do. There are people who will volunteer to help out. Of course, there will be failures, people who fall through the cracks, and continuing sad stories. But good stories could be increased tenfold quite quickly and success feeds upon success in this kind of thing, where the demonstrated individual progress is very persuasive to others.

The key commitment in this area needs to be made by the federal government. The provinces have the established programs in all of these areas but they do not have the money. They all take the position that Indians, wherever situated, are Ottawa's problem. In return, Ottawa takes the position (with some exceptions) that, once an Indian is off the Reserve, things are up to the provinces. The only way to break this impasse is for the federal government to step up with the money; they do not have the programmatic expertise (nor do Band governments) but the provinces do and will accept the responsibility if adequate cash is available.

Suppose genuine assistance of this kind were to cost $50,000 per assisted person per year, everything in, in addition to existing (inadequate) resources. Make the initial target the aboriginal and particularly Indian residents of the poorest urban neighborhoods of the western cities, who live in conditions apparent to ordinary urban Canadians. In 2001, there were almost 200,000 people of aboriginal identity in the urban centers of Vancouver, Edmonton, Calgary, Saskatoon, Regina, and Winnipeg (Statistics Canada, 2003). Many are not in poor neighborhoods but suppose around one quarter[32] need significant help and we could realistically hope to provide special services to 10% per year (these are "ball park" numbers for illustrative purposes). Helping 5,000 people per year would cost $250 million. This is not nothing but it is also not a lot in terms of our accumulated responsibilities. And—this is very important—the outlay is not endless. People become self-supporting citizens and the special cost (for that person) is over.

Suppose, then, the new special program takes in 5,000 persons per year and peaks for a few years at 25,000 persons total per year. The annual cost at that point becomes $1.25 billion. We can afford it. We have a trillion-dollar economy; we should in theory be spending over $7 billion per year on foreign aid, according to international goals, though we are not, not even by half. We are currently, by contrast, spending $10 billion on our own third world, Indian Affairs, every year in perpetuity, for very slow progress. Additional special effort is required.

But there is a big positive to be noted here. The payback for the cash required for "additional special effort" is genuine "economic development." This I define as activity that will develop the capacity of persons, individuals, rather than what is often mere subsidized Reserve or corporate shell games. Helping individuals is very different from the RCAP's notion of collective "economic development," which by history promises mostly nothing but more promises. This difference is especially so if many of the individuals concerned stay in productive jobs, which will in the nature of things probably be in the mainstream.

This kind of interim arrangement is what is required for the essential goal of this paper, which is to afford choice to every Indian person. One choice for them may be life on the Reserve, in a parallel society; that choice is already seriously funded. But, if their other choice is to take their place in the larger world, that option must be made real and not left a phony bit of politically correct smoke.

The details for the kinds of programs to be put in place are for professionals and clients working together to figure out. Education is an especially important case and many of the details there have been worked out. See, for example those described in chapter 4 of *Creating Choices* (Richards, 2006). They are sensible and straightforward, not expensive and highly worthy of experiment. It is important to understand that none of the accommodations and opportunities for Indians wishing to enter the mainstream is of itself a

32 John Richards (2001) estimates that about 30% of the urban aboriginal population live in ghetto-like, very poor neighborhoods.

revolution. Most of these things have been quietly experimented with for a long time but there has never been the public determination and the major funding required to achieve a critical mass of success. That would indeed be a revolution.

Oversight of Band governments

Pending restructuring of Indian governments by way of treaties—where that is desired and possible—there are numerous and important "interim arrangements" possible in this governance field as well. Earlier the problems that can arise when small governments hold large powers were described, problems exacerbated by a lack of oversight, the standard situation, given the delicacy with which bureaucrats regard any interference whatsoever in Band affairs. In small democracies, the ballot box is supposed to be a remedy but, when faced with small governments with large powers, the voter is best to go along in order to get along. In addition, in "nations" that in fact consist in total of only tens or dozens of large extended families, the dynamics of democracy are very different. And, of course, elections are not always held with any frequency in "custom" Bands, which follow, within limits, traditional rules rather than those of the Indian Act.

Ordinary laws may not be applied. Even very serious matters like allegations of fraud and mistreatment, which are referred either to the department of Indian and Northern Affairs Canada or the Royal Canadian Mounted Police, may then to be referred back and forth between the two with nothing happening. Often a reference for ultimate disposition is finally made to the very Band government being complained of!

Thus, an important interim arrangement that can be achieved by Parliament is provision for much better oversight of Indian governments. Federal, provincial, and municipal governments are all subject to intense scrutiny. Indian governments are not. This is just plain wrong. Other governments have to put up with ombudsmen and auditors-general that poke and pry into all things routinely and into complaints especially. Indian governments are not so pure that they should be exempt from these ordinary checks and balances.

The current federal government attempted to put open accounting for Indian government into its "Accountability Package" in the Spring of 2007. Disgracefully, the combined opposition frustrated this in an evident pandering for votes on the one hand and general anti-government negativism on the other. This is not a partisan matter. It is central to good government, which is in turn central to the lives of those living on Reserve.

Interim arrangements with respect to private property for Indians, at least with respect to housing, are long overdue. Again, this is not re-inventing the wheel: "Certificates of Possession" have long been a part of the Indian Act and the general concept is given at least lip service by the System and all political parties. But nothing much seems to happen; again, Parliament should act. No system will achieve total support but the perfect should not be made the enemy of the good. Bands that wish to rule out even minimal private property rights should be allowed to do so—the property is, after all, communal in law at the moment—but the choice should be required to be made by affirmatively opting out of a general scheme put in place by Parliament, and that choice should be by referendum for all collective members, not just the Chief and Council, who have a vested interest in retaining control of housing.

This raises another general governance question: how to find ways to give more voice to individual Indians rather than controlling Councils. Routine government by referendum is not feasible for any group but exploring ways for a bit more direct democracy would be good in an area where one can rightly be skeptical, on the record, of the efficacy and honesty of representative democracy in many cases. But, it must be asked to what extent is it right and proper that the mainstream should attempt to regulate the internal democracy of Indian governments.

Tom Flanagan (2006, December 20) has given advice on this matter.[33] He wrote that it is not enough just to transfer powers to Indian governments; in addition, "[t]he highest priority should be democracy." He called for an independent electoral agency to guarantee democratic elections, allowing media to cover meetings of Indian governments, and timely publication of budgets and expenditures. In addition, he argues for a degree of self-funding through local taxation and legislated property rights. Flanagan writes:

---

33 Flanagan's view matters not only because of his powerful arguments but also because of his very close connection with the current Prime Minister and federal government, both elected just less than a year before this article appeared. That government had moved to include Indian governments in its "Accountability Act" but the opposition parties combined to exclude such application. As a result, in an interview reported just four days before the Flanagan's article was published, Minster Prentice stated that the climate was not right to return to this issue in the minority Parliament but that it remained government policy for the future (Curry, 2006, December 16: A21).

> In the present state of affairs the typical resident of a reserve has no assurance of fair elections, indeed no assurance that elections will even take place, given that more than half of First Nations rely on so-called "traditional" ways of choosing governments. The typical resident also has no easy method of knowing what his government is doing or spending, and no guaranteed way to own a home or operate a business on a reserve. If we saw such a situation in another country we would denounce it in international forums. Yet we take it for granted as the inevitable destiny of the 2% to 3% of Canadian citizens who are status Indians. (2006, Dec. 20: A23)

I concur with his assessment and most would nod in vigorous agreement. But, there are problems. The first is that the main "international forum" has in fact passed a Declaration about indigenous peoples that would validate exactly such a situation for states that have adopted it. (Canada has not adopted it, despite the demands of the current opposition in Parliament.)

Second, such legislation might not be valid if found to be contrary to the intent of s. 25 of the Charter, which shields "any aboriginal treaty or other rights or freedoms that pertain to the aboriginal peoples of Canada" from Charter guarantees (the above democracy) that apply to the rest of us. It is true that in *Corbiere v. Canada (Minister of Indian and Northern Affairs)* (a case in which off-Reserve Indians were found to have voting rights in the roughly half of Bands where elections follow the provisions of the Indian Act rather than "custom") the court ruled on a matter of democracy relating to Indians, but it was as between Indians and the Court therefore used an analysis based upon s. 15 (equality).

In this ruling, the court specifically said that s. 25 had been little argued and was not engaged here but added, even so, that "the contextual approach to s. 15 requires that the equality analysis of provisions relating to Aboriginal people must always proceed with consideration of and respect for Aboriginal heritage and distinctiveness, recognition of Aboriginal and treaty rights, and with emphasis on the importance for Aboriginal Canadians of their values and history" (*Corbiere*, para. 54).

Even assuming that Flanagan's approach would survive a challenge based upon s. 25, would it be right for the mainstream to impose such rules? He argues that the right to do so stems from two factors: (1) the fact that mainstream taxpayers contribute a substantial fraction, often 100%, of the Indian governments' budgets; and (2) a general view that such things as accountability and transparency are so fundamental to good governance that they should be required of all governmental institutions in the country.

I think if we truly believe in holding out the option of a parallel society as one of the choices for individuals, we need to *mostly* reject the second argument, exactly as (by Section 25) we have insulated Indian governments from much of the force of the Charter. Many people will find this a distressing conclusion but either we believe in Indian exceptionalism or we do not. However, note the word "mostly." There are limits. The limit for the framers of the Charter was gender equality. They were not prepared to allow Indian governments to breach this principle.

Similar logic applies to the first argument, which is a variation on the "piper and the tune" position generally taken by those contributing funds to any enterprise. If it is really the position of the mainstream that cash subsidies allow the imposition of rules, then why not impose all of the rules of the mainstream? But that is not the position, either constitutionally or in practice, that our governments have taken.

How to square this circle? I think one can return again to the principle of individual choice, in this case exercised collectively. It seems to me that the proper response of Parliament to Flanagan's challenge is to pass model democratic legislation (including the services of the Chief Electoral Officer of Canada) and allow any Indian collective to opt out of such a model by way of majority vote in a referendum. One might even adopt the device used in s. 33, the "notwithstanding clause," whereby the opting out must be renewed every five years by another vote or end.

Along this line, Menno Boldt (1993) in his chapter on "Leadership" makes a strong case for improving participatory processes, especially for Indian constitution making. In traditional Indian societies, he writes, this sort of thing was a part of the general way of things, but is not necessarily the case today, and so,

> the most important benefit that could come from a participatory constitution making process is the empowerment of lower-class Indians. Indian elites today are in a position where they can, if they choose, rule without the popular support of, and without accountability to band/tribal members; that is, they can take advantage of the powerlessness and apathy of their people and continue to rule over their people in collaboration with, and through the powers and resources delegated to them by, the [Department of Indian Affairs and Northern Development]. (1993: 159)

Boldt also makes that case that surviving as Indians in an actual sense, rather than as a mere institutional and legal fiction, absolutely requires serious attention to internal due process and the elevation of the ordinary Indian to a position of greater power. This is another factor that should be constantly borne in mind by responsible leadership in a parallel society.[34]

In the conclusion to that chapter, he makes a telling observation: "The Indian elite class argues its readiness for self-government on the basis that it is more competent than the [Department of Indian Affairs and Northern Development] to administer on-reserve programs and services. But traditional Indian government was not based on an effective elite group. Government by consensus requires an effective people" (1993: 162). This is, in fact, a higher standard of democracy than common in the mainstream. Possibly, things have improved since Boldt wrote in 1993 but the work of Helin and Allard reminds us that the issues are ongoing.

Conclusion

The message of this chapter is twofold. Treaties and governance systems can lead to very important changes and perhaps reformed progress. The standard must be the usefulness to the individual. And major change, definitely for the good, can be made by governments without waiting for treaties at all and, at the same time, be beneficial to all Indians, not simply those on Reserves.

34 I am not here suggesting that Boldt and Flanagan would agree on the route to better governance. I am guessing that Boldt would probably resist an external imposition of rules, like that suggested by Flanagan.

NOTE

The new Gitxsan initiative

The Gitxsan Nation, 13,000 strong, has made a brand new, surprising, and potentially very important initiative. They have proposed an approach totally different from that of the System or the standard model for the Treaty process. Some background is essential here. The Treaty process in British Columbia is structured around the reality of Indian Act Bands and the general insistence is that negotiations must be conducted by such a Band or group of Bands. The Gitxsan have refused this approach, for an important reason.

While the Gitxsan are indeed registered as members of a number of Indian Act Bands in the Skeena–Bulkley-Valley area, they have successfully insisted that their negotiators will not be Band appointees but rather the Gitxsan Hereditary Chiefs. It was the Chiefs who were the successful plaintiffs in the famous *Delgamuukw* case, and it is they who (on behalf of their nation) carry the *Delgamuukw* rights.

At present, the elected officers of Indian Act Bands in the area receive government money and deliver the usual services, but it is the Hereditary Chiefs who claim and seem to hold the real political power. This is on a traditional and voluntary basis, very importantly centering on clan and "feast" meetings on all important social occasions. The structure is strong enough to have survived in identity and culture over the 132 years of the Indian Act.

The standard treaty model insists upon an elected governance structure for the entity recognized by the treaty. The Gitxsan want to preserve their model of hereditary[1] governance. No progress was being made and talks were broken off over the issue in 1996. However, it was impossible to ignore the rights of the Chiefs after the court case. Nevertheless, progress has been hung up on the governance issue.

---

1 The "hereditary" adjective does not imply the old idea of an absolute monarchy, say, and does not begin to capture the complex array of checks, balances, and acceptance of responsibility in Gitxsan practice, including procedures for removal if required.

The federal and provincial governments take the view that since the standard treaty model confers coercive powers on the new treaty government (and of course all governments in the end rest upon the ability to resort to coercion), with some of these powers being in areas where the treaty nation is essentially sovereign (in the sense of not being subject to any over-rule by either Ottawa or Victoria), such coercive powers must be justified by the assent of the governed. That, to Ottawa and Victoria, means a democratic constitution and elections.

In a breakthrough moment in early 2008, the Chiefs decided that the way to cut through this impasse was to decline any of the coercive powers ordinarily conferred on Indian governments by the treaty process and instead to live as ordinary Canadian and British Columbia citizens, governing their own internal affairs on a voluntary basis. Their sole claim thus became their "*Delgamuukw* rights" over the lands and resources of their 33,000 square kilometers of traditional territory recognized by the Court.

Governments have yet to react as at this writing. The Gitxsan, remarkably, have taken their case to the public in large advertisements in the *Vancouver Sun*, the *Globe and Mail*, and other newspapers, and on television. The detailed language of the advertisements issued by the Gitxsan Chiefs' Office is so important as a new concept as to be worth quoting.

> More than 30 years ago, the federal Deputy Minster of Indian Affairs came to the Gitxsan territory in northwest BC and declared, "Canada was ready to negotiate" on the topic of land claims. In the early 1990s, BC and Canada created the BC Treaty Process. Since 1994, the Gitxsan have participated in that process. After 14 years of negotiations, there remains no treaty between the Gitxsan and the Crown under the BC Treaty model.
>
> Governments have long said that settlements must respond to local conditions and traditions. We agree, and in that spirit propose a specific Gitxsan approach to our future relationship with the governments of Canada and BC that reflects our governance traditions.
>
> We propose a new plan, which we believe would be very welcome to our neighbours and the Canadian public generally.
>
> *Underpinning positions*
>
> A. The Gitxsan are prepared to pay income and sales taxes just as other Canadians.
>
> B. The Gitxsan are not interested in the "parallel society" concept which drives the standard treaty model. Instead the preference is for governmental services delivered by governments (mostly provincial)

as is usual in most of Canada. The laws and services currently delivered by Indian Act Band Councils can be better and more efficiently provided by federal and provincial entities as for all other British Columbians. We will naturally expect a voice in the mode of delivery to the Gitxsan.

C. The Gitxsan are not interested in the concept of "treaty settlement lands." The economic value of our collective inherited interests over the entire 33,000 square kilometres of traditional territory is to be realized by the process of "accommodation" articulated by the Supreme Court of Canada. In practical terms this will presumably be effected by a combination of our own investment, arrangements with external investors and revenue sharing agreements with governments.

D. Ratification, properly done, may pose some complexities, and require explicit recognition by the federal and provincial governments that the eight local "Bands" and the concept of "Gitxsan" are not identical ideas. Some provision will be required for the non-Gitxsan currently under the authority of Band governments, which will disappear. We suggest that this is an appropriate responsibility for Canada, the architect of the current Band structure.

Principles

1. *We come to the table as committed Canadians, paying our taxes and contributing to the country.* We seek no special status or parallel society. We wish to live as ordinary Canadians in our own way in a multicultural society. Further, we wish to pay our own way.
2. *While history has given us a special relationship with the Crown and the federal government, we wish to take our place as full citizens of British Columbia, paying for and receiving health, education and social services from the province in the same way as any others.* We believe the federal government should transfer money formerly given to Band governments for these purposes to the provincial government upon acceptance by the Province of those responsibilities.
3. *Our claim, and our only distinct claim, is to the inherited collective rights of our ancestors including those confirmed by the Supreme Court of Canada* in its *Delgamuukw* decision (1997). That interest entitles us to a shared decision making in the development of our territory and a share of the wealth that it generates, as well as fair treatment by governments in all matters. *The details of this is what we wish to negotiate.*

4. The result should be far less complex than the standard Indian government model. *We have no wish to duplicate existing service organizations.* At the same time, we stand ready to perform local services for ourselves and our neighbors under contract and by agreement when that is the most logical way to proceed.
5. *We understand that this is different from the standard BC Treaty policy.* We have no views on what is right for others and wish all parties well according to their own needs. *Our approach is what we believe is right for us, and for our neighbours.*

(Gitxsan Chiefs' Office, 2008, July 10: [advertisement]; emphasis in original; see Gitxsan Treaty Team, 2008, for a full description of the Alterative Governance Model.)

Anyone who has followed the progress of the standard treaty model will understand what a revolutionary approach this is. In one bold move, it deals with most of the "in principle" questions raised in this chapter and in chapter 4.

For governments, the three big questions will be the following. First, exactly what do "*Delgamuukw* rights" mean in practice? Second, will this really resolve the land question in the Gitxsan area? Third, what will be the impact on other treaty tables? The first can be answered by negotiation and, if this is successful, the second can be answered by an affirmative referendum among Gitxsan members. The response to the third question will depend upon the reaction to the Gitxsan approach from other Indian negotiators and from the public. This will be watched with interest and concern by all other Bands at the treaty table, as a very direct alternative to the System model that may find considerable public support.

CHAPTER 6

Where to from here?

"If you don't know where you're going, you'll end up somewheres else."
Yogi Berra

Sometimes it is easier to see the distant future than the near term. The "distant future" is an equilibrium, a steady state, the way you think the river will flow when it has negotiated the tumbles and rapids and entered into the broad plain. This future is imaginary country of course but it is simpler to imagine the destination than the complicated twists and turns of the journey. Life is like that, and so is science. Scientists and mathematicians recognize that the most difficult things to understand by far are those involving turbulence, chaos, boundaries, and transitions. The problems encountered while traveling down the river on the way to a peaceful flow at the end involve avoiding capsizing and death in the rapids, or entrapment in midway swamps, or stagnant back eddies. In Indian policy, we are still in those zones. Before planning how to negotiate the transitions, let us first a look at the likely future. There is merit in this because one can sometimes avoid turbulence in the river by simply portaging around it. In the same way, there may be quieter, less dangerous shortcuts to where we are going to go.

The future

History is determined by great currents, remarkable individuals, and accidents. The shorter the time frame, the more difference is made by individuals and accidents. But these are inherently unpredictable, whereas the great currents are easier to read. What are they? The categories I will canvass include economics, culture, and politics. Others might say, "No, demographics are destiny," or argue that technology is more influential. It is hard to disagree; they all have to be factored in.

In predicting the future for the Indian people of Canada, the first observation is that size matters. The population is small—around 700,000 depending upon definition, split into numerous cultural and geographical groups.[1] The world as a whole has a population of about 10,000 persons for every Canadian Indian. The 10,000 individuals are going to overwhelmingly influence the one. Agreed: the Indian birth rate is (for now) at least 1.5 times higher than that of other Canadians[2] and indigenous people elsewhere constitute a theoretical set of allies in the face of the 10,000. But these are grace notes. The national and planetary numbers are just too large by comparison. The world will prevail. In due course, Canadian Indians will no longer be significantly distinguishable from the general population, just as, given the forces of immigration, all Canadians will look much like the rest of the world. These are highly reliable forecasts.

The economy is where we earn our creature comforts, amass our retirement security, and garner the financial and other resources to live the kind of lives we want to live. There is no reason to expect that Indians generally will opt for a lesser economic participation and success than others. Hence, the market and all of its ways will be influential, moderated only by politics.

The market economy has effects that both "homogenize" and allow extraordinary diversity. Homogenization arises from the simple fact that the market is in its nature transactional, and the more intense the transactions

---

1 A recent court case in British Columbia, *McIvor v. The Registrar, Indian and Northern Affairs Canada* (See The *McIvor* decision, p. 30), now appealed, could raise this number by 200,000 or more. This would have important political consequences, in the sense of raising fears of diluting the patrimony per Indian, on the one hand, and causing the public to see the question as a larger one than previously thought, on the other. This would raise perception of cost and likely result in their insisting the governments take a "harder line" during negotiation.

2 The growth rate of the Status Indian population is seven times greater than the Canadian rate, excluding immigration (Gour, 2005). The aboriginal birth rate is about 1.5 times larger than the Canadian birth rate (Statistics Canada (2003): Aboriginal Peoples of Canada: A Demographic Profile). Breakdowns by reserve residence have not been found.

between individuals, the more likely they are to adopt standard practices and views, as a simple matter of convenience and efficiency. But, of course, the payoff for this is access to the whole immense world of options, opportunity, and experience.

Culture is who we are. We all accumulate cultural views as we go through life but there is simply no doubt but what some approaches are more likely than others to attract adherents. One need not agree that blue jeans and American music are the peak of cultural aspiration in order to recognize that they are in the ascendancy around the world. One need not agree that a suit and tie is the best attire to note that senior politicians in every society gradually adopt that dress. "Okay" is understood everywhere.

Canadian Indians are heirs to a considerable amount of native culture, differing according to tribe and location, a source of deep strength and pride to some and of little consequence to others. But the ratios remain unchanged. Culture is produced by human beings and the ratio of 10,000 to one applies here as well. Since it is unlikely that people will deliberately exclude the rest of the world from their lives (the Amish and Hutterites are rare exceptions), one can say with great assurance that just as Indians will enter fully into the world economy, they will do the same with culture.

Anthropologists and other experts can more precisely discuss the degree of current cultural overlap between Indian and mainstream Canada, but it is certainly very, very large, and growing. Television, the internet, and so on admit of no other outcome. All of this is standard. In the modern world, we mostly all become more like each other.[3] Whether this is good or bad, it is.

Politics has made a difference, for the worse and, latterly, for the better. That too is likely to change in the direction of homogeneity. To explain: for most of the time since European contact, Indians have been treated differently. First, it was as important savages. Next, they became a nuisance, to be isolated. Then, they became seen as citizens, but "citizens minus," to turn a modern phrase around. Latterly, they have been seen as "citizens plus." And, they are still seen as a collective and (unthinkingly) without differentiation

3 As a statistical note, that does not mean that the range of human diversity is compressed. In technical terms, while the standard deviation from the mean of the distribution may shrink, in our modern world the distribution universe itself will grow immensely larger (with increases in absolute population and also in individual capacity through wealth, education, and technology) and so the diversity of the outliers will increase.

in general, notwithstanding the fact that over 50% of Status Indians (and a much larger percentage of aboriginals) have "gone to town."

Trends in the mainstream

In the mainstream, the ideas of "the individual" as the unit of value distinct from the state or collective and notions of "equality" continue to be elaborated throughout our political culture, our workplaces, and our legal system. Differential treatment of Indians as part of a collective is discordant with this basic set of values.

The voter base of the mainstream is changing. Reference has been made before to "white guilt." But this sense of guilt is noticeable only in the politically correct descendants of the European "settler society." While this group still controls government and the media, that is changing quickly in our multicultural and immigrant society. "White guilt" is important in two ways. Guilt cries out for restitution and, more importantly, guilt clouds judgement. Persons more recently arrived in Canada, lacking this feeling of guilt, will have harder questions to ask about the old policy as they gain increasing influence.

The mainstream is increasingly a "rights based" or "rights claiming" society, especially in the shadow of the Charter. At first blush, one might think that an emphasis on minority rights would assist the cause of the "parallel society" but a bit of thought reveals that the notion of a parallel society is in fact a severe threat to minority rights in general. One parallel society may suggest to the much larger mainstream that maybe it should be a parallel society, too. In other words, as Cairns fears, the common bonds of citizenship may become too weak to continue political support for the Indian parallel society, which is not self-sufficient but rather symbiotic.

It is only a strong and unified single society that can and will make the effort to defend minority rights. Collapse the center and the idea of equality and one returns to a rights jungle. (This of course is why vast the majority of American black activists, excepting such as the Nation of Islam, have always rejected the "separate but equal" doctrine.) The danger of collapsing the center was powerfully captured by Jeffrey Simpson, who was mainly writing of the much less pervasive "parallel society" of faith-based schools and the impact this issue had on the loss of the Ontario election the day before by John Tory's Conservatives: "They did not appreciate that the more diverse Ontario becomes, the more determined is the majority to oppose what they consider public preferences that might further separate or segregate people" (2007, October 11: A27). He compared that to the debate about "reasonable accommodation" in Quebec—similar sentiments being expressed in that province—and went on to say, "[t]he one exception might be parallelism for aboriginals. But aboriginal sovereignty has been pushed by courts and political elites (aboriginal and non-aboriginal) in the teeth of public opinion that strongly prefers a more integrationist approach" (2007, October 11: A27). The worries are obvious.

In an equally powerful but rather more dangerous way, the growing individualism of Western society in general, the "me" generation, seems at this point in history to be fostering an increase in selfishness and less concern with others. In part, this is because our society is now so complex that it is harder to understand the fundamental institutions and implied contracts—the value of the larger collective, in fact—that we should all treasure and worry about, as the never-automatically-secure underpinning of our liberties. The schooling system, which used routinely to engage these values, now devotes less time to civics and history, if only because there are so many other new things to learn about.

Developmental economics is playing a part as well. A major current lever of Indian politicians is their ability to demand that they be consulted about major developments that are on territory that they claim belongs to Indians. This includes most of British Columbia and, notwithstanding treaties, due to recent court decisions is now being seen all over the country. Sometimes the claim goes beyond consultation to the giving or withholding of permission, to simple tollgating, or to actual ownership of the lands concerned. It is never possible to know, in advance of a court decision or governmental response to direct action, how the claim might turn out in law. The uncertainties are considerable and the costs and delays in dealing with this reality result in payoffs for the Indian side but also a quiet buildup of impatience and resentment on the mainstream side.

All of these trends work against the seldom stated but fundamental assumption of the Indian System that "you owe us," an assumption broadly accepted by the mainstream. If that background attitude falls apart, the political support for the parallel system collapses in due course.

Trends in Indian politics

Internal trends are working against the System as well. First, as described earlier, there is a major exodus from the Reserve, held in check for now but in the long term probably not to be stopped.[4] The outside world is just too attractive.

4 This statement is notwithstanding the numbers in given in Clatworthy (2001), which, although they show a larger percentage of Status Indians on Reserve by

The parallel society absolutely depends upon Reserve-based populations. That was the central focus of the Royal Commission on Aboriginal Peoples (RCAP). Scholars have written interesting books on non-territorial societies and one can make a case the Jews throughout the ages or the overseas Chinese more recently fit that description. But these, and faith-based social organizations that have endured, are all based on self-finance and voluntary adherence to cultural norms. The Indian System, by contrast, wishes to build its parallel society buttressed by mainstream law and cash. It is very hard to see the mainstream society agreeing to Chiefs exercising governmental powers over Band members living off Reserve (in downtown Toronto, say) and using funds generated by mainstream taxpayers.

In addition to the decline in the Indian population on Reserve, the feminist movement will be an important long-term force for change. The evidence tends to be anecdotal rather than collected but there is a pattern of women leading demands for accountability in Indian governments across the country, and especially in the West. There is a strong matriarchal tradition in many tribes and this may be a continuation of that, or there may be more modern elements in addition. There is the general success of the feminist movement in Canada over the past century, and beyond that, there is the realty of single-mother families in Indian country.

Families led by a single mother account for almost a quarter of all Status Indian families,[5] so this is a very material influence. Concern for the future of one's children is a very powerful force. There will clearly be an ongoing tension in the minds of Indian mothers as to whether the Reserve or the outside world—or, more likely, an ability to live in both—is the best way forward for their children.

Governmental policy can have a particular effect here, one way or another. Education poses a threat to the System, which is one of the reasons progress is so slow. To quote John Richards again: "Band leaders have powerful incentives not to place a high priority on high-school education; the educated youth leave the Reserve" (personal communication, March 2008, by permission). Now, educational progress among Canadian Indians is

---

2100, also indicate that the absolute numbers will be little changed. Of course, predictions looking 100 years out in this area are little more than scenarios based on defined assumptions.

5 This is twice the rate for other Canadians. In urban areas, 38% of Indian families with children are headed by single mothers (Hull, 1996).

far too slow, but it is happening. What will be the results? The early results were tended to reinforce the System as educated young Indians found willing employers therein as managers or lawyers, with the added bonus of serving their own people. But there is a limit to how many lawyers or administrators the Reserve can employ. Increasingly, new law graduates, medical people, educators, and social workers will have to find work in the mainstream, and engineers, software developers, tradespeople, retail and finance employees, and so on all have to go where the work is—which is mostly not on Reserve. So education and the world of work—surely good things, hard to oppose—in fact undermine the notion of a parallel society.

The default scenario for the next 50 years

If the above trends are extrapolated, the future in longer term seems pretty clear but, as Keynes said, "In the long term, we are all dead." What about the next 50 years? If there are no major changes in existing policies, it is likely that there will be a significantly successful rear-guard action against structural change, a continuing elaboration of the parallel society, growing financial costs to the mainstream, and a continuation of existing circumstances for Indians with gradual improvements in education and in infrastructure and governance on the Reserves. Given the inertia of our political system, the dangers for politicians taking action in this area, the lack of political payoff for risking change, the flaws in our courts and Constitution, the incentive structure in the Indian System, and the sloth of our media, persistence of the status quo is likely; that is the way to bet.

For individual members of the mainstream in their material lives, this is really a matter of indifference. Yes, there are costs but they are not large in the scale of things. It takes a real moral concern for one's fellow man to invest much energy in this field, even to the extent of trying to learn much about it. That is a part of the difficulty: learning is not easy.

An inherently complex social problem is made all the more difficult by the incentives bearing on those most knowledgeable to conceal, obfuscate, promise, plead, shame, and mislead in order to extract maximal resources for their own solution, the parallel society. An open, honest, and informed discussion is the enemy of the status quo. Detailed disclosure of Indian government operations and results is an enemy of the status quo. And taking the position that Indians are somehow different from other human beings is central to maintaining the status quo.

Indifference, incentives to maintain the status quo, secrecy: it makes for a strong and perfect iron triangle, most resistant to attack. Pierre Trudeau approached this triangle with a bulldozer. He proposed to simply break it. The approach was not assimilative nor did it lack compassion; no one who has actually read the White Paper could believe that. And had the approach been instituted, it would have worked, in the sense that for better or for worse we would not be talking about this issue today. Integration with the mainstream would be well advanced, educational and employment advances would be paying off, emotions would have cooled, and the turbulence of transition would be, not forgotten, but history.

That approach was not sustainable in the Canada of 1970. It is even less possible today. Change, if it is to come, must be chosen, not imposed. Will such change come of itself? In this survey of the possible future, I return again to the book of Calvin Helin and this time, reluctantly, to disagree with him. Helin devotes most of three chapters to the argument that the mainstream population is aging, the aboriginal population is growing more quickly and is younger, that Canada desperately needs more workers, that many aboriginal businesses are doing well, and that therefore there is almost a self-curative economic process in place that makes it in the interests of everyone to make sure that good economic things—that is, aboriginal employment—happen. Thus, a rising tide will lift all boats, if we have any common sense at all.

I have no disagreement with these arguments but would argue that, for Indian policy—not "aboriginal" but "Indian," the subject of this book—the picture is much darker, at least for some. Those who choose to escape the parallel society—to "go to town"—will indeed benefit from the economic trends identified. But such developments are against the interests of the System and the Reserve. Since governments pay virtually all of their attention and all of their money to the support of the parallel society, and since integration with the mainstream (which is where the jobs are) is likewise against the interests of the parallel society, my guess is that Indians in that world will continue to be isolated and further, that the money to support this will continue to be extracted by the System for the foreseeable future, unless the Helins and Allards of this world can break the grip.

This will be very difficult. The other Iron Triangle of the media, the law, and the System is just too tough for politicians to challenge. There is no political upside and the Chiefs and allied organizations (not to mention opposition political parties) are immediately on your case. So governments will continue to support the (eventually, but not soon) dwindling populations on isolated[6] Indian Reserves for the foreseeable future.

---

6 Urban Reserves present a more optimistic case.

Help for individuals in the meantime

Natural economic forces will automatically help those living off Reserve, but not those on Reserve. But if people—Indian and mainstream—do want to choose change for everyone, there is another way. It will not lead to a revolution: the end result, the long-term future will be the same. But it will provide a serious short-cut to that long-term future, offering the possibility of much improved choices for Indian people between now and then. The choices mostly remain up to them, not the mainstream.

If one adopts the position of this book that our primary concern should be individuals and their choices and that the collective is merely instrumental,[7] the responsibility of the mainstream society is conceptually pretty simple. It is:

- to underwrite a minimum social-safety net;
- to remove barriers to equality of opportunity; and
- to actively foster equality of opportunity.

In other words, to help individuals make the most of their individual lives. While the words are simple, the implications are not.

For instance, is the minimum safety net simply to be available or is it to be imposed? The latter position, for example, could involve significant geographical migration from isolated areas where an adequate safety net and equality of opportunity, by urban standards, are not possible in practice.

Kashechewan

In Kashechewan, for example, the explicit choice to move to an urban area, which was the recommendation of the expert who studied the situation and consulted the residents, obtaining their general approval, was not taken up by the government. The position of the System that isolation was preferable prevailed, as the Band apparently changed its collective mind. Kashechewan is unusual in that the choice was so starkly put. But the default decisions over recent decades to leave people in obviously difficult geography and circumstances are really unmistakable in result and motive. One is less

7 One must be clear that this is not a statement about culture, which is more than instrumental. A culture has free-standing value to its supporters, and many of the strongest supporters of Indian culture are non-Indian. But in the end it is supported by individual choice.

likely to be criticized by the System for doing nothing if that preserves the status quo. The details can be tragic.

The Kashechewan First Nation community consists of around 1,500 and 2,000 people (the exact number is unknown though a consultant guessed 1,550 to 1,700) and lies on a flood plain on the Albany River some 480 kilometers north of Timmins. This is isolation. The Reserve was created in 1905. The community made headlines in October 2005 when mass evacuations by air were required following sickness and a discovery of *E-coli* bacteria in the water. The community had been under a boil-water advisory for two years.

Former Ontario Minister Alan Pope was appointed to investigate since, "[p]roblems with deteriorating and inadequate housing and community services, water quality and flooding have lead [sic] to numerous evacuations at public expense and public debate over the quality of life for the members of the KFN and the need to relocate to a safer location" (Pope, 2006: 2). Mr. Pope found a budget in disarray, heavy indebtedness, and a stand-off with the INAC as a result. The dikes were in bad shape, and engineering reports contradictory.

On health care: "Community based services ... are incomplete, inconsistent and inadequate ... public health efforts, community health programs, mental health programs, medical practitioner's presence and availability, laboratory and investigative services are inconsistent, spotty and often non-existent" (2006: 6).

Housing was

> not only inappropriate for local temperatures and climate conditions [and] obviously ... assembled or constructed without proper supervision or inspection ... Homes in the community were often poorly maintained by the occupants with no sense of responsibility for their own living conditions ... [Kashechewan First Nation] ... has no housing standards or by-laws, nor personnel with any responsibility for enforcing housing or living standards. (2006: 7)

About the water plant: "it is clear that inadequacies and operational deficiencies have existed for some time" (2006: 8). The location of the sewage outfall could contaminate the water intake in some circumstances. Policing is minimal and "[t]here is a significant problem with vandalism, reckless driving and other out-of-control conduct" (2006: 9). Fire services were inadequate.

School services were declining. "[The elementary] school is closed due to health and safety concerns, site contamination and vandalism. It will not re-open any time soon. Elementary and secondary school students share ... attendance and curriculum are reduced accordingly" (2006: 10).

"Prospects for economic development look bleak ... and ... [t]o remain in isolation with no access to income or employment opportunities is to sentence this community to despair and poverty" (2006: 11). This is neither a pretty picture, nor an unusual one for isolated Reserves.

The consultant carefully surveyed the community in meetings and in house-to-house visits: "A significant majority of community members believe that the best interests of themselves, of their children and families, and of the entire community are served by a relocation ... to a new Reserve" (Pope, 2006: 15). The "majority" wanted to move south, split between Smooth Rock Falls (on the Trans-Canada highway) and Timmins, an Ontario town of about 40,000 with decent community services. After consideration, Mr. Pope recommended a new Reserve near Timmins, with the Band retaining ownership of the existing Reserve for summer and other uses.

The government offered to finance the move to Timmins at about $200 million. For whatever reason, the Indian government commissioned a new report surveying the community, which said that only 5% wanted to move to Timmins, and most people wanted to move to a new location up-river at a $500 million cost for construction of newly requested (by the authors of the new report) facilities such as a paint-ball park, ski hill, swimming pool, bowling alley, hotel, radio station and a movie theatre. It is understandable why one would vote for this. It is also to be noted that all of these can be found already in Timmins.

The government balked at that and the upshot is improved facilities at the old site. There is no reason to believe that the new facilities will improve the lives of the people. As Mr. Pope said, "To remain in isolation with no access to income or employment opportunities is to sentence this community to despair and poverty" (2006: 11). This vignette squarely puts the issue of subsidizing and maintaining misery.

In this context, recall the thought experiment in the first chapter about a nameless Brazilian tribe. The best way to preserve a culture is to isolate it; that is also the best way to impoverish the individuals living in that collective, both culturally and economically. Is that a moral thing to impose or even to finance? Again, removing barriers to equality of opportunity and actively fostering it may result in that opportunity being taken. That, in turn, could lead to changes in lifestyle, to the advantage of the individual and the diminution of the collective.

The individual

I have no doubt that the individual is the proper focus of our efforts and the remainder of this chapter will explore how mainstream society can fulfil the three parts of its responsibility. The intent is wholly constructive. There is no wish to denigrate any existing institution, nor any choices individuals might wish to make. They may, for example, choose to subordinate their own lives to the interests of the collective. That is a perfectly valid individual choice but not, I submit, an estate that others should impose, as is the practice at present.

There is no wish to be unfair to the Indian System, which the mainstream has to acknowledge as a creature of its own making. When people build their lives on laws and an incentive structure fully under the control of the mainstream and, more particularly, of governments, they are entitled to some security—in some cases security of continuity—and to compensation where that is not possible. Except in times of national emergency or genuine *force majeure*, governments must pay for their mistakes and that payment can only come from the taxpayer. (It would be good if taxpayers better understood this cost-of-mistakes factor in all areas of public policy.) Indeed, genuine progress in Indian affairs has little hope of success unless it can enlist the willing support of much of the System. There are no bad people here—at least, no more so than in any other large group of human beings. There is no lack of compassion and much experience that can assist with improving an unacceptable state of affairs.

Recommendations must not seek to eliminate Indian rights. These rights are the property of their owners and may be traded off by them if they wish but are not to be expropriated by others. Anyone in the mainstream who has difficulty with this idea should clearly understand that these particular property rights stem in part from ancient British common law, and in part from Canadian law, including our Constitution. They did not come out of nowhere. One may object to some of the court decisions involved but, unless one is prepared to evade the rule of law—too high a price in this case and almost always—then one must simply accept it. The constitutional position of Canadian Indians is a fact. Proposals for improvement must build upon those foundations. The centerpiece of new Indian policies should be that their adoption will not be imposed by the mainstream, but rather taken up by individuals.

More choice, not less

The expansion of individual choice must be the addition of new options; not eliminating the old ones. For that reason, the Reserve system and the Industry and the parallel society will continue into the foreseeable future.

Only individuals, by their future actions, will tell us whether the new options will gradually displace the old or not.

Guarantees will continue, as they will for all Canadians, as everyone has access to a "safety net." But the structure of guarantees should not push the individual in one direction or another, as is currently the case. And the guarantees must also be so structured as not to overpower incentives, for nothing is more destructive of the human spirit than a free ride. We all have a claim on our country but that claim does not come without a corresponding responsibility. No collective, ancient or modern, can survive and prosper without that basic rule.

To repeat, the overall description of a new approach is simple: the touchstone is the individual, not the collective. From this it follows that the Indian tribe is not of paramount importance; that status is reserved for the Indian *individual*. The tribe is merely an instrument that may be employed more, or less, or not at all. It also follows that Indian culture is not of paramount importance (except in a free-standing artistic and scholarly sense); that paramount status is reserved for the Indian person, who then uses that culture as a tool, or an enjoyment, or an identity or not at all, as he or she pleases.

What does this mean in practice? It means leaving the parallel system in place but adding a new choice of a system that would offer to treat Indians as ordinary Canadians, with some special "add ons" to meet historical challenges.

- In education, provide for a voucher system to be administered by parents, not the collective, allowing the education of the child at a place of choice of the parents at any available school in the province.

- In welfare, make funding available for income support according to local provincial standards, to be administered by the Province.

- In health (a non-cultural matter), provide funding for the provinces for complete health-service delivery with on-Reserve locations as negotiated with Band governments or accessible external facilities otherwise.

- In child care, replace a parallel system that is politically correct but also scandalous in many parts of the country with the standard provincial system.

- In matters of general on-Reserve governance, economic development, housing, municipal services, and so on, bring accountability to Indian governments by sending much of the funding now sent for these purposes to Chief and Council instead to individuals for "tax back" by Chief and Council as approved by the local on-Reserve voters.[8]

Is this the same as the failed White Paper? No. The White Paper contained a fatal flaw, a denial of the past, the repudiation of a contract. It failed to offer the continuing choice of the System.[9] That choice must be preserved. While denying the long-term usefulness of the parallel society, one can still recognize that not to offer that option in holding out the idea of individual choice is in effect to offer a Faustian bargain to the Indian individual: give up who you are for membership in the wider world. That is in fact a false choice, an unnecessary condition.

But, the reader may say, how can you argue for the preservation of places where poverty is widespread given the lack of economic opportunities; where education is poor, family violence, incest, and substance abuse common, suicide rates four to six times the average; where government operates by cronyism and family compact; where diabetes is endemic and general health poor, housing is in decay; where private property is absent; which are at a third-world level on the UN Human Development Index? Why do you keep that on offer as an option? The response is that those conditions are not what is on offer; the offer is a choice to make the best of a claimed right to a parallel society and to improve these things if you can by way of connections with the wider world. Our moral obligation arises out of the fact that we have created that parallel society and we are hung with the consequences.

That does not mean, however, that this is likely to last forever. The opening up of new options can be described as a two-track process. The first track is empowering individuals by giving them the best available tools to work with the world. Some of this may be direct and some may be indirect, that is, by way of parents (or the family) or the collective. The second track is reshaping mainstream institutions to make them more welcoming and open to Indian aspiration when that choice is taken and also to remove roadblocks and perverse incentives, which still include some racism and much ignorance.

---

8 I am indebted for this concept to Jean Allard (2002) of Manitoba.

9 —though it did envision support for Indian culture.

Empowering individuals

We know quite a lot about the elements necessary to empower individuals. First is security of the person, with all that implies as to health, housing, and love. This includes shelter from the malign influences of tangible threats like substance abuse and intangibles like gang membership. Second is the sense of self-worth, with the associated parameters of hope and aspiration. Third is the toolkit for life, primarily education. But that simple word spans such a huge range of possibility. And, fourth, is access to opportunity.

It is an obvious understatement to say that none of the four elements (with the exception, one would hope, of love) are normally available in adequate measure on remote and isolated Reserves. And, it is stating a very inconvenient truth to say that, in the very nature of things, the four elements simply cannot be brought to isolated Reserves in adequate measure. Of course, the goals are not new, especially in such matters as housing and health. The sums spent to date to these ends have been both enormous and woefully ineffective. Much of the expenditure may have been wasted or inefficient but the attempts have been made, in good faith, in a very major way, and too often the outcomes are simply unsatisfactory to anyone.

The obvious choice is a stark one: isolation or engagement with the mainstream, which means moving to town or close to town. Whether the move is to be made by individuals or by Reserves is an open question; either is possible, though the latter will be resisted as a threat to the System. That choice can only be made by individuals and their families but we fail Indians just as we would fail any Canadian by failing to offer it. Isolated communities are "parallel societies" by necessity. In settled rural and urban areas, the parallel societies are created by the policy of government and the System, and the community can become isolated *de facto* as a separated society, focused inwards towards the tribe and often, to victimhood, the terrible past, and dreams of future settlements. By force of geography, urban Reserves may not show such a dramatic absence of security, hope, education, and opportunity but, by definition, the parallel society remains a smaller thing than the mainstream.

What are some of the operational means of providing the four elements necessary to empower individuals, especially for children? All societies bootstrap themselves upwards through their children. In Canada, we leave this responsibility in very large measure to the parents or the extended family. Only rarely does the state feel it necessary to "apprehend" children in order to look after their welfare. But, this is not the case for Indians. In British Columbia, where Indians constitute about 2% of the population, about 50%

of children "in care" are aboriginal. This is just shocking. Sixty percent of "street kids" in Vancouver are aboriginal (Smith, Saewyc, Albert, MacKay, Northcott, and McCreary Centre Society, 2007). Fortunately, the "in care" group is still the exception and the parental responsibility is still the norm. But there is clearly a case here for more community involvement for those in care, and this is a fact well recognized by all concerned, though there remains debate over whether Indian children must be cared for by Indian agencies exclusively, as has been the recent trend.

For whatever reason, professionals and academics handle this issue with kid gloves. But the media are increasingly leading on the issue. In a powerful column in the *Globe and Mail*, Margaret Wente (2007, October 13) reported on a series in the *Winnipeg Free Press* about the transfer of responsibilities for the care of aboriginal children in Manitoba from the provincial authorities to aboriginal agencies. Chaos ensued and the children suffered, as they were removed from or denied adequate mainstream fostering and placed in what often turned out to be terribly unsuitable aboriginal homes simply because of the racial connection. Wente stated that aboriginals make up about 25% of the population of Manitoba under age 19 but that

> aboriginals and Métis make up 85% of the 7,200 kids in care ... Nobody wants to say the hard thing: The vastly disproportionate number of native kids in care is the result of widespread social collapse. No one can claim to have the answers. But blaming the white man will no longer do. And white guilt over the sins of the past has simply made matters worse. It has created a deadly double standard that tolerates widespread abuse and neglect of children—as long as they're aboriginal, not white. (2007, October 13: A27)

This is a significant moral issue. The standard watchword is that the interests of the child come first. In the case of the System, the interest of the collective's retaining control of the child in sometimes inadequate or even unsafe locations is put first. Those advocating the primacy of the interests of the collective over the individual in this area need to answer for these outcomes. And mainstream politicians have to reflect upon their over-riding duty to all children, unless and until courts order otherwise.

Elsewhere, in the great majority of cases where the family unit is still functioning, even if not always "intact," there is a strong case for direct assistance in order to empower the individual. There are two main avenues.

1. Put educational choice into the hands of parents

The first is that educational choice should be in the hands of the parents and for that to be a reality the parents will need to be provided with financial resources in the way of vouchers, to be spent at a school of parental choice, which may or may not be on a Reserve or under collective control. If the school chosen is far from home, there must be adequate additional provision for shelter—again at the parent's choice, we are not talking government "residential schools"—as required.

2. A modified and transitional Guaranteed Annual Income (GAI)?

The second avenue would be to provide direct payments to persons. More than half of federal funding for Indian purposes flows through Indian governments, Chiefs, and Councils (the rest is for administration, health care, and so on). The proposal by Jean Allard of Manitoba, previously cited, is worth supporting in principle: a diversion of a very significant fraction of these funds—the total being in excess of $5 billion—from Band governments to individuals. Allard's rationale begins with the fact that, in most of the Numbered Treaties, there was provision for "Treaty Money" to be paid to individuals; $5 per year was the usual amount, with more for Chiefs and "headmen." Allard reasons that at that time an acre of land was worth about $1 and that a similar acre is now worth $1000 and suggests that the Treaty Money should be increased in a similar way.

The idea has been elaborated considerably by John Richards (2003) and both of us served on the Treaty Annuity Working Group, a special committee of the Social Planning Council of Winnipeg, which investigated the idea. The differences are in the details, which of course are very important in plans that are intended to give constructive incentives as bearable costs. Allard would pay $5000 per annum to all Indians. I agree with roughly that number but, like Richards, would pay the sum only to adults. I would add a voucher system for children's education and leave open the possibility of either paying a lower annuity rate to those living off Reserve or at least not "stacking" onto provincial plans. In addition, any special urban assistance of the kind proposed in the previous chapter would have to be taken into account, again to avoid "stacking." The details are worth a small book in themselves.

There is at least one similar, though smaller, plan in existence, namely the James Bay and Northern Quebec Agreement: Cree Hunters and Trappers Income Security Program. This plan is intended to sustain a traditional way of life by paying cash for hunting instead of welfare, has about 1,600 adults enrolled (with a bonus for children) and pays about $15,000 per year. I have not seen any independent studies on the outcomes.

If one accepts this idea of "treaty money" as an authentic reflection of the actual intent of the original settlement, the payments should be made whether the individuals concerned are on Reserve or not, both because today's individuals are descendants of the treaty signatories and as a practical matter, in order to facilitate mobility. Of course, Band governments would still need money to provide services. They could maintain their cash flow by imposing taxation on those of their members on Reserve up to the amount diverted. This is not just a shell game. Taxpayers are far more likely to hold governments accountable than mere clients. You will feel more strongly about the use of money taken away from you than money you never had.

What are the arguments in principle and practice that might possibly justify such an idea? The principled arguments in favor are that the concept would empower the individual and open choices. The justification for affording some such payment to Indians and only to Indians would be that it is a time-limited transitional assistance scheme to persons injured by our historic policies. The "time-limited, transitional" approach is essential in order to avoid perpetually emphasizing even further the difference between Indians and ordinary Canadians. The practical argument in favor is that it would have a good chance of usefully changing incentives and have a low (if any), additional overall financial cost.

There are several things to be said about this proposal. The first is that it would be expensive for Ottawa, though not on a net basis. As argued above, payments to all Indians—a sort of a partial, low-level, Guaranteed Annual Income (GAI)—would have to be expanded to take in the off-Reserve population. Thus if, say, $2 billion were diverted from Councils (around $5,700 per on-Reserve person per year or $8,800 per adult over 16,[10] roughly an additional $2 billion would be needed for current off-Reserve persons, were payment to be made at the same level. There is, however, a strong argument for a lower payment to those living off Reserve, as the tax-back rate would

10 Author's calculations based on 2006 data, estimates only. For the purposes of this calculation, the number of eligible persons on and off Reserve is taken as the average between the Census number of Registered Indians (623,000) and the Departmental registration forecast for 2007 (770,000). The proportion of persons aged 17 and over is interpolated from Census data at 65%.

be much lower.[11] (For off-Reserve Indians, generally more affluent, there would also be an offset to the Treasury through the inclusion of the payment in taxable income.)

In considering this proposal, it is well to remember that we already have a *de facto* GAI for poor people in Canada by way of the welfare system. In the case of the GAI proposed for Indians above, the GAI payment would not be "stacked," but rather instead counted as a portion of the welfare otherwise payable. This would thus not be "new money" but an intergovernmental transfer wrapped in an arguably more dignified box.

To achieve minimal net fiscal impact, the tax claw-back could be structured in the same manner as the OAP, completely recovered when a person's income is around $60,000. Sunset provisions could be included as well; indeed, if one agrees that our policies should not single out Indians but rather provide for equal treatment except where otherwise required by law, then a sunset provision is essential. The idea is "transitional."

The minimal amount of "new money" for this plan does not mean that there would be no impact. The adult Indian individual would have a guaranteed $8,800 per annum in pocket. This would enhance both mobility and accountability, the latter because the tax-back rate on Reserve would necessarily be high, and the individual would get that bill personally. There is nothing like paying for something to induce a concern about the services received in return. Having the cash would encourage mobility as it would follow the individual, providing a minimal monthly stipend wherever he or she went, with transitional provisions easing the difference between rates on and off Reserve. Further, since there would be a net new cost for the federal government and a net reduction (by way of lower urban welfare payments) for the provinces, it should be possible to induce the latter to re-direct the funds saved into settlement services for urban Indians requiring them.

The second thing that must be said about this proposal is that GAI schemes are in themselves controversial. Experiments in Canada and other countries have yielded mixed results in terms of outcomes and incentives. The response to that point is that the perfect should not be made the enemy of the good and it may well be that a GAI in this circumstance would have merit. In addition—and this is very important—this is not a traditional,

11 This is because Band Councils would either have to cut services dramatically or impose a high rate of taxation on the monies transferred to individuals, formerly flowing directly to Councils. This factor does not apply off Reserve.

"full blown," GAI. The annual amounts should be sufficient to empower and assist but not enough to support or corrupt.

The third thing is a major policy question. Are children to be included in the per-capita payment? In my view, the answer should be no, as long as the educational voucher discussed elsewhere is generous and applicable from (say) kindergarten level. There should be no specific payment for having children: the money should be exclusively for educating them as standard welfare payments take non-educational child-support needs into account.

The fourth thing is that this partial GAI idea—as with the educational vouchers—will be highly controversial. It will be attacked as an assault on the size and power of the Reserve system, since it would afford mobility to persons of all ages. It is reasonable to estimate that if choice is offered, some will take it up. But the intent is not an attack on the parallel society, but rather the empowerment of the individual. Nevertheless, the case will be made, and the best response—a response grounded in fairness—is to offer the increased resources needed for the parallel society to compete effectively with the mainstream as individuals make their choices, where that need can be demonstrated and the resources used productively. The only goal here is to level the playing field for individual choice.

The collective starts out with a built-in advantage in this competition—the advantage of cultural familiarity, family ties, tradition, inertia—all powerful forces. With these advantages, it is also fair to say that another route for the empowerment of the individual—other than the mainstream—can be by way of improving the services offered by the collective. The results might be quite surprising. Competition can change results amazingly.

These two general approaches are very much at the conceptual level. They will require detailed thought and elaboration by expert professionals in education and health, governments, scholars, and the Industry before major implementation. They may in the end be rejected. In that case, other avenues must be found because, without question, the empowerment of the individual is a missing key in a majority of Indian cases, notwithstanding many success stories.

The off-Reserve world—reshaping mainstream institutions

The second track is the reshaping of mainstream institutions and the removal of roadblocks and perverse incentives. These are questions within mainstream control. There is therefore no excuse for inaction. One part of what is required is entirely a matter of government policy. In other words, it can be done tomorrow, by our elected representatives. The other part—a very important part—relates to the law, which creates many of the "roadblocks and perverse incentives."

Policy

While insisting upon the obligation of the state to hold out the genuine choice of the parallel society, I would argue that the real and necessary change (for the parallel society is already government policy) is to make the option of greater interaction with the mainstream a genuine one. Since almost all of the government services provided to ordinary citizens flow from provincial and local governments, the opportunity for Indian relationships with those governments must be made as real and attractive as the now largely federal relationship. Some of the more traditional Chiefs feel very strongly that their ties are with the Queen but it is a constitutional reality that the Crown acts through the provinces as well.

Once any person is off the Reserve, there is no reason in theory that this provincial citizenship should not be apply more fully. The problems are in practice and in finance, above all the latter, which makes the situation all the more disgraceful, because anything like these problems that can be solved by the mere application of money should be solved. Now. As earlier noted, the federal government by and large takes the position that Indians living off Reserve are not its financial concern. They do provide health and education-subsidy programs but such are minor compared to the need.

The real need is for provincial programs, "enhanced" with federal money, that are as generous to Indians as they would be to, say, an immigrant from Asia. In the immigration business they call this a "settlement" responsibility. The adaptation of the newcomer must be eased by special programs and attention. The same responsibility exists to aid the "settlement" of those Indians—by no means all—who require special help with housing, schooling, training, job search, health, social assistance, drug problems, and so on. For instance, Helin puts forward excellent proposals about settlement initiatives for urban Indians (2006: ch. 15): such things as the simple provision of information to on-Reserve people who would move if they knew how, urban housing and other support services and, above all, successful experiments in education such as the Grandview/?Uuquinak'uuh Elementary School in Vancouver. All are common sense, practical things that can be done.

Provinces do not adopt these "settlement" techniques by and large, though they do try, mostly using the standard approach involving social workers, welfare, and the justice system. They should explicitly accept this additional responsibility to aid the "settlement" of Indians coming off Reserve. But, the only way it will happen—this is a political reality—is if the federal government is prepared to pay for it. So that commitment should be made. Earlier in this paper, I estimated the cost: it is in the billions per annum. Also mentioned was the payback: it is in the tens of thousands of persons living productive lives, and multiplying year by year while the problems correspondingly decline. In this sense, I do not disagree with the conclusion of the RCAP that it is an economic thing to spend a great deal of money in this area. The disagreement lies as to where it should be spent. I say that a great deal of it should be in the outside world, not the parallel society.

It would be wrong to say that none of this is being done. There are small programs, there are experiments, and there is good will. But there is not, as yet, big dollars. That is one missing ingredient. It is not the only one. Also required is extended and strong political will, which may well be the scarcer resource. Once again, I will defer to the professionals in how these programs should be designed. That part will flow, once the decision is taken to empower the Indian individual in the outside world, at the initial expense of Ottawa. In other words, social opportunity can be arranged by the simple application of good will and money. Legal equilibrium will be much more difficult to arrange.

Law

Since at least *Sparrow* in 1990, the courts, led by the Supreme Court of Canada, have been busily engaged in social engineering in this field. It is sophistry to say that they have simply been interpreting the law. They have been making the law. As previously noted, the Supreme Court is indeed supreme, above Parliament even, in Indian law. The law is what the Court says it is. There are so many judgement calls involved that, on a spectrum of zero (indicating no special Indian rights beyond the statute and common law) to 10 (indicating the invention—my word—or the recognition—theirs—of all of the necessary grounding for a parallel society), they have scored at least a 5. They could have been anywhere between zero and ten. That latitude exists.

It would be wrong to criticize motives. Management of Indian policy in Canadian history has been, however well intended, near criminal in effect. Judges have therefore wanted to put a thumb on the scales on the side of the Indian, and they have done that. Such is only human. But litigation is a very blunt and inefficient instrument. For example, it customarily creates winners and losers. It can also create enduring resentments. But it is sometimes necessary to break logjams, in which case one can only hope for wisdom and balance. The net effect of litigation to date has been to add a clearly very large but unquantified amount of legal power to Indian collectives, while subtracting the same indefinable amount from governments. Many people feel intuitively that is a good thing but the result, so far, has been to increase complexity and uncertainty and reduced accountability.

Private entities are caught in the middle, and find the new rules vague and confusing. Mainstream society is based upon the predictable order of laws passed by governments that it elects. It is not used to the unpredictable law-making of courts. (Normal litigation is quite a different thing, much less important, much more routine and predictable.) The judicial making of Indian law is in such an early stage that uncertainty reigns. And uncertainty is the enemy of stability in the lives of ordinary persons and of progress, investment, and so on. So these things slow down tremendously while the costs from delay and of acquiring information and increased certainty go up. The net economic outcome is a powerful dampening effect.

A new seat at the table of power

This kind of social and legal uncertainty is not an entirely new phenomenon. In abstract terms, what has happened is that a new player has been seated at the table of society, with a so far unclear, but clearly large, basket of powers. Two historical precedents commend themselves, namely the growth of the trade-union movement throughout the twentieth century and the growth of the environmental movement over the past generation. Both developments saw significant power shifts and a new status quo.

The trade-union question is pretty well mature these days. A considerable body of labor law and practice has been developed, as well as specialized, efficient, and expert institutions like Labour Relations Boards to deal with almost all questions, removing them from the slow, clumsy, and less expert courts. The labor movement itself, at least in the Western world, has long since peaked and is in a long-term and slow decline. It is not without continuing value as a social force but has been superseded in most of the private sector, dominant now only in the monopoly sector of government.

By contrast, the environmental movement is clearly still on the upswing.[12] The result has been the institution of a large and growing body

12 This is often at a cost to union jobs, one of the little ironies of history, as it is the old, high-impact, and unionized heavy industries that tend to be most discouraged and displaced to other parts of the world, or replaced by non-union high-tech processes.

otherwise segregated districts and schools), relations between whites and blacks were essentially run by the court for a generation. A large part of this was because of very strong anti-black racism, which simply does not exist to any comparable degree in the Canada *vis-à-vis* Indians. This fact should make the Canadian accommodation easier. But there is another factor which makes it more difficult.

The courts in Canada have in fact handed Indians something very different than blacks were afforded in the United States. The drive of Martin Luther King and his colleagues was to become equal in American society; the mandate of the Canadian courts to Indians is to be separate and different in Canadian society. The American courts see all Americans as individuals; the Canadian courts take the same perspective except for Indians, whom they see as members of a collective. This makes an immense difference. Without sacrificing culture, the black player sought to gain status as an ordinary American. The Indian player is offered status as a different sort of Canadian, with special rights. The incentive for the Indian player then is—and most human beings would follow this incentive—to test the limits of that new advantage. That is precisely what is going on.

Trade unions, environmentalists, and Indians

It is interesting to compare the similarities and differences among the three sets of "new players," trade unions (as they once were), environmentalists, and Indians. All came from a position of relative powerlessness in the face of mainstream society and its major actors, governments and other large organizations. All have as their major lever to attain their objectives an ability to frustrate the activities of the major actors. This is not to say that there is no room for or motive for co-operation among the parties, and indeed in a healthy and mature relationship co-operation will be the usual mode. It is simply to note the underlying reality. Just as the power of a government relies ultimately on its monopoly on the use of force, so the powers of these three new players rely ultimately on their ability to throw a wrench in the gears.

But then the incentives of the three groups begin to differ. Trade unionists have tangible incentives—better money, work rules, union security—to take job action and ultimately go on strike. But their members also bear a personal cost in such action and this cost increases with time. When the pain is equalized all around, the strike is settled. There are automatic stabilizers at work. Everyone suffers. This is an example of balanced and symmetric power.

Environmentalists opposing development of this or that kind have no direct personal incentives such as money to motivate their tactic and they are under no internal pressure of time whatsoever to settle. Indeed, quite the contrary: every day a given development is stopped is a "win." Thus there is no automatic regulator to the standoff from the environmentalist side, as there is in the disputes between labour and management. There is, however, a time pressure on the developer's side (whether that be a person, a firm, or a government) in the sense that, for these people, time is money and getting something done is better than getting nothing done, up to a point. There is therefore an incentive on the developer to make concessions, up to that point, while there is no corresponding incentive on the opposing side. This is a description of an asymmetric power arrangement, which is not a healthy one. That is why approval systems have been developed by governments to balance the interests in environmental disputes and ultimately permit development, or not, but in any case to bring a resolution within a reasonable time frame.

The Indian player in the new reality has the best of both the union and environmentalist positions. The Indian player can seek to receive a tangible personal (that is, collectively personal) payoff such as cash, land, or future work rules (e.g., indirect employment such as committees, or direct employment) or royalties, and so on. In this, we see the incentive pattern for a trade union but without the balancing factor, since for the Indian player there is no new cost however long negotiations may continue. Life goes on just as before.

In this sense, the Indian player also has the environmentalist player's immunity from time pressure, though not quite to the same degree, as there can be a positive payoff for eventual local development, where this is almost never the case for the environmentalist. At best there is mitigation.[17] So clearly here we have another asymmetric power arrangement and it is another irony of history that the Indian, so long oppressed, is distinctly on top in this one.

As to the other players, the private sector is thoroughly confused and worried. It hates uncertainty. It looks to government to resolve that. Such, after all, is the prime function of government, to bring and preserve order. But governments are deeply afraid of this issue. They are afraid of the courts. They have no idea how far Indian power might be expanded and are afraid to know. In litigation and negotiation, the tendency is to drag things out

17 The foregoing illustrates why the assumed natural alliance between Indians and environmentalists is an unstable one. The parties seek different objectives. While each party may find the other temporarily useful in pressuring developers or governments, in the long run more basic objectives will prevail.

and exercise extreme caution. The finance departments of governments are worried about dollars: it is clear that the cost may be immense. Far better to delay the problem until someone else's watch.

Governments are also afraid of the voters. They know that there is a huge slug of white guilt to be dealt with, so they dare not take hard lines on Indian questions. But they also know that, as the voters come to appreciate the true dimensions of the question and the probable cost of solutions, they are going to be very unhappy. So again, obfuscation and delay put off the evil day of reckoning.

Governments are especially afraid of Indians. Oka, Gustafsen Lake, Caledonia, these have been traumatic events for less-than-courageous ministers. The Indian victories in court do not seem to end. The negotiating demands do not go away. Delay is again the easy political answer. But it is the wrong one.

Indian power

Now, in this new reality, let us examine the positioning and mind-set of the players in what the Americans would call "Indian country." Those Canadians who think this does not affect them should consider that until otherwise specified by the courts, "Indian country" potentially includes over 90% of British Columbia and the Atlantic, parts of Quebec (note *Delgamuukw* and *Haida Nation v. British Columbia (Ministry of Forests)* for this first group), and essentially all of the Prairies and most of Ontario and Quebec where covered by treaties (note *Mikisew Cree First Nation v. Canada (Minister of Canadian Heritage)* and *Platinex Inc. v. Kitchenuhmaykoosib Inninuwug First Nation*). Some urban or long-occupied parts of Ontario and Quebec are probably exempt from this statement (though note the contrary case of the Caledonia occupation in progress as at this writing). The geographical coverage is huge.

The Indian position with respect to developments in these areas[18] is, as noted above, one of asymmetric power. There is a clear right of consultation in any claimed territory (title need not be proven; only claimed), which consultation may be more or less elaborate, more or less lengthy, and require

18 And "developments" need not be new action on the ground. British Columbia cases have established that distant and unrelated activities such as the transfer of cutting permits or the sale of company shares can be caught up in the required consultation and mitigation process.

more or less mitigation of impact—or even permission—according to rules that are still very amorphous. The right to consultation does not constitute the right to a veto—*Haida* makes that clear—but does impose serious delays and potentially large costs, whether in cash, land, reduced developmental activity, or some other form of payment. So expansive is the potential that recently in British Columbia an enormous mining project (the Kemess North expansion of Northgate Mining in northern British Columbia) was turned down by an environmental review panel, which found that there was no environmental veto but that Indian objections gave rise to a "social" concern. In other words, limits are still being tested.

In treaty lands, a recent development is that of *Platinex*, which affects a prospective mining development in north-western Ontario. Even though the treaty dates to 1929, the Kitchenuhmaykoosib Inninuwug First Nation (KI) has claimed additional land on the grounds that its population is now larger.[19] Since logically the new lands could be claimed anywhere in a rather large treaty area, the KI have been able to stop the drilling of a few exploratory holes—nothing more than that—by the subject mining company, notwithstanding seven years of discussion. A reading of the case does not reflect at all well on the tactics of the company, which behaved in an arrogant manner, but neither does it reflect well on the KI, who do not appear to have negotiated in good faith. (Good-faith negotiations are expected by the courts from both sides.) Nor does the Province of Ontario look well in this matter, nor indeed does the federal government. The delays in responding to the KI claims have been unconscionable. KI filed its current formal claim seven years ago (though this issue has gone on much longer than that) and the federal government has not yet taken any position on it. In latest developments, the Court had decided to micro-manage the relationship in what may become a usual mode.

These two cases are illustrative of the power of the Indian position. Many more current examples could be given, such as recent attempts by a Prince Rupert band to frustrate port expansion for the Pacific Gateway project and the before-mentioned injunction obtained by the Musqueam to temporarily stop the sale of major federal buildings in Vancouver. The Musqueam have also successfully stopped the sale of the University Golf

19 This question alone has major national implications as it is easy to see that this idea of growing land for a growing population, if accepted, would re-open every settlement in Canada. The idea of subtracting land from falling populations has not yet been broached.

Course from the Province to the University of British Columbia, and it appears they will gain title to that land. The Innu of Labrador have successfully bargained on further proposed development of the Churchill River, and delayed and extracted a major settlement in respect of the Voisey's Bay nickel project. There is every likelihood that an active aboriginal bar will multiply the cases exponentially, often by way of seeking injunctive relief, that is, by stopping developments.

There are two sorts of thing going on here. One is right and proper; the other is bad for everyone. The good sort of thing is the ongoing attempt to improve relationships, work together, and also to redress historic injustices according to law. Not everyone by any means agrees with the direction Indian law has taken but the law is the law and unless we are revolutionaries we cannot abandon it. And of course, the Supreme Court having the immense flexibility it does, the future course of Indian law may change as it is further elaborated. In furthering these "good things," consultation and accommodation are good ideas, and "good faith" is the best idea of all.

The bad sort of thing that is going on is when asymmetric power and uncertain conditions are used as background conditions for blackmail and tollgating, in order to extract cash or other concessions as a condition of people simply getting about their legitimate business with no adverse impact upon Indian interests. The power of delay, or eternal studies, of court injunctions, repeatedly postponed meetings, vague demands, the invention of "sacred" status, blockades in defiance of court orders and similar tactics is immense. The intelligent solution for the person trying to do business is simply to swallow hard and pay up or go away, but this is bad for everyone else.

It is bad for those employing such tactics, because they are immoral and therefore corrupt those who use them. It is a "sort of" answer to say that the white man has been immoral for one hundred years of more but it is a wrong answer for everyone. And it is bad for the overall society, because these kinds of tactics greatly increase the cost of doing such business as is done, delays other development, and completely forecloses some projects or scares off some investors who would otherwise have contributed to the well being of all Canadians, Indians included.

The difficulty is that it is nigh impossible for the outsider to tell whether what is going on is "good" or "bad" in any given case. For a time, and without inside knowledge (which insiders almost never see it as being in their interests to divulge) it can be difficult to tell whether similar tactics are either "good" or "bad," and in part the distinction depends upon motive. This is clearly an unsatisfactory situation.

The biggest problem is uncertainty. The size of Indian power is undefined; the rules are unknown; the protocols are fluid; the case law is evolving. Who should do what? There is not much the private sector can do. It just has to get along as best it can. Less is done, at greater expense.

There is not much different that one can expect from the Indian side. While far from monolithic, the various collectives are, each in its own way, doing their best to push to the limits what might be possible with their new powers. They cannot be blamed for this, anymore than one can blame a union for getting what it can. If anything, even more activity should be welcomed, as a way of forcing governments to see their duty. More Indian litigation would be good, because litigation will help clarify the current uncertainties. Governments have been afraid to do this. In that context, the controversial cases of *Platinex* and *Tsilhqot'in Nation v. British Columbia (William)* are welcome, whatever the eventual results.

The main responsibility lies with those who have the main power and those who set the agenda, and this means governments, both federal and provincial, and the courts. The courts with their traditional disinclination to make decisions in this area, rather always encouraging the parties to negotiate, have really been ducking their duty. By analogy to the *Brown* case in the United States, they have let the genie out of the bottle. In Canada, they are going to have to do the Canadian equivalent of the American court's supervision of busing. *Platinex* will be a leading case here, because the judge has done exactly that. The parties have been unable to negotiate in good faith. He has knocked their heads together, issued orders as to what they should have negotiated, and imposed those orders. If they do not negotiate what is left, he will issue further orders. That kind of approach brings reality to what can otherwise be eternal dithering or tollgating.

The Plaintiff in *Tsilhqot'in Nation v. British Columbia (William)* asked for the same sort of thing, not to resolve all of the issues, simply a current declaration of aboriginal title with leave to apply to the court as ongoing questions arise. This was not granted. However, whether the courts want this or not, they will be unable to avoid such supervision, having set the stage and then left it full of uncertainty. They will either finally have to deal with the wreckage as they have done in earlier cases, or expert tribunals will need to be established.

Governments have to do more. They have developed some protocols of what is meant in an operational sense by "consultation" but they have failed to take the legal steps necessary to have those protocols blessed by the courts. That simple development would add immensely to certainty.

For greater certainty, questions involved in the design of consultation protocols could be determined and eventual packages ratified by reference to the SCC (by Ottawa) or the provincial Courts of Appeal (by provincial governments).

Governments should be proactive on questions of title. Where they disagree with the Indian side and the dispute has lingered too long, they should simply litigate, seeking a declaration of clear title (that is, with no aboriginal burden) or by other means. There has been too much reluctance to do this. Yes, litigation may take a few years, though far less once precedents are established. But negotiations by the BC Treaty Commission have been underway for 14 years and may once again bog down post *William*. By contrast, comprehensive and determined litigation could have given final answers over that length of time. Governments have shown no stomach for such an approach to date.

Eventually—not too long, one would hope—expert non-judicial bodies like environmental assessment panels can and should be established. Indeed, in the best of all worlds, all such questions of permitted land use should be determined by a single agency in any given province or area. This would undoubtedly take co-operation between federal and provincial governments, which is already beginning to happen on the environmental side.

It is not outside of the realm of possibility that the wheels may fall off: that co-operation will not be forthcoming, litigation will produce slow and confused results, or court decisions may produce outcomes that the mainstream political system is simply not prepared to countenance. This would be most unfortunate but there is a fallback position available. Section 35.1 of the Constitution Act, 1982, reads as follows:

> 35(1) The government of Canada and the provincial governments are committed to the principle that, before any amendment is made to Class 24 of section 91 of the "Constitution Act, 1867," to section 25 of this Act or to this Part,
>
> (a) a constitutional conference that includes in its agenda an item relating to the proposed amendment, composed of the Prime Minister of Canada and the first ministers of the provinces, will be convened by the Prime Minister of Canada; and
>
> (b) the Prime Minister of Canada will invite representatives of the aboriginal peoples of Canada to participate in the discussions on that item.

This clearly contemplates potential amendment to constitutional sections touching Indians and makes it clear that consultation is required. It also makes no provision for Indian veto, only consultation. The federal and provincial governments together are probably free to amend the constitution in this area if required. This would likely be done by using the "7 and 50" formula rather than unanimity, but even possibly Section 43, which provides for an amendment affecting only one province and requiring the assent of only that province and Ottawa, might be used in unusual cases like British Columbia where the unsettled land component is so huge. In any case, prior consultation in good faith with Indian representatives would certainly be required.

This power *in extremis* is not unreasonable. Constitutional amendment is very difficult, as it should be. But in the end, the will of the majority will prevail in a democratic system. It is much to be hoped that we do not reach this point. The parties and the courts will likely be more sensible than that. The fallback of a constitutional amendment should perhaps be seldom mentioned but never forgotten.

The hoped-for alternate future is that dispute resolution will be handled routinely by accepted, reasonably certain, and rapid procedures, and that most matters touching Indians and their desired futures will be decided one at a time by the individuals concerned. That is how the rest of Canada and the Western world works, and it works quite well. In the end, that is the central message of this essay. Indians have been oppressed in the past, and special attention and support is owed to overcome continuing difficulties stemming from that.

Indians today have some special rights, title, and privileges that are matters of law (if still somewhat undefined) and are collective and/or personal property, to be exploited, traded off for other things, or managed in any other way by the owners. Beyond that special ambit, closely determined (for too much privileged distance in any part of society is socially disruptive), Indians should be ordinary citizens, living such lives as they decide. Too much legal uncertainty remains, and it should be expeditiously reduced.

Indians in the future, it is my argument, should determine their individual lives by individual choice (which may be to adhere to a collective or join the larger mainstream or seize elements of both worlds), and it is for the rest of us to make those choices real in a manner that is fair to Indians and to the mainstream as well. Perhaps only in Canada could such an unusual project work: the expansion of individual choice to opt into a collective based on ethnic characteristics and heritage available only to a few, rejecting many of the values and law and authorities of the mainstream state, and yet legally empowered and financed by that state.

But then, Canada has become a most unusual country. Except for the geography, we have changed almost beyond recognition in the past 50 years. The usual explanations of what binds us—British or French ancestry, the railroad, the CBC, "Canadian culture," anti-Americanism—all of these things together do not come close to explaining the Canada of today. We are defined rather by two new things.

The first is a gigantic, mutual insurance policy that guarantees that Canadians will support each other in all of the things necessary for life: peace and order, income, heath, education, food, and housing. People are then free to get on to make what they will of their lives, based upon that security. That is the Canadian deal, we are rich enough for that, and we are so insistent upon it that we can admit of no exceptions. We will not have people reduced to beggary or starvation or even serious discomfort, even if they are directly responsible for their state. We agree to have "free riders," up to and including entire regions, to ensure that none are left behind. Why? Perhaps because that would cause the rest of us discomfort.

The second is an extraordinary tolerance of individual and group behavior, stretched to the limits and beyond, including of things that most lands would class as undermining the viability of the state itself. The United States styles itself the most robustly individualistic nation in the world but we leave them behind in our tolerance. Few of us would dream of sporting a bumper sticker saying, "Canada, love it or leave it!" We do have stickers that say, "Support our troops," but the wish is for the soldiers, not the mission.

Canadians would not for an instant contemplate a civil war to save the union from secession. Quite the contrary: we are the only country in world to have spelled out exactly how to separate, in the *Clarity Act*, considered a great feat of statecraft. It may have been American television that popularized that useful statement, "Whatever ...", but Canada has adopted it as a national creed. Our multinational policies accept with equanimity large ethnic areas where Canadians can live their lives according to languages and values that do not originate here. This too is quite foreign to Americans for, while such enclaves exist in their country as well, they are considered as anomalies to be cured rather than end points to be enjoyed.

So it is too with Indian policy. While it is quite true that Americans have "reservations," they tend to be more integrated with the mainstream and the subsidies tend to be disguised as in the quasimonopoly on casinos afforded to the tribes. More importantly, it is inconceivable that new law increasing the separation of American Indians would be contemplated by the Congress today.

Nearing the end of this essay, I return briefly to the philosophical question of a "multinational state," if that is what we are. As the reader will know, I am sceptical, but I also fully accept that our own history—the history overwhelming shaped by the mainstream—requires us in fairness to behave toward Indians, at least *pro tem*, as if we were indeed such a state. But that said, I do not accept that the parallel society is the best solution, though I explicitly accept that we must leave it on offer. What I do believe strongly is that subsidiarity is capable of finessing many of the "in principle" and symbolic problems arising from our general concern for equality.[20] The reader will recall that subsidiarity calls for decisions to be made at the lowest possible level with the capacity of dealing with any given issue. When applied to organizations of the scale and circumstances of Indian communities, it allows for site-specific and capacity-specific solutions of the kind that cannot come out of great constitutional schemes.

Another way of looking at the outcome of a vigorous application of the principle of subsidiarity to the organization of government in Canada is that it tends very much to "live and let live." When powers are devolved as much as possible consistent with capacity, the tendency is for decision-making to move closer to the citizen. The discipline of political science might describe this as federalism with "deep decentralization." Subsidiarity is not opposed in principle to higher bodies setting standards and providing financing for the lower but this must always be justified and the maximum flexibility allowed. As applied to Indian government, the approach calls for maximum disentanglement, plus vertical and horizontal coordination mechanisms for the inevitable entanglements that remain. And, of course, sometimes the best theoretical resolutions along the lines of this model must be constrained by the necessity of keeping things simple enough that citizens are equipped to maintain accountability.

This is not re-inventing the wheel; it is common in practice and needs to be acknowledged. Here is an example from *Six Perspectives on Treaty Making*: "The 'Namgis Nation has an accord with the Village of Alert Bay, which has resulted in a $7 million wastewater site. The two governments each have

20 Subsidiarity is also a principle that holds great promise in easing the relationship of the federal government with the provinces, and of the provinces with municipalities.

two representatives on a development board that meets regularly to talk about common issues" (British Columbia Treaty Commission, 2006: 20). Such small victories happen everywhere.[21]

This practical approach does not fit well with demands for constitutional "rights and sovereignty" because the essence of subsidiarity is that it must always be ready to change in response to changing political, economic, and technological realities. Constitutional litigation does not allow this. It is brittle, rigid, and not based in on-the-ground practicality, no matter how much the Court may do its best to nuance words.

But "live and let live, with accountability" is in my view a much-shared Canadian principle that should be allowed much more operational space. It admits of experimentation and, therefore, of progress. Accountability admits of monitoring and the shutting down of mistakes. Both of these are good things, and both are unsettling to governments. But this is worth a lot of exploration if the good will can be found.

It is too soon to know if the current Canadian experiments in these matters will work, whether we are leaders in a new kind of nation on the planet or whether our very tolerance will weaken necessary bonds and end up in separation. It probably does not matter much, because the new fragments would be very similar to the old, mostly replacing Ottawa with local capitals but continuing the same polices, better done.

These underlying facts, plus the fact that the number of persons involved is small, mean that the "parallel society" policy being systematically advanced by governments and the System is within the tolerance of Canadian institutions and values. The significant question, which can be answered only by the individuals concerned, is whether that option offers the best life choices to Indians. The only insistence of this book is that that choice be informed and truly available, without the rules being rigged one way or another. In other words, that people should be free.

⚘ ⚘ ⚘

It is in a way disappointing to end this essay endorsing the above compromises with the fundamental principle of individual equality before the law, and therefore suggesting so many different policies for Indians *per se*. That is

21 The same report also has a section on the Nisga'a Nation some six years into its term but speaks only about the Treaty, without any mention of how it has improved (or not—we do not know) the lives of ordinary people.

because it is in my opinion wrong, wrong, wrong to treat different Canadians differently in political and legal terms on the basis of culture or heritage or race or color or whatever. But such differential treatment is what our constitutional law and our history mandates. In this book, I have tried to work fairly and in good faith within that scope. But I disagree with the scope and with the constitutional mandate. Constitutions can be wrong. That is why they have provision for amendment.

We need a sunset clause, a new day. We should in due course consider a constitutional amendment that removes all reference to Indians from the Canadian constitution and law in, say, 50 or 100 years. This should be done without changing any property rights at that time, with any remaining special privilege thereby effectively expropriated to be fully compensated as a quit claim. There has to be an end to old history or it so encrusts the future that too many options are foreclosed. The people who pay in the end for differential treatment are individuals, Indians above all.

This will not happen in my lifetime if Canada survives as a political unit. But one way or another, eventually it will happen. We will all be equal in our political status and free to work out our varied lives. Even now, that should be the guiding star.

The Indian land question in British Columbia

by Paul Tennant

Nations and Indians

In early British Columbia, the word "nation" was commonly used in its "other" meaning, one forgotten by most Canadians today. The Oxford Canadian Dictionary (1998 edition) gives it, still valid today, as "a group of Aboriginal people with common ancestry who are socially, culturally, and linguistically united." This usage bears no implication of nation-statehood. Early traders and officials used "nation" both for local village communities and for whole peoples (all persons having one distinct identity based on linguistic and cultural tradition). As they learned English, BC Indians used "nation" in the same way, and they still do. Here I use "first nation" for local community and "tribal nation" for Indian people (e.g., Haida, Shuswap). Each of BC's 200 first nations exists also as an Indian Act band. My use of the synonyms "Indian" and "aboriginal" follows contemporary usage. In BC, persons having Indian status under the Indian Act are called "status Indians," while "non-status Indians" are persons having Indian ancestry but lacking Indian status. Until it was amended in the 1980s, the Act granted Indian status to any woman marrying a status Indian man and withdrew status from any status Indian woman who married a man lacking such status. Children of these intermarriages inherited their mother's status or absence of it. Over the generations, Indian women "married out" at substantial and increasing rates; thus the general BC population includes many thousands of non-status Indians.

Chronology

1760 The future British Columbia is home to several hundred thousand people in some 30 tribal nations and many hundreds of communities.

1763 British Royal Proclamation of 1763 recognizes Indian "Nations or Tribes" as owning, under British sovereignty, the lands they occupy in the region of North America "lying to the Westward" of the Atlantic watershed.

1774 Spanish reach Vancouver Island, followed by James Cook in 1778. Fur trade and epidemics of European diseases begin.

1840s Having come overland with Canadian fur traders, Roman Catholic missionaries, many French speaking, are well established among interior Indian peoples and those in the most southerly coast areas adjacent to the Fraser River mouth. More northerly coastal reaches, less touched by the overland trade, have few missions.

1846 In the Treaty of Oregon, the USA acknowledges British sovereignty over what will become BC.

1849 Vancouver Island becomes a colony with Hudson's Bay Company, under James Douglas, in charge of settlement. Indian population is now less than half original numbers. Douglas, born to a "free colored" woman in a Caribbean colony, is married to a native Indian woman from Canadian territory.

1850–54 Soon made Governor of the colony, Douglas arranges treaties with 14 Indian communities on the Island. These "Douglas Treaties" acknowledge pre-existing aboriginal land ownership, by purchasing title, and provide that rights to fish "as formerly" and to hunt on unoccupied treaty lands shall continue.

1850s Preferring that Indians become Protestants and learn English, Douglas recruits British missionaries for the remaining coastal areas.

1856–64 White public opinion accepts pre-existing Indian ownership and supports more purchases of land title. Island Assembly urges Douglas to purchase remaining Indian lands and allocates money for the purpose.

1858 Mainland becomes new colony under Douglas; his instructions from the Colonial Office assume that he will sign more treaties.

1860–64 Instead of treaties, Douglas implements his "system"; it seeks Indian assimilation but with dignity and individual equality. Indians are granted preemption (homesteading) rights equal to those of Whites, but get only small reserves, intended as way stations to assimilation.

1864 Douglas retires. Joseph Trutch gains control of Indian land policy; he regards Indians as inferior savages.

1865 Indian population has declined to 40,000.

1866 The two colonies are united as British Columbia. Trutch remains dominant. The Legislature prohibits land preemption by Indians. Trutch reduces size of existing reserves; allows a maximum of 10 acres an Indian family in new reserves. Indians protest.

1870 Asserting that the Douglas treaties had been mere friendship pacts, Trutch becomes the first official to deny existence of aboriginal land title in BC. Dominant white view is now that Indians had been primitive nomads and that the land had been essentially empty until discovered by Whites. Official BC policy henceforward assumes that British sovereignty had created unencumbered Crown title.

1871 Trutch is instrumental in arranging "Terms of Union" with Canada. Indians and "lands reserved" for them are now under Canadian jurisdiction. Trutch lets Canadian officials assume that BC has extensive treaties and reserves as substantial as in Canada. Thus the Terms ignore the land issue while guaranteeing a reserve policy "as liberal as that hitherto pursued" by BC, in effect entrenching Trutch's precedent of 10 acres per Indian family.

1872 Trutch, John A. Macdonald's main BC ally, is appointed BC's first lieutenant-governor.

1872 Legislature removes right of Indians to vote in BC elections.

1870s East of the Rockies, Government of Canada arranges the major prairie treaties, which acknowledge original Indian title and provide reserves of 640 acres per family.

1870s Coast and Interior Salish chiefs hold large protest assemblies that gain prominent attention in the Legislature and, under the headings "Indian Land Question" and "Indian Land Claims," in newspapers. The Indian demands are equally for [1] a principled acknowledgement of original land occupation and ownership; and [2] treaties that transfer land title to the Crown and guarantee adequate reserves.

1874 Canadian officials urge reserves of 80 acres a family; BC refuses.

1875 Opposition motion passes in BC legislature compelling publication of *Papers Connected with the Indian Land Question, 1850–1875* (British Columbia, 1875/1987). Trutch prevents legislative debate on larger reserves.

1876 Governor-General Lord Dufferin urges BC to acknowledge Indian title.

1880s Christian missions and Department of Indian Affairs (DIA) are now well established in BC, and educating and "civilizing" Indian children by removal from home and family is underway.

1884 Canadian Parliament outlaws the potlatch, the major social, economic, and political institution of the coastal peoples.

1887 Nisga'a and Tsimshian chiefs travel to Victoria to demand recognition of title, negotiation of treaties, and provision for self-government within Canada. Premier Smithe rejects any notion of original Indian title, saying "When the whites first came among you, you were little better than the wild beasts of the field."

1887 Fearing Indian rebellion on the land issue, BC and Canada create a public commission of enquiry, which hears repeated Indian demands for treaties and self-government. Commissioners reject demands and depict Indians as disloyal and simple-minded tools of white agitators.

1890s A new source and type of leaders emerges among coastal peoples. The new leaders are not elders, nor in all cases from chiefly families. They are young men who have been educated in a local Protestant mission school. While still fluent in their own Indian language, they are also fluent in spoken English and able to read and write. They inform and represent, and come to lead, their peoples in pressing claims and complaints upon BC and Canadian officials. They are "neo-traditional." Among interior peoples with the Catholic missions, no comparable leadership develops.

1899 Canada unilaterally extends Alberta's Treaty No. 8 into the northeastern BC using federally owned land for reserves at 640 acres per family.

1906 Salish chiefs hold large assembly at Cowichan and send three chiefs to London to request treaties.

1906 The Royal Proclamation of 1763 is now basic to BC Indian political thought, as is faith that British justice will remedy Canadian and BC injustice.

1907 Nisga'a chiefs form "The Nisga'a Land Committee."

1909 Neo-traditional leaders on the coast form the Indian Rights Association. Interior Salish chiefs form the Interior Tribes of BC. For both, the issues are title, treaties, and reserve size.

1912 BC Premier McBride and the new federal Conservative government sign an agreement under which a joint commission will settle the

BC Indian land question, but only by examining reserve size. Title and treaties are to be ignored.

1913–16 The joint commission hears repeated Indian demands for treaties and larger reserves. Indians fear that reserves will be further reduced. Commissioners and federal officials repeatedly reaffirm the Indian Act's guarantee that reserves cannot be reduced without Indian consent.

1913 The Nisga'a send a petition to the British government affirming their loyalty to the British Crown and asking that the Royal Proclamation's promise of treaties and self-government be fulfilled. The petition is widely discussed and endorsed by BC Indians.

1914 The federal government offers to support BC Indian land claims in court, providing that it selects, and pays, the Indians' lawyers. Indians reject the condition.

1916 The joint commission recommends enlarging some reserves by adding a total of 136 square miles (appraised at an average of $5.10 an acre and generally unfit for agriculture) while removing 74 square miles (appraised at more than five times the value of the additions and almost all of it suitable for agriculture or sought for urban expansion). The federal Minister of Indian Affairs again reaffirms, in Parliament, that any cut-offs require Indian consent.

1916 Representatives of several tribal nations, most of them coastal, form the Allied Tribes of BC, the first organization claiming to represent all BC Indians. Peter Kelly (Haida) and Andrew Paull (Squamish) are the main leaders.

1916–20 Believing that cut-offs will occur, the Allied Tribes holds protest meetings. Coastal chiefs openly hold potlatches, thus defying the Indian Act. Federal officials in BC recommend police suppression

1920 The Minister introduces, and Parliament passes, a bill authorizing cut-offs without Indian consent. Simultaneously, the BC provincial police conduct a wave of potlatch arrests; some chiefs are convicted and jailed.

1921 In London, in a case arising in Africa, the Judicial Committee of the Privy Council, still the highest court for Canada, rules that aboriginal title throughout the Empire is a pre-existing right that "must be presumed to have continued unless the contrary is established." Canadian federal officials resolve to prevent the BC Indians from getting their claims into the courts.

1924 Reserve cut-offs are carried out. Among BC Indians, they become second only to denial of original title as a symbol of government and white deceit and immorality.

1925 Allied Tribes petitions Parliament for an enquiry.

1927 Liberal federal government agrees to a parliamentary inquiry, hoping to use it as a means of keeping the land claims from the courts. Inquiry rejects the validity of claims and thus the need for treaties. Parliament amends Indian Act to prohibit "any Indian" from making any claim against the Crown without the permission of the Canadian government.

1927–47 BC Indian political activity fades, in part because a conflation of the potlatch prohibition and the 1927 amendment leads to the widespread, but false, Indian belief that it is illegal even to mention land claims in any gathering of more than two persons.

1947 Indians gain BC voting rights as a by-product of enfranchisement of other racial minorities.

1949 Frank Calder, a Nisga'a hereditary chief and graduate of a Protestant residential school, is elected to the BC Legislature. His riding covers all four Nisga'a villages but extends over a much wider area, whose mainly white voters give substantial support to Calder and his party, the Co-operative Commonwealth Federation (CCF).

1949 Appeals to the Judicial Committee from Canada are abolished.

1951 With the Judicial Committee out of the way, and convinced that BC Indian political action is now a thing of the past (and also concerned about UN human-rights criticism) the federal government has the Indian Act amended to remove the prohibition of land claims as well as the provision prohibiting potlatches.

1952 Calder and other north-coast chiefs promptly begin discussing ways to proceed on land claims. George Manuel (Shuswap) begins political organizing in the southern interior.

1955 Guided by Calder, the Nisga'a chiefs form the Nisga'a Tribal Council; a major purpose is to gain settlement of the Nisga'a land claim. The Council is the first BC Indian organization to consist not of chiefs or delegates but of the people. Membership is automatic for all adult Nisga'a (including off-reserve and non-status) with each having one vote in Council Assemblies.

1958 Guided by the Nisga'a example, the Nu'chah'nulth (formerly "Nootka") create their tribal council.

1960 Manuel outlines the claims of interior Indians to a Parliamentary committee. The claims are identical to those put forward in the 1870s.

1960 Indians are granted the federal franchise. Phasing-out of Indian residential schools begins—for the purpose of achieving faster and more effective assimilation.

1965 Two Nanaimo Indians are arrested for hunting on unoccupied treaty land. BC's lawyers argue that the Douglas agreements were not treaties but, just in case, they present a new argument: that the Proclamation of 1763 did not extend all the way westward in North America but only as far the British had "discovered" in 1763. The Supreme Court of Canada rejects both arguments in ruling that the Douglas treaties are treaties with binding effect. The case and the ruling trigger the emergence of aboriginal rights as serious issue in Canadian courts.

1969 Encouraged by the Nanaimo case, Calder leads the Nisga'a in taking their claim to court. The BC Supreme and Appeal Courts rule that Indian title never existed. BC Chief Justice Davey accepts the Proclamation as inapplicable and states that the Nisga'a could have had no concept of title, as they "were undoubtedly at the time of settlement a very primitive people with few of the institutions of civilized society, and none at all of our notions of private property."

1969 The Canadian government presents to Parliament a formal statement of its intentions in Indian policy. In conventional parliamentary usage, such statements of intention are called "white papers." This one sets out the government's plan for achieving the full and final assimilation of Indians into mainstream society. Indians have neither been consulted nor informed. Indians across Canada need no prompting to see that "white paper" literally means "white policy." Among Indians the white paper becomes an enduring symbol of white misunderstanding and prejudice.

1969 In BC, chiefs from about one third of first nations, and from a majority of tribal nations, meet and form the Union of BC Indian Chiefs (UBCIC), intending it to oppose the white paper and to proceed with land claims. Soon non-status Indians from all parts of the province, organized by Butch Smitheram (non-status Okanagan), meet and form the BC Association of Non-Status Indians (BCANSI), intending it, in large part, to gain Indian Act benefits, notably housing and education, for non-status Indians. In effect, it seeks equal but separate treatment.

1970s The UBCIC and BCANSI obtain substantial federal funding—the UBCIC from the Department of Indian Affairs; BCANSI through the new multicultural program. Each opens a head office in Vancouver and hires a large headquarters staff, consisting mostly of young Indian high school graduates, some of whom work part-time while attending university. Employees of the two organizations mingle in much after-work socializing .

1972–75 BC's first New Democratic Party government agrees to consider return of cut-off lands but asserts that settling land claims is a federal matter.

1973 In the *Calder* case, the Supreme Court of Canada rules that Nisga'a did hold aboriginal title to their land before BC was created. On whether Nisga'a still have title the judges split evenly; thus, legally, the Nisga'a lose. But, respecting the reasoning of the judges who hold that title continues, Prime Minister Pierre Trudeau changes federal policy. Canada will now negotiate to settle Indian land claims but only one claim at a time in any province.

1974 The Province of Quebec and the affected Indian communities conclude the James Bay Agreement. Similar agreements are later reached in both northern territories. All embody the principles that BC Indians demand in treaties.

1975–80 Tribalism based on traditional linguistic and cultural identities re-emerges and solidifies as the dominant social and political force among BC Indians. The Union weakens and develops no claim.

1976 Led by Bill Lightbown (Haida) BCANSI rejects the separate-but-equal approach in favour of creating one organization uniting all BC Indians, status and non-status. Among those influencing the change is 28-year-old Bill Wilson (Comox), recent law-school graduate and the second BC Indian to become a lawyer. He and Lightbown view tribal nations, not Indian Act bands, as the foundation components of BC Indian identity and as the only legitimate building blocks for province-wide political action. BCANSI opens its membership to status Indians (thus allowing Wilson to join) and changes its name to United Native Nations (UNN), with "nations" meaning tribal nations. As its first act, the UNN elects Wilson as its President. For the next quarter century he will be the pre-eminent political thinker and strategist among BC Indians.

1976 The Federal government starts negotiations with Nisga'a. BC declines to participate.

1976–81 The Social Credit government proceeds on cut-off lands issue. Negotiations start in 1981. Cut-off lands are later returned or paid for at current value.

1980s A new generation of Indian leaders emerges. Like the "neo-traditional" leaders in the previous century, they are young, but there are now both men and women, and they come from all parts of BC. Through employment in Vancouver in the 1970s with UBCIC or BCANSI, or both, they have gained political knowledge and organizing skills, and developed a network of province-wide contacts. Most have attended university; some have professional degrees (they find law and education most appealing). Few know their grandparents' language but almost all strongly identify with their traditional tribal nation and almost all have a lively sense of historic injustice. All feel an Indianness inherent in all BC Indians, whether status or non-status, and admire Calder and Manual as its personification. The and most influential of these new leaders is Bill Wilson, who continues as President of the UNN; other new leaders include George Watts (Nuu'chah'nulth), Joe Mathias (Squamish), Miles Richardson (Haida), and Steven Point (Sto'lo).

1982 BC's Social Credit Attorney-General denies that Indian title ever existed but presents a brand-new, back-up argument: the 1871 federal agreement to pay for BC's liabilities *existing at Union* requires federal government to pay for any present-day surrender or transfer of title.

1984 In the *Guerin* case, brought by the Musqueam, the Supreme Court of Canada reaffirms that aboriginal interest in the land in BC is a "pre-existing legal right" derived from aboriginal practice and not from any British or Canadian action.

1985 The BC Court of Appeal halts logging on Meares Island pending court case on Nu'chah'nulth land claim. Judges observe that claims have been ignored and that negotiations would be appropriate.

1985 A new Attorney-General states: "You start negotiating land claims and you're down the Neville Chamberlain route."

1985 *Vancouver Sun* public opinion poll indicates that 75% of those with an opinion support negotiations.

1985 A federal task force recommends the federal government alter its policy of negotiating only one claim per province. Government ignores report.

1985–89 A recurrent pattern is evident: (1) After years of preparation, a tribal nation or, more often, several neighboring first nations present a formal land claim to the federal government, with a copy to BC; (2) Ottawa and BC do nothing; (3) BC allows new or continuing resource development on the claimed land; (4) new generation leaders organize a protest blockade designed to gain, and gaining, national and international television coverage; (5) on camera, the leaders present their case eloquently, enabling the general BC public, for the first time, to hear about land claims directly from Indian leaders (6) the leaders apply for a court injunction to stop the development; (7) BC courts grant the injunction, in effect suspending provincial authority over development.

1988 Bill Wilson and others create the BC First Nations Congress (FNC), intending it as a coordinating forum for land claims strategy, action, and eventual negotiations. The term 'first nations" acknowledges what is now apparent: contrary to Wilson's hopes, only a few tribal nations (notably the Haida) will be able to present a unified land claim. Wilson is elected FNC chairman. The Haida and several other tribal nations do participate.

1989 At Wilson's initiative, the inaugural "Industry/First Nations Conference" is held at Whistler (BC). Leaders of BC's major forestry, mining, and fishing companies discuss land claims amicably with tribal nation leaders.

1989 In the *Delgamuukw* (Gitksan-Wet'suwet'en) case before the BC Supreme Court, BC government lawyers repeat the standard provincial arguments and assert that BC Indians have been treated fairly.

1989 BC forms the Native Affairs Advisory Council. Premier Vander Zalm and Minister of Native Affairs Jack Weisgerber meet with some tribal nations to discuss Indian demands.

1990 In *Sparrow* case (Musqueam), Supreme Court of Canada recognizes aboriginal food-fishing rights in non-treaty areas, subject only to conservation requirements.

1990 To demonstrate solidarity with Mohawks protesting at Oka in Quebec but also to pressure BC to recognize title and to negotiate, a number of southern interior bands mount road and rail blockades. The Union of BC Indian Chiefs, its support now centering in the same area, proposes a province-wide framework treaty.

1990 Premier Vander Zalm announces that the province will negotiate land claims but will not acknowledge pre-existing title. The federal government agrees to drop its policy of negotiating only one claim at a time in any province .

1990 To reflect more clearly its not being just another Indian organization, but being instead a relatively small entity composed of delegates meeting periodically, the First Nations Congress changes its name to "First Nations Summit" (FNS). Wilson remains its leading figure.

1990 In October, to discuss how negotiations will proceed, the FNS meets with Prime Minister Mulroney and, the next day, with the entire BC Cabinet, in public session, in Vancouver. Wilson, for the FNS, proposes that a "tripartite study group" composed of members chosen by BC, Canada, and the FNS prepare detailed recommendations. Mulroney and the BC Cabinet agree. In December, the tripartite BC Land Claims Task Force is established. Still underway, the Nisga'a negotiations will not be affected by any new arrangements.

1991 In *Delgamuukw*, Judge Allan McEachern of the BC Supreme Court rejects present-day aboriginal title and right to self-government. Endorsing traditional White views, he depicts the claimants as descendants of primitive peoples who had neither law nor government.

1991 The New Democratic Party forms provincial government under Mike Harcourt. The Ministry of Native Affairs becomes Ministry of Aboriginal Affairs. BC becomes a full participant in Nisga'a negotiations.

1991 The Claims Task Force unanimously recommends a "British Columbia Treaty Process" having negotiations on a claimant-by-claimant basis, supervised and coordinated by a tripartite Claims Commission as "keeper of the process," and with equal involvement by BC and Canada. The term "first nation" would be applied to any Indian group whose claim is accepted by the Commission. There would be a six-stage process, commencing with a first nation's statement of intent, followed by several steps of actual negotiation, culminating in an "agreement-in-principle" that would become the text of the treaty when ratified by the "first nation," by the BC Legislature, and by Parliament. The FNS, BC, and Canada endorse recommendations. In the next few years the Task Force recommendations are at times referred to in negotiations as "the bible."

1992 The BC government formally recognizes both aboriginal title and an inherent right of aboriginal peoples to self-government. BC is for the first time ahead of the federal government in meeting aboriginal demands.

1992 Prime Minister Mulroney, Premier Harcourt, and Wilson (for the FNS) sign agreement to establish a negotiation process and a five-member BC Treaty Commission.

1993 Treaty Commission membership appointed. It is now generally accepted that BC treaties will include aboriginal self-government as well as settlements of land claims.

1993 BC Court of Appeal partially reverses the McEachern judgement, ruling that aboriginal title did exist and that a limited form (that of non-exclusive use and occupancy) continues to exist in non-treaty areas. This is the first time that any court in Canada has recognized present-day aboriginal title. The Court denies any aboriginal right to self-government.

1993 In December, the Treaty Commission begins operation and receives some 40 notices of intent; one is from the Haida tribal nation, a few are joint notices from several neighboring first nations, while most are from individual first nations.

1994 The new federal Liberal government of Jean Chretien adopts the policy that section 35 of the Constitution includes the aboriginal right to self-government.

1994 For idiosyncratic reasons largely irrelevant to mainstream Indian claims, some interior Indians hold protest blockades and then mount an armed standoff with RCMP at Gustafsen Lake.

1995 Seventy percent of BC's first nations, either alone or jointly with neighbors, have given intent to negotiate. Among tribal nations only the Haida and several others having only a few component first nations have given intent.

1996 The NDP is re-elected in BC; the Reform Party tries but fails to make land claims a major campaign issue. The Liberal Party under Gordon Campbell form Official Opposition.

1997 The Supreme Court of Canada completely reverses McEachern's judgment, ruling that aboriginal title is a present-day right to the land itself. It invalidates the BC lower courts' rulings on self-government but gives no ruling of its own.

1998 The Alliance of BC Interior First Nations formed, with area and groupings of support largely similar to those of Union of BC Indian Chiefs. While opposed to the BC treaty process, these interior groups deal amicably with BC ministries to gain services and benefits.

1998 Nisga'a Final Agreement signed by Nisga'a, BC, and Canada. BC's Opposition Liberal Party strenuously objects, especially to the self-government provisions and to the absence of voting rights for non-Nisga'a residents in Nisga'a local government elections.

1999 BC Legislature approves the Nisga'a Agreement after the NDP government uses closure to end Liberal filibuster. Liberal Opposition Leader Gordon Campbell and fellow MLA Geoff Plant, a prominent lawyer specializing in aboriginal issues, initiate a personal court challenge to the validity of any Nisga'a Treaty (*Campbell et al. v. AG BC/AG Cda & Nisga'a Nation et al.*). The BC Supreme Court rejects their views and requires them to pay the Nisga'a's court costs.

2000 Parliament approves Nisga'a agreement; it thus becomes a Treaty, the first in modern BC.

1995–2000 The Ministries of Forests and of Mining, which together regulate almost all resource development in the province, include a small but increasing number of Indian officials with relevant specialized university degrees. At regional levels, consultation with local first nations, based on Ministry acknowledgement of aboriginal rights and interests, becomes required standard practice.

2000 Campbell promises a Liberal government would hold a referendum on treaties and would appeal *Campbell et al. v. AG BC/AG Cda & Nisga'a Nation et al.*

2001 Liberals win landslide victory in May election (Lib. 77, NDP 2). Geoff Plant becomes Attorney General with responsibility for BC's treaty negotiation and for administering the referendum.

2001 Premier Campbell reassures the First Nation Summit, by promptly meeting with it, by pledging to continue the treaty process unchanged (thus regardless of any referendum outcome), and by announcing there will be no appeal in the court case.

2001 After extensive public hearings, a legislative committee, with its Liberal majority, recommends specific wording for 16 referendum questions and for a conciliatory preamble promoting reconciliation.

2002 Campbell and Plant reject the Committee's recommendations, substituting their own eight questions, which the Legislature approves.

Their wording is not conciliatory to aboriginal sentiments and there is no hint of seeking reconciliation. However, except for one question asking voters to reject aboriginal self-government, the questions are worded so that a vote of "yes," which the government recommends, will in fact endorse the principles and practices that the NDP government had been pursuing.

2002 Responding to the criticism that a "referendum on rights" will damage the treaty process, Plant states the "referendum will invigorate a treaty process that's urgently needed in the province."

2002 Public discussion is lackluster prior to the May referendum. Opponents of the treaty process do not attack the content of the questions. About one third of eligible voters mail in their ballots. More than 80% of the voters vote as the government had asked, rejecting self-government but endorsing the status quo in treaty negotiation.

2003 Ministry of Forests introduces pre-treaty "interim measures" allowing first nations to harvest local timber on Crown lands that will likely revert to the them in their treaty and also on unlogged portions of areas already licensed to private companies. The policy proves enormously popular and successful, as much from its principled acknowledgement of aboriginal interests as from its providing local employment. It also prevents the conflicts that led previously to blockades and injunctions. It eventually involves more than half of BC's first nations and more than 80% of those in forested areas.

2003–04 Campbell and Plant refer often to reconciliation. Plant sees it leading to "a new relationship based on mutual respect." Politically active Indians generally see the Liberal government as having become adequately conciliatory in practice if not in word. With the treaty process continuing unchanged, Indian political activity and interest subsides at the province-wide level and turns to local treaty preparation. Wilson leaves Vancouver and the United Native Nations to work for his own and neighboring communities in their preparation.

2005 Liberals re-elected with reduced majority (46 Liberal, 33 NDP). NDP Leader Carole James becomes Leader of the Opposition. A former senior official in the BC Ministry for Children and Families and most recently employed by the Carrier-Sekanni Tribal Council, she is the daughter of a Saskatchewan Métis, and is married to a BC Indian and former RCMP officer.

2005 New, stand-alone, Ministry of Aboriginal Relations and Reconciliation is created, with Tom Christensen, an MLA on good terms with Indian leaders in his Okanagan riding, as Minister. He states that the government's goal is to be a good partner with aboriginal British Columbians as they attain their full potential, and that the BC will achieve its full potential only if they are full partners.

2007 On Campbell's recommendation, Steven Point is appointed BC's first aboriginal Lieutenant Governor. Since law school he has been chairman of his Sto'lo tribal nations council, a Provincial Court Judge, and a Chief Commissioner of the BC Treaty Commission.

2008 Only two treaties have been achieved in the BC Treaty Process (by the Tsawwassen First Nation and by a group of five Nuu'chah'nulth first nations). An additional few seem imminent. Some 40 negotiations continue at varying stages. Increasingly, participants and the Treaty Commission itself identify difficulties, notably land disputes between adjacent first nations and the slowness of the process itself, but see no feasible solutions.

References

Alfred, Gerald Taiaiake (2005a). *Wasáse: Indigenous Pathways of Action and Freedom*. Broadview.

Alfred, Gerald Taiaiake (2005b). Wasáse: Indigenous Pathways of Action and Freedom—First Words. *CTHEORY*. <http://www.ctheory.net/articles.aspx?id=444>, March 1, 2005.

Allard, Jean (2002). Big Bear's Treaty: The Road to Freedom. *Inroads* 11: 110–71. <http://www.bigbearstreaty.ca/Inroads_11_Allard.pdf>.

Anderson, T., et al. (eds.) (2006). *Self-Determination: The Other Path for Native Americans*. Stanford University Press.

Arneil, Barbara (1996). *John Locke and America: The Defence of British Colonialism*. Clarendon Press.

Assembly of First Nations (1991). *First Circle on the Constitution: First Nations and the Constitution*. Discussion paper. AFN.

Assembly of First Nations (2005, June 27). *AFN National Chief Phil Fontaine Meets with Federal-Provincial-Territorial Ministers to Discuss First Ministers Meeting: National Chief Challenges Ministers to "Close the Gap" between First Nations and the Canadian Population within Ten Years*. Press release. <www.afn.ca/article.asp?id=1546>.

Assembly of First Nations (2005, June 28). *Bill C-31 Twenty Years Later: AFN National Chief Calls for First Nations Control of First Nations Citizenship*. Press release. <http://www.afn.ca/article.asp?id=1548>.

Bickerton, James and Alain-G. Gagnon (eds.) (1999). *Canadian Politics*. Third edition (Broadview).

Blatchford, Christie (February 2, 2008).Canada's Native Reserves Deserve Foreign Correspondent Treatment. *Globe and Mail*: A2.

Boe, R. (2002). Future Demographic Trends May Help Canada's Aboriginal Youth. *CSC Forum* 14, 3. Correctional Service of Canada.

Boldt, Menno (1993). *Surviving as Indians: The Challenge of Self-Government*. University of Toronto Press.

Borrows, John (2003). Measuring a Work in Progress: 20 Years of Section 35. In Ardith Walkem, ed., *Box of Treasures or Empty Box: Section 35 and the Canadian Constitution* (Theytus Press): 225 ff.

Breaker, R., and B. Kawaguchi (2002). *Infrastructure and Funding in First Nations Education: A Literature Review and Summary Recommendations*. Minister's National Working Group on Education.

Breathour, Patrick (2008, March 14). Chief Louie's Community Manifesto: Work Early, Work Hard, Work for the Band. *Globe and Mail*: 53.

British Columbia (1875/1987). *Papers Connected with the Indian Land Question, 1850-1875*. Government Printer; reprinted 1987, Queen's Printer for British Columbia.

British Columbia, Ministry of Aboriginal Relations and Reconciliation (1991). *Report of the British Columbia Claims Task Force* (June 28). <http://www.gov.bc.ca/arr/reports/bc_claims_task_force.html>.

British Columbia, Ministry of Aboriginal Relations and Reconciliation (2007). *A Guide to Aboriginal Organizations and Services in British Columbia 2007/2008*. Queen's Printer for British Columbia. <http://www.gov.bc.ca/arr/services/down/guidetoservices_2007.pdf>.

British Columbia Treaty Commission (2006). *Six Perspectives on Treaty Making: 2006 Annual Report of the BC Treaty Commission.* <http://www.bctreaty.net/files/pdf_documents/BCTC06AR-FINAL.pdf>.

British Columbia Treaty Commission (2008). *Negotiation Update.* <http://www.bctreaty.net/files/updates.php>.

Buchanan, James, and Gordon Tullock (1962). *The Calculus of Consent: Logical Foundations of Constitutional Democracy.* University of Michigan Press.

Cairns, Alan (2000). *Citizens Plus: Aboriginal Peoples and the Canadian State.* University of British Columbia Press

Cairns, Alan (2005). *First Nations and the Canadian State: In Search of Coexistence.* Institute of Intergovernmental Relations, Queens University.

Cairns, Alan, and Tom Flanagan (2001). An Exchange. *Inroads: A Journal of Opinion* 10: 101–123. <http://www.inroadsjournal.ca/pdfs/Inroads_10_Cairns_Flanagan.pdf>.

Calderisi, Robert (2006). *The Trouble with Africa: Why Foreign Aid Isn't Working.* Palgrave Macmillan.

Canada (1969). *Statement of the Government of Canada on Indian Policy.* White Paper. "Published under the authority of the Honourable Jean Chrétien, PC, MP, Minister of Indian Affairs and Northern Development, Ottawa." Cat. no. R32-2469. Queen's Printer. Available in HTML at <http://www.ainc-inac.gc.ca/pr/lib/phi/histlws/cp1969_e.html> and in PDF at <http://www.ainc-inac.gc.ca/pr/lib/phi/histlws/cp1969_e.pdf>; these versions are searchable, but not paginated.

Canada, DIAND (2002). *Registered Indian Population by Sex and Residence 2001.* Catalogue No. R31-3/2001E. <http://www.ainc-inac.gc.ca/pr/sts/rip/rip01_e.pdf>.

Canada, DIAND (2006). *Registered Indian Population by Sex and Residence 2005.* <http://www.ainc-inac.gc.ca/ai/rs/pubs/sts/ni/rip/rip05/rip05-eng.pdf>.

Canada, Indian and Northern Affairs Canada (2004a). *Fact Sheet: The Nisga'a Treaty.* <http://www.ainc-inac.gc.ca/pr/info/nit_e.html>.

Canada, Indian and Northern Affairs Canada (2004b). *Basic Departmental Data* 2003. <http://www.ainc-inac.gc.ca/ai/rs/pubs/sts/bdd/bdd03/bdd03-eng.pdf>.

Canada, Indian and Northern Affairs Canada (2006a). *Canada's Position: United Nations Draft Declaration on the Rights of Indigenous Peoples—June 29, 2006.*

Canada, Indian and Northern Affairs Canada (2006b). *Registered Indian Population by Sex and Residence* 2005. <http://www.ainc-inac.gc.ca/ai/rs/pubs/sts/ni/rip/rip05/rip05-eng.pdf>.

Caro, Robert A. (2002). *Master of the Senate.* Vintage Books.

Clatworthy, Stewart (2001). *Re-assessing the Population Impacts of Bill C-31.* Four Directions Project Consultants, Winnipeg. <http://www.ainc-inac.gc.ca/pr/ra/rpi/index_e.html>.

Clatworthy, S., and M. Mendelson (1999). *A Statistical Profile of Aboriginal Youth in Canada, 1996.* Human Resources Development Canada.

Clemens, Jason, Jonathan Hayes, Mark Mullins, Niels Veldhuis and Christopher Glover (2005). *Government Failure in Canada, 2005 Report: A Review of the Auditor General's Reports, 1992–2005.* Fraser Institute. <http://www.fraserinstitute.org/researchandpublications/publications/3099.aspx>.

Clemens, Jason, Charles Lammam, Milagros Palacios, and Niels Veldhuis (2007). *Government Failure in Canada, 2007 Report: A Review of the Auditor General's Reports, 1992-2006.* Fraser Institute. <http://www.fraserinstitute.org/researchandpublications/publications/4988.aspx>.

Clemens, Jason, Mark Mullins, Niels Veldhius, & Christopher Glover (2004). *Government Failure in Canada, 1997–2004: A Survey of Reports from the Auditor General.* Fraser Institute. <http://www.fraserinstitute.org/researchandpublications/publications/2948.aspx>.

Cornell, Stephen (1999). *Keys to Nation Building in Indian Country*. Udall Centre, University of Arizona.

Cornell, Stephen (2002). *The Harvard Project Findings on Good Governance*. Speaking notes for address to Self-Government: Options and Opportunities, Speaking Truth to Power III (March 14–15), BC Treaty Commission. <http://www.bctreaty.net/files/pdf_documents/dr_cornell_speech.pdf>.

Cornell, Stephen, and Joseph P. Kalt (1998). Sovereignty and Nation Building: The Development Challenge in Indian Country Today. *American Indian Culture and Research Journal* 22, 3. Also available at <http://www.ksg.harvard.edu/hpaied/docs/CornellKalt%20Sov-NB.pdf>.

Cornerstone Planning Group (serial). *BC Media Monitor: First Nations Edition*.

Coyne, Andrew (2006, December 7). *What Does "Citizen" Mean?* <http://andrewcoyne.com/columns/2006/12/what-does-citizen-mean.php>.

Crowley, Brian Lee (1995). Property, Culture and Aboriginal Self-Government. In H. Drost, B.L. Crowley and R. Schwindt, *Market Solutions for Native Poverty: Social Policy for the Third Solitude* (C.D. Howe Institute): 58–97.

Curry, Bill (2006, December 16). Ottawa Shelves Reform Plans on Native Governance. *Globe and Mail*: A21.

Diamond, Jared (1999). *Guns, Germs and Steel*. Norton.

Dworkin, Ronald (1985). *A Matter of Principle*. Harvard University Press.

Easterly, William (2006). *The White Man's Burden*. Penguin.

Farris-Manning, C., and M. Zandstra, (2003). *Children in Care in Canada: A Summary of Current Issues and Trends with Recommendations for Future Research*. Child Welfare League of Canada.

Flanagan, Tom (2000). *First Nations, Second Thoughts*. McGill-Queen's University Press.

Flanagan, Tom (2006, December 20). Bring Democracy to Indian Reserves. *Globe and Mail*: A23.

Foster, Hamar, et al. (2003). *Trespassers on the Soil:* United States v. Tom *and a New Perspective on the Short History of Treaty Making in Nineteenth Century British Columbia*. 139/139 B.C. Studies. University of British Columbia.

Four Directions Consulting Group (1997). *Implications of First Nations Demography: Final Report* (August 5). DIAND. <http://www.ainc-inac.gc.ca/pr/ra/execs/index_e.html>.

Friesen, Joe (2008, January 18). Audit May Lead to Charges against INAC Office. *Globe and Mail*: A6

George-Kanentiio, Douglas (2006). *Iroquois on Fire: A Voice from the Mohawk Nation*. Greenwood.

Gibson, Gordon (1999a). *Comments on the Draft Nisga'a Treaty*. Public Policy Source No. 18. Fraser Institute.

Gibson, Gordon (1999b). *A Principled Analysis of the Nisga'a Treaty*. Public Policy Source No. 27. Fraser Institute.

Gibson, Gordon (2000). *Principles for Treaty Making*. Public Policy Source No. 38. Fraser Institute.

Gitxsan Chiefs' Office (2008, July 10). [advertisement] *Vancouver Sun*.

Gitxsan Treaty Team (2008). *Alternative Governance Model: "Gitxsan Reconciliation."* Gitxsan Chiefs' Office. <http://www.gitxsan.com/Governance.pdf>.

Globe and Mail (2005, October 12). Separating Races Is Not the Answer. [Editorial] *Globe and Mail*: A22.

Gour, C. (2005). *Basic Departmental Data 2004*. Canada, Department of Indian Affairs and Northern Development.

Grey, Julius (January 6, 1993). [op. ed.] *Montreal Gazette*.

Health Canada (2000). *Pro-Action, Postponement, and Preparation/Support: A Framework for Action to Reduce the Rate of Teen Pregnancy in Canada.*

Health Canada (2003). *Acting on What We Know; Preventing Suicide in First Nations.*

Hawthorn, H.B., (ed.) (1966/67). *A Survey of the Contemporary Indians of Canada.* 2 vols. Queen's Printer.

Helim, Calvin (2006). *Dances with Dependency.* Orca Spirit.

Hirschman, Albert O. (1970). *Exit, Voice and Loyalty.* Harvard University Press.

Hull, J. (2001). *Aboriginal Single Mothers in Canada, 1996: A Statistical Profile.* Canada, Department of Indian Affairs and Northern Development.

Hunter, Justine (2007, November 3), Landmark Deal Causing Concern. *Globe and Mail*: A11.

Irwin, Hon. Ronald (1994). Speech presented to the federal provincial/territorial meeting with Ministers and Aboriginal leaders.

Isaac, Thomas (2006). *Aboriginal Title.* Native Law Centre, University of Saskatchewan.

Kymlicka, Will (1995). *Multicultural Citizenship: A Liberal Theory of Minority Rights.* Oxford University Press.

Latimer, J., et al. (2004). *A One-Day Snapshot of Aboriginal Youth in Custody across Canada.* Department of Justice.

Liberal Party of Canada (1993). *Creating Opportunity: The Liberal Plan for Canada.* The "Red Book." Official Election Platform.

Mann, Charles C. (2005). *1491: New Revelations of America before Columbus.* Knopf.

Mitchell, William C., and Randy T. Simons (1994). *Beyond Politics: Markets, Welfare and the Failure of Bureaucracy.* Westview Press.

Morse, Bradford W. (1999). The Inherent Right of Aboriginal Governance. In John Hylton, ed., *Aboriginal Self-Government in Canada: Current Trends and Issues* (Purich): 16–44.

Mrozinski, Lisa J., Minster of the B.C. Attorney General, Aboriginal Law (2007). Provincial Regulation of Aboriginal and Treaty Rights. Paper presented to the Pacific Business and Law Institute.

Office of the Correctional Investigator of Canada (2006). *Annual Report of the Office of the Correctional Investigator of Canada* 2005-2006. <http://www.oci-bec.gc.ca/reports/ar200506_e.asp>.

Pelzer, A.N., ed. (1966). *Verwoerd Speaks: Speeches 1948–66*. Johannesburg: APB Publishers.

Pope, Alan (2006). *Report on the Kashechewan First Nation and Its People*. October 31, 2006. <http://www.ainc-inac.gc.ca/nr/prs/s-d2006/kfnp_e.html>, as of 07/02/2007.

Rawls, John (1971). *A Theory of Justice*. Oxford University Press.

Richards, John (2001). *Neighbours Matter*. C.D. Howe Institute.

Richards, John (2003). *A New Agenda for Strengthening Canada's Aboriginal Population: Individual Treaty Benefits, Reduced Transfers to Bands and Own-source Taxation*. C.D. Howe Institute.

Richards, John (2006). *Creating Choices: Rethinking Aboriginal Policy*. Policy Study 43. C.D. Howe Institute.

Romanow, Roy, John Whyte, and Howard Leeson (1984). *Canada... Notwithstanding: The Making of the Constitution 1976–1982*. Carsell/Methuen.

Royal Commission on Aboriginal Peoples [RCAP] (1993). *Focusing the Dialogue*. Discussion Paper #2. RCAP.

Royal Commission on Aboriginal Peoples [RCAP] (1996a). *People to People, Nation to Nation: Highlights from the Report of the Royal Commission on*

Aboriginal Peoples. Cat. no. Z1-1991/1-6E. <http://www.ainc-inac.gc.ca/ch/rcap/rpt/index_e.html>.

Royal Commission on Aboriginal Peoples [RCAP] (1996b). *Report of the Royal Commission on Aboriginal Peoples*. Indian and Northern Affairs Canada. <http://www.ainc-inac.gc.ca/ch/rcap/sg/sgmm_e.html>.

Schwartz, Bryan (1986). *First Principles, Second Thoughts: Aboriginal Peoples, Constitutional Reform and Canadian Statecraft*. Institute for Research on Public Policy (IRPP).

Scott, Jacquelyn Thayer (2006). "Doing Business with the Devil": Land, Sovereignty, and Corporate Partnerships in Membertou, Inc. In Terry Anderson, Bruce Benson, and Thomas E.Flanagan (eds.), *Self Determination: The Other Path for Native Americans* (Stanford University Press): 242–72.

Simpson, Jeffrey (2007, October 11). When You Light a Match Near a Toxic Mix of Education and Religion ... *Globe and Mail*: A27.

Smith, A., E. Saewyc, M. Albert, L. MacKay, M. Northcott, and The McCreary Centre Society (2007). *Against the Odds: A Profile of Marginalized and Street-Involved Youth in BC*. The McCreary Centre Society. <http://www.mcs.bc.ca/retrieve.cfm?Document=Against_the_odds_2007_web.pdf>.

Smith Melvin, Q.C. (2000). *Some Perspectives on the Origin and Meaning of Section 35 of the Constitution Act, 1982*. Public Policy Source No. 41. Fraser Institute.

Standing Senate Committee on Legal and Constitutional Affairs (2006). *Proceedings of the Standing Senate Committee on Legal and Constitutional Affairs*, Issue 10: Evidence, September 27. <http://www.parl.gc.ca/39/1/parlbus/commbus/senate/Com-e/lega-e/10eva-e.htm?Language=E&Parl=39&Ses=1&comm_id=11>.

Statistics Canada (2001). *2001 Census of Canada*. <http://www12.statcan.ca/english/census01/home/Index.cfm> (updated: August 11, 2008).

Statistics Canada (2003). *Aboriginal Peoples of Canada: A Demographic Profile, 2001 Census*. Cat. No. 96F0030XIE2001007.

Statistics Canada (2005). *Projections of the Aboriginal Populations, Canada, Provinces and Territories, 2001 to 2017*. Catalogue No. 91-547-XIE.

Statistics Canada (2008). *2006 Census of Canada: Aboriginal Peoples.* Release No. 5 (January 15). <http://www12.statcan.ca/census-recensement/2006/rt-td/ap-pa-eng.cfm>.

Taylor, Charles (1993). Shared and Divergent Values. In Guy Laforest (ed.), *Reconciling the Solitudes: Essays on Canadian Federalism and Nationalism* (McGill-Queens University Press): 155–86.

Taylor, Charles (1996). Why Democracy Needs Patriotism. In Joshua Cohen, (ed.), *For Love of Country: Debating the Limits of Patriotism* (Beacon): 119–21.

Tomuschat, C. (1983). Protection of Minorities under Article 27 of the International Covenant on Civil and Political Rights. In R. Bernhardt et al. (eds.), *Volkerrecht als Reschordnung Internationale Gerichtsbarkeit Menschenrechte: Festschrift fur Hermann Mosler* (Springer): 949–79.

Tully, James (1999). Aboriginal Peoples Negotiating Reconciliation. In Alain Gagnon and James Bickerton (eds.), *Canadian Politics*, third ed. (Broadview): 411–39.

United Nations (2007). *Declaration on the Rights of Indigenous Peoples.* General Assembly Sixty-first session, Agenda item 68 (September 13). United Nations.

Vancouver Sun (2007, July 27). [editorial] *Vancouver Sun*. Available at <http://www.tsawwassenfirstnation.com/media/jul27vs_2007.php>.

Wente, Margaret (2007, October 13). White Guilt, Dead Children—in the Name of Political Correctness. *Globe and Mail*: A27

Legislation and case law

Benoit v. Canada 2003 FCA 236.

Calder v. Attorney-General of B.C. (1973) 34 D.L.R. (3rd) 145.

Campbell et al. v. AG BC/AG Cda & Nisga'a Nation et al., 2000 BCSC 1123.

Canadian Charter of Rights and Freedoms, Part I of the *Constitution Act, 1982*, being Schedule B to the *Canada Act 1982* (U.K.), 1982, c. 11. <http://laws.justice.gc.ca/en/charter/>.

Charlottetown Accord: Consensus Report on the Constitution, Charlottetown (August 28, 1992). Final text Consensus report on the constitution.

Corbiere v. Canada (Minister of Indian and Northern Affairs) [1999] 2 S.C.R. 203.

Delgamuukw v. British Columbia [1997], 3 S.C.R. 10101.

R. v. Drybones, [1970] S.C.R. 282

George III. *Royal Proclamation of 1763* [Royal Proclamation, 1763 (U.K.) R.S.C. 1985 Appendix II, no. 1].

Gladstone v. Canada (Attorney-General) (2005) 1 S.C.R. 325, 2005 SCC 21.

Guerin v. The Queen (1984) 2 S.C.R. 335 (1984)

Halfway River First Nation v. British Columbia (Minister of Forests) (1999) 178 DLR (4th) 666, 1999 BCCA 470.

Haida Nation v. British Columbia (Ministry of Forests) 2004 SCC 73 [2004] 3 S.C.R. 511.

Health Services and Support – Facilities Subsector Bargaining Assn. v. British Columbia, [2007] 2 S.C.R. 391, 2007 SCC 27.

McIvor v. The Registrar, Indian and Northern Affairs Canada, 2007 BCSC 827.

Mikisew Cree First Nation v. Canada (Minister of Canadian Heritage) 2005 SCC 69.

Mitchell v. MNR., 2001 SCC 33 [2001] 1 S.C.R. 911.

Montana Band of Indians v. Canada (Minister of Indian & Northern Affairs) 51 D.L.R. (4d) 306, [1988] 5 W.W.R. 151, [1989] 1 F. C. 143, 59 Alta., L. R. (2d) 353, 18 F.T.R. 15 (Federal Court Trial Division).

Platinex Inc. v. Kitchenuhmaykoosib Inninuwug First Nation, ON S.C. files 2006 CanLII 26171, 2007 CanLII 16637, and 2007 CanLII 20790. The series of actions is ongoing as at this writing.

R v. Kapp, 2008 SCC 41.

R. v. Kapp, SCC 31603, Dec. 11, 2007.

R. v. Marshall [1999] 3 S.C.R. 456 (*Marshall I*).

R. v. Marshall [1999] 3 S.C.R. 533 (*Marshall II*).

R. v. Marshall; *R. v. Bernard* [2005] 2 S.C.R. 220, 2005 SCC43.

R. v. Pamajewon, [1996] 2 S.C.R. 821.

R. v. Powley, 2003 SCC 43 [2003] 2 S.C.R. 207.

R. v. Sparrow (1990), S.C.R. 1075.

R. v. Van der Peet (1996) 2 S.C.R. 507.

Sga'Nisim Sim'Augit (Chief Mountain) v. Canada. In progress, BCSC, action no. L000808.

Tsilhqot'in Nation v. British Columbia 2007 BCSC 1700. Commonly referred to as "*William*."

ABOUT THIS PUBLICATION

Distribution
This publication is available from <http://www.fraserinstitute.org> in Portable Document Format (PDF) and can be read with Adobe Acrobat® or with Adobe Reader®, which is available free of charge from Adobe Systems Inc. To download Adobe Reader®, go to this link: <http://www.adobe.com/products/acrobat/readstep2.html> with your browser. We encourage you to install the most recent version.

Ordering publications
For information about ordering the printed publications of the Fraser Institute, please contact the publications coordinator

- e-mail: sales@fraserinstitute.org
- telephone: 604.688.0221 ext. 580 or, toll free, 1.800.665.3558 ext. 580
- fax: 604.688.8539.

Media
For media enquiries, please contact our Communications Department

- 604.714.4582
- e-mail: communications@fraserinstitute.org.

Website
To learn more about the Fraser Institute and to read our publications on line, please visit our website at <http://www.fraserinstitute.org>.

Disclaimer
The author of this publication has worked independently and opinions expressed by him are, therefore, his own, and do not necessarily reflect the opinions of the supporters, trustees, or staff of the Fraser Institute. This publication in no way implies that the Fraser Institute, its trustees, or staff are in favor of, or oppose the passage of, any bill; or that they support or oppose any particular political party or candidate.

ISBN
978-0-88975-243-6
Printed and bound in Canada.

Date of issue
January 2009

Editing, design, and production
Lindsey Thomas Martin

Cover design
Bill Ray

SUPPORTING THE FRASER INSTITUTE

To learn how to support the Fraser Institute, please contact

- Development Department, Fraser Institute
  Fourth Floor, 1770 Burrard Street
  Vancouver, British Columbia, V6J 3G7 Canada

- telephone, toll-free: 1.800.665.3558 ext. 586

- e-mail: development@fraserinstitute.org.

ABOUT THE FRASER INSTITUTE

Our vision is a free and prosperous world where individuals benefit from greater choice, competitive markets, and personal responsibility. Our mission is to measure, study, and communicate the impact of competitive markets and government interventions on the welfare of individuals.

Founded in 1974, we are an independent research and educational organization with locations throughout North America and international partners in over 70 countries. Our work is financed by tax-deductible contributions from thousands of individuals, organizations, and foundations. In order to protect its independence, the Institute does not accept grants from government or contracts for research.

菲沙研究所的願景乃一自由而昌盛的世界，當中每個人得以從更豐富的選擇、具競爭性的市場及自我承擔責任而獲益。我們的使命在於量度、研究並使人知悉競爭市場及政府干預對個人福祉的影響。

Nous envisageons un monde libre et prospère, où chaque personne bénéficie d'un plus grand choix, de marchés concurrentiels et de responsabilités individuelles. Notre mission consiste à mesurer, à étudier et à communiquer l'effet des marchés concurrentiels et des interventions gouvernementales sur le bien-être des individus.

تتمثل رؤيتنا في وجود عالم حر ومزدهر يستفيد فيه الأفراد من القدرة على الاختيار بشكل أكبر، والأسواق التنافسية، والمسؤولية الشخصية. أما رسالتنا فهي قياس، ودراسة، وتوصيل تأثير الأسواق التنافسية والتدخلات الحكومية المتعلقة بالرفاه الاجتماعي للأفراد.

Nuestra visión es un mundo libre y próspero donde los individuos se beneficien de una mayor oferta, la competencia en los mercados y la responsabilidad individual. Nuestra misión es medir, estudiar y comunicar el impacto de la competencia en los mercados y la intervención gubernamental en el bienestar de los individuos.